SECRETS FROM MY SILENT EDEN

Secrets From My Silent Eden

Paul W. Ogden

Published by
Bookstand Publishing
Morgan Hill, CA 95037
Record 3957_1

In a few cases, names have been changed to protect the identities of those involved.

ISBN 978-1-61863-605-8

Printed in the United States of America

Dedication

This book is dedicated to Jonathan H. Ogden and his wife, Dorothy W. Ogden.

For eleven years, my deaf brother unknowingly prepared the way for my arrival. He taught everyone in the family how to reach out and communicate.

PREFACE

Throughout my life as a professional educator, I have been asked this question by my students, colleagues, associates, and press representatives, some of them hearing, some deaf: "How have you done it?"

I now wish to fully respond to those who have asked the question.

Whether hearing or deaf, saint or sinner, believer, agnostic, or atheist, I hope the following pages give you joy, laughter, hope, guidance, sensitivity, encouragement, and inspiration.

When I was in graduate school, I fell in love with the painting portrayed on the cover of this book. I first saw it on a poster in a faculty member's office. At that moment and every time since, whether on a poster, in a book, or when I viewed the original at the National Gallery of Art in Washington D.C., Monet's *Artist's Garden at Vétheuil* drew me in.

I delighted in the sensation of being in the garden, of feeling embraced and supported. It reminded me of the Garden of Eden, a place where life begins, a place where people live in harmony and peace. It also brought back memories of my family—my mother, father, and brothers, who lovingly gave me my first lessons in communication. As I grew up, I sensed that all of us seek such a garden, a place where we can understand and be understood, a perfect world for living and loving. For me, it depicts a world of perfect communicating.

None of us are perfect communicators. But when I enter into Monet's garden, I find the courage to try again, to reach out to others in an attempt to love and achieve mutual understanding. I hope this book will inspire a little of that same courage in you.

Contents

Introduction 1

1. Terms of Communication 7

2. Our Relentless God 29

3. Made for Intimacy 49

4. All People, All Nations 67

5. Christians and Communication 85

6. Love in Action 99

7. Daring to Doubt 115

8. Finding Faith 127

9. The Truth of the Matter 145

10. God's Love Letters 165

11. To Forgive Is Divine 181

12. Heavenly Conversation 205

13. Broken Blessings 223

14. True Contentment 241

15. The Mystery of God 259

Secrets from My Silent Eden 275

Notes 277

Acknowledgements 285

About the Author 287

Butterflies 289

INTRODUCTION

I sat in the twelfth row of the Stonewall Jackson High School auditorium, a speck in a sea of fellow students adorned in traditional black robes and topped by mortar boards. I was nineteen years old and finally about to receive my high school diploma.

I felt as though I'd come to the end of a long chapter in my life. The crowd in Charleston, West Virginia, that turned out for the ceremony was huge. Five hundred students were graduating, and their families and friends were there to celebrate. The guest speaker was a congressman with a boring speech. Normally, as class co-valedictorian, I also would have delivered a speech, but I was graduating at the height of the Vietnam conflict. West Virginia Senator Jennings Randolph had forbidden student graduation speeches throughout the state, apparently to prevent anyone from inciting a riot by expressing antigovernment sentiments.

I didn't mind. I was just thrilled to be done with high school and moving on to the next adventure. A newspaper reporter had recently interviewed me and published an article about my achievements. Now I felt like a racehorse trapped at the starting gate. I couldn't wait to get my diploma and be with my family and friends at the graduation party planned for me. I was surrounded by friends—we weren't required to sit in alphabetical order—and joined them in passing notes and making gestures to each other (many had to do with drinking) as we waited. Teachers with stern expressions walked up and down the aisles to maintain order.

Finally, it was my turn to go up to the platform. It was a long walk through the crowd, up the steps, and across the stage. I shook hands with school officials and the congressman, received my diploma, and eventually returned to the steps and back to my seat.

It wasn't until twelve years later that I discovered the rest of the story. I was with my mother in her modest apartment in a retirement center in Oakland, California. We enjoyed the view of thick green vegetation out her patio window as we reminisced about earlier times. She brought up my high school graduation and the "wonderful display of appreciation they gave you."

I frowned. "What display?" I said. "What are you talking about?"

"Why, when you walked up on stage to get your diploma," she said. "The whole crowd rose up, two thousand people cheering and clapping. A lot of them were crying."

I was flabbergasted. Apparently the newspaper article had gone straight to the hearts of many people in Charleston. I'd been so busy concentrating on getting to the platform and receiving the diploma that I hadn't noticed the reaction of the crowd.

Perhaps the confusion is understandable. I didn't see the crowd because I was watching my feet on the steps and then the people on stage. I didn't hear their applause because I was born with sensorineural hearing loss in both ears. Either the hair cells of the cochlea in my inner ear or the auditory nerve that transmits signals from my inner ears to the auditory cortex of my brain are damaged (I've never learned which). I have never heard a sound and have no notion of the quality of speech or other sounds.

I am profoundly deaf.

This is not all that defines me, however. I am also outgoing and inquisitive. I enjoy people and learning about the world around me. From my earliest days, this combination of qualities stirred within me a passion to understand and master—as much as possible—the art of communication. It has propelled me toward a lifetime of study of the subject and a career in teaching others about it, including more than thirty years as a professor of Deaf Studies at California State University, Fresno.

I suspect that communication is important to you too. After all, our ability to send and receive messages and interact with others has everything to do with our satisfaction and success in life. You and I long to be understood—by our friends, our bosses, our parents, our children, and most certainly by our boyfriend, girlfriend, husband, or wife. Nothing is more frustrating than trying to express a vital message or your innermost thoughts and realizing that your coworker, teenager, or lover isn't getting it—or worse, that he or she isn't even trying to understand!

When communication succeeds between you and another person, however, it unlocks the potential of the relationship. You discover points of common delight. Ideas pour out and build on each other. A bond forms. Even when you disagree, communication creates a connection that often leads to mutual trust and respect. An effective exchange allows you to see circumstances from another's perspective. And when communication flows at an intimate level, it can open the door to love.

As important as good communication is to our human relationships, however, my life has shown me that it's even more critical in our relationship with the Lord. What happens when we pray for God's help in a crisis and hear no answer? What do we do when we sense that God is distant and leaving us to fend for ourselves? So often, our response is anger, disillusionment, and doubt. On the other hand, during periods when we sense the Lord's guidance and presence, when we discern His voice and direction, we feel encouraged and strengthened. Our prayer life is more vibrant. Our worship is more meaningful. Our faith deepens.

I do believe there are times when the Lord is purposefully silent. But I can't help wondering—at moments when God seems far away, is He truly distant or is His message simply not getting through? Is He speaking and we're not "hearing"? Is our faith falling away for the simple reason that we're failing to communicate?

I am the author of a book for parents of deaf children called *The Silent Garden*. When I imagine this silent Eden, I picture something like paradise, a place with perfect communication. No breakdowns. No confusion. No barriers to understanding. No floundering for words. In my mind, I see where this smooth interaction takes place. It is located on top of a hill with spectacular views of a nearby blue ocean and more distant, snowcapped mountains.

In my garden, I don't hear the waves crashing—I feel the spray of water on my face. I don't hear the wind—I feel the breeze in my hair. I don't hear the seagull cry—I see it swoop across the sky into a magenta sunset. I don't hear a friend call my name—I feel his touch on my shoulder and see his wave of greeting. I am connected to everyone and everything. Best of all, I am in continual, joyful conversation with my Lord and Savior. He understands me completely, and I Him.

My experience as a deaf person and as a human being struggling to understand God, faith, and my purpose in this world has taught me that successful communication is at the core of an abundant life and a thriving faith. It's taken me a long time to absorb this lesson. In many ways, I'm still learning it. Yet I've picked up a few "secrets" along the way that I believe can dramatically improve *your* life and faith. Some will be so familiar they won't seem like secrets at all, but by presenting them within the context of communication, I hope they will provide fresh insight.

This book tells my story, but it is also much more. It is for anyone—believer, doubter, seeker, atheist, agnostic—who wants to discover more about how to relate with people and with our God. My prayer is that it will speak to you no matter where it finds you on your journey.

I invite you to join me as we explore it together.

1

Terms Of Communication

If you wish to communicate with me, define your terms.

Voltaire

It was a sunny afternoon in June, six months after our perfect wedding on a California beach. Anne, my beautiful new bride, and I were spending the summer at my brother's home in Berkeley while he and his family traveled. Custom-built in 1920, the house was nestled in the city's north hills and featured three bedrooms, wood floors, a huge and ornate fireplace, and a view of San Francisco Bay from the back deck. It was a wonderful setting for what should have been an idyllic first summer for a pair of newlyweds.

Idyllic, however, was not the word that came to my mind that day. *Insane* was closer to it.

I felt pressured, stressed, and grief-stricken. My father had passed away unexpectedly just three weeks after our wedding. A student I'd worked closely with had recently committed suicide. I was dealing with a series of health issues, including fatigue and mood swings caused by what I later learned was low blood sugar (hypoglycemia). Most pressing at the moment was work on my dissertation, which I desperately hoped to finish that summer so I could earn my Ph.D. in educational psychology and deafness from the University of

Illinois at Urbana. The project involved more than three hundred pages of text, tables, and research data about the experiences of adults who'd been educated at private schools. It was a daunting task, one I wasn't sure I could complete before beginning my second full academic year in my new job as coordinator of Deaf and Hard of Hearing Services at the College of the Sequoias in Visalia, California.

And then there was my wife.

I'd met Anne in Atlanta at a youth leadership conference sponsored by a national nonprofit organization. Though I was dating another girl at the time, I'd noticed Anne almost immediately—the way she smiled, talked, and laughed. She was expressive with her face and hands as she talked and gestured. She was easy to lipread. As a deaf person and someone who'd decided to make teaching about communication my career, these were things I valued highly.

Our first date was two years later, at a Christmas party in Pasadena, California. When our host passed around a magazine article describing how Anne was one of the first hard of hearing† registered nurses in the country, several of the guests commented on her amazing accomplishments. I, however, was looking at the photo that accompanied the article.

[1]"No, that's not what's amazing," I said. "What's amazing is how pretty she is. She's beautiful!"

---

[1] [† Footnote: The word *deaf* is used in two ways, depending on the user. Professionals such as medical doctors and audiologists use the word to refer to severe hearing loss, as opposed to *hard of hearing,* which can be minimal to quite serious but is correctable to some extent with the use of hearing aids or cochlear implants. People in the Deaf community, on the other hand, use *deaf* to identify themselves as members of a specific subculture. They are proud of this identification and do not perceive it as a pathological label in any way.]

The first date led to a second. We enjoyed each other's company and found we had much in common. We'd both given our hearts to Jesus Christ earlier that year. And we both believed strong communication was one of the foundations of a successful relationship. Our conversations flowed so smoothly that it seemed obvious we were meant for each other.

Somehow, though, all that seemed to change as soon as we married. Part of it was the grief and stress from dealing with the death of my father. Another part was the fact that Anne had decided to quit smoking, cold turkey. She also had an increasingly difficult relationship with her mother. And still another big factor was my dissertation. To Anne, my sudden, single-minded focus on work meant that I no longer cared about her. She didn't understand why I couldn't set it aside for a time and just relax. For me, the project was so intense and absorbing that I couldn't turn it off, even when I wasn't at my desk. We argued about it constantly.

That wasn't all. Two days earlier, Anne had been so upset with me while cooking in the kitchen that she forgot to allow our pressure cooker to cool. When she pried open the lid, scalding water exploded into her face. It was a terrifying moment. I rushed Anne to the emergency room, which we followed with a visit the next day to a plastic surgeon. We were relieved to learn that the burns would heal naturally and leave no scars.

After caring for Anne and making little progress on my dissertation, however, I felt more stressed than ever. I even resented Anne and her accident for taking time away from my work, which added a measure of guilt to everything else.

The exploding pressure cooker was a metaphor for our marriage. Everything was about to blow.

I was in my brother's study: a damp basement room with a low ceiling, one tiny window, and rows of books about the history of theater and languages. My green-tinted Smith-Corona classic, a manual typewriter, sat in the middle of a desk, surrounded by papers that appeared to be strewn about carelessly. Only I could make sense of them—and even I was having trouble doing that at the moment.

I scratched my head. The totals for one of my tables weren't adding up, but I couldn't figure out why. Something was way off. *Now what?* I thought. *How am I ever going to get this done?* I was rechecking the figures when I noticed Anne next to me. She stood with her arms crossed.

"Now you're going to neglect me again," she said. "I feel like I'm a widow."

For days, I'd buried my feelings and frustrations. I was like a volcano ready to erupt. Now the lava began to flow.

"You're bothering me!" I said, signing with savage hand motions. "You don't want me to get my Ph.D.? You want me to give it up? All right, I'll give it up for you. I'll just stay with my master's degree and forget everything else. Forget all the work I did at Illinois. Is that what you want?"

Anne's eyes returned fire. "No, that's not what I want!" she said. "I just want you to acknowledge me once in a while. You make me feel like I don't exist. Is that so hard to understand?"

We fought like this for the next two hours. Then Anne began to cry. I felt like doing the same—or worse, like just giving up. Had it been a mistake to marry Anne? Should I just leave? No. I knew in my heart that marrying Anne wasn't a mistake, that I loved her deeply, in a way I'd never experienced before.

We'd been so optimistic only a few months earlier. We were ready to embark on the journey of life together. We were soul mates, bound by our mutual goals and interests. As new Christians, we looked forward to growing closer to God and each other as we moved forward in our faith. Perhaps most important of all, we enjoyed a relationship based on openness and strong communication.

Anne truly was a great communicator, expressive and straightforward. I considered myself an expert on communication. My deafness had forced me to develop my ability to send and receive information in ways other than speaking and hearing. I'd studied people, ideas, and communication for years in college, taking classes in psychology, philosophy, existentialism, and sign language. I'd made communication my vocation. I had trained to teach others how to teach the deaf, as well as to instruct parents on how to communicate with their deaf children.

But if Anne and I were such wonderful communicators, why did we fight all the time, usually over the same things? Why didn't she understand my situation? What was I not understanding about her? What in the world were we doing wrong?

Balloon Moments

When communication flows freely between you and the important people in your life, it generates a sense of satisfaction and peace. It instills an impression of safety and confidence, encouraging creative expression and boldness to say what might otherwise be left unsaid. We are not spirits, nor are we telepathic. We are physical beings encased in shells of bone, muscle, and skin, and as such any effort to put forth an idea must be tentative. We're like a child who releases his helium-filled balloon into the sky, never quite knowing where our expression will land or how it will be received or interpreted.

Perhaps this is why one of the most rewarding feelings in life is that of being understood, of being *known*. When the balloon comes back to us, something almost miraculous has taken place. We release an idea into the world and discover to our delight that it was correctly interpreted and returned. Even better, we occasionally receive a new balloon along with the old. This is the beginning of meaningful exchange, and when it works our collection of balloons grows large enough to lift us up and carry us to a new and wonderful place. We long for these "balloon moments."

Communication doesn't always work this way, however. Frequently—perhaps more often than not—we release our balloon and watch it drift away, never to be seen again. Worse, we observe someone catch our balloon and then carelessly, or purposely, pop it in their hands. The result is frustrating or worse. If you've ever asked your friend or spouse to pick you up for an important meeting and then were left waiting because they wrote down the wrong time, you know what I mean.

Sometimes our misguided attempts at communication are humorous. Advertisements in newspapers and magazines like these, for example, don't quite express the meaning intended by the writer:

- Dog for sale: eats anything and is fond of children.
- Tired of cleaning yourself? Let me do it.
- Stock up and save. Limit: one.
- Used cars: Why go elsewhere to be cheated? Come here first!
- Our experienced mom will care for your child. Fenced yard, meals, and smacks included.
- Illiterate? Write today for help.[1]

When miscommunication arises in the midst of tragedy, however, it's no laughing matter. In 2006, an explosion trapped a group of twelve miners underground near Tallmansville, West Virginia. Relatives gathered at a local church to await updates on the crisis. Hours later, they broke out in laughter, song, and shouts of gratitude when it was announced that eleven of the twelve miners had survived. But three hours after that, the chief executive officer of International Coal Group delivered a different message: in reality, only one miner had been found breathing. The rest were dead. The CEO had to tell the shocked and furious families and friends that the initial word from the rescue team, that the miners had been discovered and were being checked for vital signs, had somehow been garbled by the time it reached company officials on the surface. It was a terrible miscommunication.[2]

If an accurate exchange of information is this difficult to achieve, how then do we discover the sweet spot of successful communication? How do we stay there when we find it? How important, truly, is effective communication to our life and faith?

Perhaps the answers begin with a better understanding of the art of communication.

Getting It Right

The ways we communicate with each other in the twenty-first century are changing rapidly. Much of this is driven by advances in technology. Cell phones are replacing landline telephones. Email has nearly eliminated the practice of writing letters. Business is conducted by fax. Texting, tweeting, and social media allow us to stay in contact with friends old and new on a continual basis.

The trend is toward speed and quantity. We have the ability to send a message to hundreds or even thousands of people instantly. We become impatient if we can't reach someone immediately. We strive to enlarge our email mailing lists and "friend" counts on Facebook. Perhaps by necessity, the depth of our exchanges, at least in the electronic world, is shrinking. As society moves at an increasingly dizzy pace, fewer of us take the time to talk, write, or read at length. Some would argue that we lose as much as we gain from technological innovation.

We may debate the merits of these shifts, but one thing has not changed: the fundamental need to communicate effectively with the rest of the human race. When President Barack Obama and his team negotiated a nuclear arms reduction treaty with Russian President Dmitry Medvedev in 2010, both sides relied on the experience and skill of translators to accurately transmit their messages. When sixteen-year-old Abby Sunderland attempted that same year to become the youngest person to sail solo around the world and a storm disabled her boat and satellite phone, her rescue depended on the signals transmitted from a pair of emergency beacons.

Similarly, the success of a business rests on accurate and seamless communication. Jack Welch, the former General Electric chief executive officer, tells the story of an investment meeting with Steve Klimhowski, an employee of Northwestern Memorial HealthCare. Klimhowski was so informed and passionate about Northwestern's mission, Welch says, that after just five minutes together, he realized that Northwestern's leaders had to be strong communicators in the area of company vision.[3]

Communication is just as vital in our personal relationships. We seek friends we're comfortable with, people who seem to offer easy conversation and connection. We seek a potential husband or wife that we can bond with on a deep level, someone who knows and understands us intimately, a person we can view as a "soul mate."

Brian and Kerry Nichols, a couple we know from our church, have forged this kind of relationship over the thirteen years of their marriage. They shared the following:

> While God has gifted us with a deep love for each other, the strength of our relationship hasn't come without a committed willingness to

> be both vulnerable and safe. Our greatest conversations have ridden on the critical nonverbal parts of communication: the countenance of our faces, the expression in our eyes, the tones of our voices. The words can all be right, but if our bodies betray our words with a stern look or a harsh tone, any meaningful conversation withers.

Our ability to successfully transmit, receive, and understand messages depends on our successful use of the communication pathways available to us. The spoken word is only one of these pathways, which are far more numerous and complex than most people realize. They are so important to human existence that we discover and begin to develop them even before we are born.

From the Beginning

Multiple studies have demonstrated that human beings are able to memorize sounds from the external world while in the womb, during the last trimester of pregnancy. The results of a study released in 2009 showed that the cries of newborns imitated the melody pattern of their families' native language just three to five days after they were born. French newborns tended to cry in a rising melody, while German newborns preferred crying with a falling melody. The patterns matched the characteristic differences of the two languages. It seems that humans, even before they are born, listen to the world around them and once they enter the world, attempt to imitate what they've heard. It is part of an effort to communicate and bond.[4]

The main developmental task of infancy, in fact, is to bond and gain a sense of trust with the primary caregivers. Though seemingly helpless and completely dependent on its caregivers, an infant is not simply a passive recipient of their attention. From the beginning, human development is a reciprocal process. The biological attributes and behaviors of human infants draw caregivers to them, ensuring that they receive what they need. So these little, apparently helpless human beings are actually their parents' interactional partners, equipped to obtain from them the very experiences they need in order to develop.[5]

When an infant gazes up into the face of a parent, it is a means of establishing a connection; gaze triggers gaze, and the result is the beginning of the infant's first social relationship. This process, which is crucial to the development of infant-parent bonding, is called gaze coupling.

Vocal interaction carries the bonding further. In the first few months of life, a child learns that his or her cry attracts an attentive parent. This discovery eventually provides a bridge to language. Trust grows when parents respond consistently; if a parent does not respond to the child's cries, trust is slower to develop. The back-and-forth exchange—first I make a sound, then you respond—establishes the pattern for conversation in the years ahead. Verbal communication is a dance of turn taking, and the first taking of turns is the cry and response.

By ten months of age, human babies learn to use gestures as well as cries to attract attention or make demands, and can even enjoy simple games: give and take the baby rattle, hide the baby rattle. By thirteen months babies usually shows signs of more elaborate communication patterns—babbling, singing, cooing—the first level of speech.

This is the path most babies follow. For children born without hearing, however, vocal interaction is severely limited and different. Bonding between these children and their parents requires a different approach.

Two Deaf Children

"Here he is, Mrs. Ogden, a beautiful baby boy."

The nurse handed me to my mother, Dorothy Coblentz Ogden, and she cradled me in her arms for the first time. It was

February 15, 1949, at King's Daughters Hospital in Staunton, Virginia. As she gazed into my eyes, my mother drew in her breath in surprise. Even in those initial moments, she sensed the challenging journey ahead. The clue was the loose way I held my head. It indicated I had no sense of balance, a common characteristic of babies who have hearing loss, which is often accompanied by a damaged equilibrium.

My mother picked up on my deafness because of my brother, Jonathan. I was the actually the fourth (and last) son born to Dunbar Ogden Jr. and Dorothy Ogden. My oldest brother, third in a line of Dunbars, arrived first, in 1935. David followed a year later. Jonathan was born in 1938.

As Jonathan grew, my parents noticed he seemed weaker than his brothers were at the same age. He didn't sit up when he should have been able to. My parents attributed this weakness to the fact he was born so close to his brothers. But as time went on, they noticed he did not seem to recognize sounds as he should. One day, my mother realized that whenever Jonathan saw her he thrust his arms up to her, wanting to be picked up. But when his face was turned away, he didn't respond to her even when she called him. She would be a few feet behind him and would repeat his name, yet there would be no reaction.

Still, the fact that Jonathan was deaf eluded my parents until he was about three. It took an inordinately long time before a doctor confirmed their suspicions. During the lengthy, emotional process, one doctor actually declared that Jonathan was mentally retarded. It was a difficult diagnosis for my parents to shake off, but finally another doctor ruled it out and convinced them that the problem was deafness.

In the early 1940s, there was almost no accurate information about deafness. Special public services for parents of deaf children did not exist. After Jonathan's diagnosis, my mother and father began the slow process of collecting information and skills they would need to raise a profoundly deaf child. When I was born, their experience with Jonathan equipped them to more easily prepare me for a life without sound. They understood it was vital that their deaf children be given every tool possible to communicate with the outside world.

When I came along eleven years after Jonathan, my mother knew what to do immediately. Hearing babies soon recognize the sound of their own cries and link the response of caregivers to their vocalizations. They learn that if they cry long and loud enough, someone will show up. In my case, however, as for any profoundly deaf baby, I could not hear my own cry or my mother's soothing voice. My mother understood that she had to rely on other methods. If I was upset, she picked me up or otherwise made sure that I could see her. She gently stroked my face, comforting me by tactile means. She made sure I would not miss out on the natural bonding process between mother and child.

When I grew older, my mother used several techniques to develop my communication ability. She cut out pictures, pasted them on cardboard, and wrote their names on the bottom. She taped labels to pieces of furniture and other practical objects, all with the idea of stimulating language. She practiced by asking me to bring her different things, forcing me to understand what she said by reading her lips. She had me work on numbers and was always printing something for me on cardboard. If I could not hear, she was determined to make me proficient at other means of communication.

A New Vocabulary

My parents' experience with Jonathan saved me from years of frustrating interaction with my family and professionals. From him, my family learned that deafness affects hearing and speech, but *not* the natural desire to communicate.

Jonathan's deafness inspired my family to focus on nonverbal communication. This made them aware of their bodies as well as their speech. They learned to sharpen their perceptions about gestures, postures, and facial expressions, and to expressively use these elements when communicating with Jonathan. By the time I came along, my family, especially my mother and brothers, were experts in nonverbal communication.

In my early years, as with any young child, much of what I needed to get across involved my feelings and curiosities. These messages came through in body language, and my family responded to me immediately. All families respond to their babies' expressive motions, but they usually treat such movements as informative only. The baby smiles: it is content. The baby cries: it is wet or hungry. Their babies' expressions and gestures give them pleasure, but it is not until the children learn to talk that many parents think of them as communicating beings.

My family had a special reason to concentrate on my vocabulary of body movements, gestures, and sounds. By learning to read my body language and my noises, they moved closer to participating in an ongoing conversation with me as valid and informative as any verbal exchange. Eventually, we developed a system of signs and signals that seemed to be born out of our subconscious.

It helped that my family was naturally physical. My mother held me and hugged me often. My brothers and father, who had been a wrestler in college, wrestled with each other and with me. We played many physical games and boxed each other around—activities that sometimes led to fights among the older boys, though they were surprisingly careful with me.

I remember playing "airplane" with my father. He lay on his back on the floor with his feet straight up, while I leaned my stomach against the soles of his feet and balanced in the air. My dad also flipped me. He lay on his back, supporting me by the shoulders with his hands, my hands on his knees while he kept my body straight up in the air. Then he would flip me over so that I would land back on my feet. He did that with all of us boys. We performed many other daring acrobatics. My mother always watched, as mothers do, with a little trepidation.

For a small boy who could not hear the warmth expressed in words and tone by mother, father, or brothers, these physical exchanges were a graphic way to communicate with me. Without the use of the spoken word, my family told me how much they loved and treasured me. They did so by "speaking" a language I understood.

Unfortunately, some parents of deaf children are less sensitive to the potential benefits of nonverbal communication. They may not notice its effect on their children or may not take the time to investigate the advantages. Sometimes this lack of awareness is a manifestation of the parents' intense wish that their child be "normal." They think, *If he could only learn to speak, he wouldn't be deaf anymore, he would be just like everyone else.* Desperately hoping that their child will learn to speak, these parents focus on the spoken mode of expression to the exclusion of other modes. This attitude leads parents to suppress their own nonverbal communication. They are so intent on helping their deaf children acquire spoken language skills that they mute their facial expressions and gestures and deprive their children of physical clues to the meaning of their spoken messages. These parents don't want to distract their child's attention from words. They forget, or don't know, that by suppressing these natural forms of expressiveness they are stripping away a large percentage of the content of normal social conversation. In addition, many of these parents find it too much work to speak frequently with their deaf children, depriving their kids of the practice they need. A few parents and educators even put a condition on their communication with deaf children, making it clear that they will do what the children want only if the children express their messages in spoken words that everyone can understand. How discouraging! Consider how you would react if someone you felt close to—a relative, say, from another country—suddenly exclaimed, "Don't talk to me in English, ever! Learn to speak my language or don't speak to me again!"

No one knows children better than their parents, of course, and each family must choose the communication approach that will be most effective for that individual child. When well-meaning parents insist that their deaf children adapt to the parents' preferred method of communication, however, they can send an unintended message: We're not willing to communicate in the manner most comfortable to you; you're not worth the effort. To their child, it may feel like rejection and create a barrier that can be difficult or impossible to overcome.

It's the same message I once received at a high school dance. When I asked a beautiful, expressive, blond cheerleader to dance with me, she didn't hesitate in turning me down. Her explanation was direct: "I don't want to dance with you because you're deaf." It wasn't because she didn't like me. She hardly knew me. She didn't want to make the effort to get to know me because I couldn't communicate using her preferred method.

The lesson applies just as much in reverse, of course. People who enunciate well and are expressive with their face and hands are easier for me to lipread and understand than others. People who mumble, look away when they talk, cover their mouth, or have a heavy mustache are difficult to lipread. In high school, if I couldn't read someone's lips, I often didn't want to bother with them. They didn't pass my test. Who knows how many friendships I missed out on because I wasn't willing to take that first step toward closing our gap in communication?

It's one thing when poor communication prevents a relationship from getting started. It's more intense, however, if you suddenly discover you can't communicate with your wife.

Different Interpersonal Styles

That first summer in Berkeley, Anne and I knew we needed help—though each of us was sure the other needed it most. Anne said I needed to go to counseling so I could learn how to deal with my health problems. I said she needed to go so we could figure out our marriage conflicts.

Soon enough, with the help of a counselor named Carla, we began to learn that we'd come into our marriage with differing expectations and differing styles of communication. I discovered that my soul mate, the person with whom I had so much in common, was my opposite in a number of ways. Today, looking back on that time, I can see six major differences in our approach to each other and our problems. Maybe you can relate to some of them as well.

1. Emotional vs. Logical

In their political views, my father was a staunch liberal and my mother a conservative. They continually shared their views and opinions about the world with all of us in the family, yet I never heard them argue about anything. We always discussed such issues in a calm manner, usually over the dinner table. My parents were rational people who were comfortable with disagreement. My father's role as a public figure, a pastor, probably further served to constrain any outbursts he might have been tempted to display. I grew up with the idea that this was how families behaved. People discussed issues in level voices, using logic and often humor to present ideas and persuade others to a specific point of view.

Anne's childhood experience was far different. If her father and mother were upset about something, it was common for them to vent their emotions in loud voices in front of the children. Before our marriage, the conversations between Anne and me took place in stress-free environments. Little was going on in our lives to raise the level of tension between us, so our conversations were calm and rational. That's why Anne's behavior was a shock to me when we started having disagreements after we married. She yelled. She paced. She banged on countertops and walls.

"I can't discuss this with you if you blow up," I'd say to Anne. "You have to calm down and sit quietly for this discussion, or I can't listen to you."

She couldn't do it.

2. Now vs. Later

Related to Anne's need to express her emotions was a strong desire to discuss important matters right away. At the end of our first date, we sat drinking coffee at the kitchen table in her apartment. Anne wrapped her hands around her mug and locked her blue eyes on mine. "So, Paul," she said, "what do you want out of this relationship?"

I leaned back with surprise. *I can't believe she asked that,* I thought. *She's very straightforward.* On the other hand, I decided, it might be nice to get everything out in the open from the beginning.

What I appreciated when we dated, however, began to irritate me after we married. If Anne brought something up and my thoughts were elsewhere or I simply wasn't sure of my opinion, I didn't have an answer for her. I needed time to think. This bothered Anne.

"Please hurry," she'd say. "Tell me what you're thinking. Don't keep me waiting." Another time when I was at a loss for words, she explained why my lack of response was so upsetting. "If you don't answer right away and tell me what's on your heart, I feel you're not being honest with me," she said. "You need to share right away."

Too often, I couldn't do it. Men and women seem to be quite different in this way. Generally, women react quicker and are more verbal.

3. Concise vs. In Depth

It's been said that the average female speaks twenty thousand words per day, while the average male finds it necessary to utter only seven thousand words per day. In our case, there were times when the ratio seemed closer to a hundred thousand to one.

During many of our discussions, I couldn't understand Anne's habit of rehashing the issue before us. She seemed to say the same thing over and over. The words weren't always the same, but as far as I could tell, the meaning was. Anne wanted to explore our problems from every angle. For me, two or three times were more than enough. When I was ready to move on, Anne was not. I believe many people share this approach.

4. Listen vs. Fix

One of the ways I tried to shorten our lengthy discussions was to offer solutions. If I could just solve the problem, I figured, Anne would be happy, we'd have nothing more to talk about, and I could get back to whatever I was doing. When the conversation went too long, my response was, "Do this. Change that."

This did not work so well, however. Instead of making Anne happy, she seemed to get more frustrated with me. It took me a long time to realize that she wasn't seeking my input. Instead of fixing her problems, she just wanted me to listen to her.

5. One-on-One Time vs. Other Priorities

Anne especially valued our time together. She was accustomed to focusing on just a few close relationships, and she naturally wanted to make her husband her top relationship priority. With me immersed in my dissertation, however, she couldn't do that. Even when we were together, my mind was often distracted. It left her feeling blocked and rejected.

I, on the other hand, had grown up in a household with frequent visitors. My father regularly invited people over—

members of his congregation, old friends, or someone he'd just met—for dinner or to talk, and I followed in his footsteps. I was used to having many friends, and thought nothing of inviting people to our home. I enjoyed sharing my time with Anne with a group of people. It felt comfortable and natural. Yet for Anne, it was another obstacle to the intimate relationship she desired with me.

6. Assertive vs. Accommodating

When Anne and I were in a restaurant and received poor service—say, the waiter was ignoring us—we dealt with the problem in different ways. Anne would wave down a waiter or even get up to find a manager and insist that someone take our order right away. My approach to changing the waiter's attitude, meanwhile, was to be especially nice when he did show up so as to (I hoped) win his cooperation.

We brought similar approaches to our marriage. In general, Anne's response to problems between us was to become more demanding. It often pushed me away. I felt she was too aggressive and unreasonable. Yet I didn't know how to confront her. I attempted to resolve issues by becoming more accommodating toward Anne, but that often didn't work either. She felt I wasn't assertive enough.

The First Secret

The long list of differences between us might have been enough to discourage anyone. I wondered if it was possible to achieve the trusting, joyful, intimate marriage that Anne and I both dreamed of. Yet I knew that I loved Anne and that she loved me. I also had seen up close how love—combined with authentic and vulnerable communication—can bridge even the widest of canyons between two people.

I already knew a couple named Eugene and Brenda when I ran into them during my second date with Anne, a New Year's Eve party in Piedmont, California. They were such opposites, it was like something out of a comedy act: he was deaf, she was hearing; he was French-Canadian, she American; he was Catholic, she Baptist; he was a teacher of the deaf, she a speech pathologist; he was white, she was black. They had recently married, and one might surmise that with so many strikes against them, their relationship was doomed to fail. Yet by the way they looked at each other and talked and laughed with each other, it was obvious they had worked through these differences so successfully that I couldn't help seeing a bright future for them. Anne and I were amazed at them, and said as much that night. "Love conquers all" was Brenda's explanation. Today, more than thirty years later, they are still happily married.

If Eugene and Brenda could do it, why couldn't Anne and I? We loved each other. We were committed to each other. Why, then, did we have so much trouble communicating? What were we missing?

What I didn't realize was that I'd forgotten one of the earliest lessons of my childhood. My mother's efforts to teach me to lipread, my father's affectionate and physical games, my brothers' consistent willingness to include me in their roughhousing, everyone's efforts to understand my sometimes halting speech—this was love expressed through the communication styles most comfortable and effective *for me.*

Though I would not have articulated it this way at the time, the first step for Anne and me toward changing our marriage was to discover a simple yet powerful secret:

Successful communication requires reaching out on the other person's terms.

What seems obvious at first becomes astonishing when we realize just how rarely we do this. When put into regular practice, however, our efforts to communicate with the important people in our lives on their level can be transforming. It can take our relationships to places we never thought possible.

To borrow from our earlier illustration, it can expand our balloon collection so that it fills the sky.

Even more significant is what this means for our faith and our relationship with God.

Anne and Paul at a pre-wedding party in Santa Barbara, California in 1978

Paul and Anne on their delayed honeymoon trip to the Pacific Northwest in the summer of 1978

Paul with his parents in Berkeley, California, a few weeks before his father passed away in 1978

2

Our Relentless God

God is calling you to a passionate love relationship with Himself. Because the answer to religious complacency isn't working harder at a list of do's and don'ts—it's falling in love with God.

Francis Chan

During my last year of graduate school at the University of Illinois in Champaign-Urbana, I lived in a comfortable apartment with a striking view of the sycamore-lined street that led into the Illinois campus. I was alone, however, and the apartment began to feel more than a trifle desolate. Except for the vibrations of my footsteps across the floor and the movement of my chair when I pulled it up to my desk in the mornings, the flat was unnaturally still. It was the perfect time, I decided, to get myself a dog.

Lox was a puppy, half Labrador and half German shepherd, a scruffy survivor rescued from the local pound. I had no experience training dogs, but as a student minoring in psychology, I was confident that my knowledge of the theories of behavioral scientists, combined with a little common sense, were all I needed.

I was right. I moved my work materials into the apartment's kitchen and confined Lox there as well. Whenever he started showing signs of having an "accident," I swooped him up and tossed him outside. Lox quickly got the message, and within two days he was scratching at the kitchen door whenever he needed to relieve himself. Teaching the command "come!" was next. I tied a rope to Lox's collar, and every time I signaled "come!" I pulled the rope to me. Lox's reward for walking to my side was a piece of cheese or raw beef. It took only a few more days for him to master this maneuver without the rope.

I didn't begin my training of Lox with a lecture about the relationship between master and animal or the social benefits of relieving oneself in acceptable ways. I recognized intuitively that I had to speak "dog." I had to communicate in ways my dog would understand. Though we may see clearly how to exchange information with animals, the results we desire can easily elude us when the target is another human being.

Socrates, as described in Plato's *Phaedo,* said that a person must communicate with others in terms of their experience. If you are a doctor and you try explaining a medical diagnosis to your patient in technical terms she's never heard before, your message won't get through. When you use lay terms she's familiar with, however—arm, leg, bone, muscle—you'll be understood. If you attempt to describe the crowded conditions on New York City streets to someone who's never been out of Minnesota and say, "It's a little like Chicago," the reaction may be a puzzled look. If you're a thoughtful communicator, you'll search for an example the person can relate to: "It's a little like the Great America mall on the day after Thanksgiving."

Successful communication requires reaching out on the other person's terms. If that's true, we must think about who we're attempting to exchange information with, identify their preferred communication style, and respond accordingly.

Most people are primarily either readers or listeners. They absorb information more efficiently one way and less so the other. In 1963, when Lyndon Johnson assumed the U.S. presidency after the assassination of Jack Kennedy, he inherited Kennedy's staff. They continued to write reports for their new boss just as they had for the previous one. But Johnson, unlike Kennedy, wasn't a reader. He was a listener. The staff's efforts were largely ineffective because Johnson was more comfortable gathering knowledge by the spoken word.[1]

Consider another illustration from the workplace. Men, in general, prefer to solve problems on their own and ask for help only if necessary. Women, in general, prefer to collaborate and will begin solving a problem by seeking others' input. This was the case for a supervisor named Jerome and a staff member named Karen who was responsible for solving a problem.

> When [Karen] enters Jerome's office, she clearly has an idea about what needs to be done but doesn't immediately say so. She presents the problem and asks Jerome what he thinks should be done. He gives the obvious solution and she agrees it is a good idea. She then moves on to implement it.
>
> She walks out of the meeting thinking she has proven how conscientious and competent she is. This, however, is not Jerome's perspective. After the meeting, Jerome quietly wonders, "Why did she come to me? What a waste of time. The solution was obvious. I'm not sure she is capable of doing this job."[2]

Karen isn't incompetent; she just has a different communication style. She could have avoided leaving the wrong impression by being direct and letting Jerome know she'd already come up with a solution to the problem. Jerome, meanwhile, could have avoided making an erroneous conclusion about Karen's abilities by recognizing her natural tendency toward inclusion. It's the wise employee—and boss—

who takes into account their colleague's experience and preferred communication style.

Parents must also be discerning when communicating with their children. When a mother or father needs to have a serious conversation with their four-year-old, they—like the doctor described above—will be most effective if they use words their toddler understands. But reaching out on the other person's terms involves much more than word choice. In the case of the toddler, the physical stance of the parent can dramatically influence the way the parent's message is received. A father who towers over his daughter as he speaks may be perceived as authoritarian or even threatening. The same father, when he drops to his knees so he can be eye level with his daughter, communicates an unspoken desire to enter her world and see things from her perspective. This is a small gesture that expresses a great deal. It is an act of respect and love.

The ways we express love is the focus of the popular book series by psychologist and author Dr. Gary Chapman. In his books, Chapman describes five "love languages" and postulates that we all have a preferred method for receiving love. These five are:

- Words of affirmation.
- Physical touch.
- Quality time.
- Acts of service.
- Gifts.

Chapman advises us to study the people we're close to, learn their love language, and "speak" to them in the way that best communicates our affection from *their* point of view (though he stresses it's important to continue expressing ourselves through all of the love languages). For parents, this means helping their children through the trials of early childhood and adolescence by demonstrating love in a manner they appreciate and understand. If a daughter's primary love language is physical touch, for example, an extra dose of hugs is called for.

When our toddlers grow into teenagers, we may find that what communicated effectively in the past isn't as effective today. A mother named Patsy described this frustration: "I've known for a long time that Teddy's primary love language is words of affirmation. I've always verbally affirmed him but now that he's fourteen, he is saying to me, 'Mom, don't say that. Mom, stop saying that. Mom, I don't want to hear that.' It's very confusing to me. I say things like, 'You are the greatest. I'm so proud of you. You are so smart. You are so good-looking.' Things I've always said."

Teddy's love language hasn't changed, but his dialect has. He's growing up, is adopting a more independent and adult view of life, and wants to be treated accordingly. He's ready to hear more mature expressions of love: "I admire the strong stand you took for racial equality…I appreciate your hard work on the lawn…I trust you because I know you respect the rights of others." He's also ready to be called "Ted."[3] The challenge for parents who want to reach out to their children on their kids' terms is recognizing the often subtle, and sometimes overt, shifts in those terms.

What does this all mean for the most intimate of relationships—marriage? During our difficult first years together, Anne and I slowly began to find out.

Making It Work

We'd managed to get a few things right. At the start of our marriage, Anne and I made it a rule to never bring up the word *divorce* even in our heated conversations. It was one small way to demonstrate our commitment to each other and to avoid planting seeds of doubt. We also tried our best to avoid the word *you*, as in, "You didn't put away the dishes." The phrase,

"It looks like someone didn't put away the dishes" conveyed the same meaning. Even better was the neutral statement, "The dishes haven't been put away."

Though we were new Christians, we were also familiar with this admonishment from the apostle Paul: "Do not let the sun go down while you are still angry, and do not give the devil a foothold" (Ephesians 4:26-27). How often we had to remind ourselves to put these words into practice! Yet it did allow us to wake up each day with a fresh start.

All three of these rules or principles helped us control the simmering anger between us. We learned from our counselor and others that there was much more we could do. One of the most significant techniques for us was giving each other the freedom to announce, "I have something to say." It was the cue for getting out a watch and setting aside ten minutes (or longer if needed) for one person to speak and the other to simply listen without interruption, correction, or giving a defense. The receiver was also expected to not take these comments personally.

This helped resolve several of our frustrations. It gave Anne the opportunity to get her emotions out. It took away the pressure on me to produce an immediate response, and also prevented me from offering quick "fix-it" solutions when Anne really wanted me to just focus on what she was saying. It gave Anne the chance to explore an issue thoroughly in words, yet I didn't feel stressed because I knew there was a time limit for the discussion.

We discovered another method for improving our communication and marriage—separation. My sister-in-law, Annegret Ogden, advised Anne to get out of the house and travel if I was working on a major project like the dissertation. Anne was initially shocked to hear this. As a new wife, she felt she should be at her husband's side. But Annegret was insistent: "That's what I do when Dunbar's writing. It's all right. It's temporary. When Paul's finished, you'll both be happy again. Trust me." In our case, it was the right advice. Anne traveled around California with a friend, which relieved the pressure on me to give Anne the attention I wanted to give her while still focusing on the dissertation.

The most significant changes we made, however, were founded on the loving act of recognizing and reaching out on the other's terms. I gradually learned when to offer solutions and when to simply allow Anne to express her feelings, even if they were accompanied by a bucketful of emotions. Anne began giving me the freedom to think on an issue for a day or two before I responded to her questions.

I also made an effort to talk with Anne first before inviting friends over, and I cut back on these social gatherings in order to spend more one-on-one time with Anne, which I realized I enjoyed immensely. Anne, meanwhile, grew more and more comfortable with my friends and with hosting people she didn't know well in our home, to the point that she now looks forward to having ten or fifteen people over for a party (though there are still times when she finds herself "peopled out").

We've also moved closer to the other's terms in the areas of assertiveness and accommodation. Once, for example, we were out for dinner at a restaurant. The overhead lighting for our booth was dark, so Anne asked our waitress to turn up the light, which she did. The light fixture in the booth next to us, however, must have been on the same electrical circuit. When the couple sitting there noticed the increase in light, they had *their* waitress turn their light—and ours—back down.

I was ready to let the situation go, but Anne was not. In the past, I might have tried to discourage Anne from pursuing the matter further or simply said nothing, implying that I felt it wasn't worth it. This time, however, I encouraged her. "If it bothers you," I said, "we should tell them to turn it back up." By supporting her assertiveness, I was communicating more than agreement. It was a way of saying to Anne, "Your feelings are important to me." We did get the light turned back up, which led to an amicable solution—the man in the next booth reached up and unscrewed his light bulb, bringing out smiles all around.

Each of these changes represented a shift that enabled Anne and me to communicate better. At the same time, they conveyed unspoken messages of love, appreciation, caring, and respect. That's the underlying implication behind reaching out in a way that is easier for the other person—that this person's feelings and comfort *matter*. Wouldn't you rather communicate with someone who shows this level of concern?

I've seen this principle at work countless times in my life, most dramatically in my own marriage. Recognizing and reaching out on another's terms is one of the fundamental methods for turning a rocky relationship into a strong one. It can forever transform communication between two people.

But just how comprehensive is this idea? Is what works for people also effective in the spirit world? What about communication between a flesh-and-blood person and the invisible, all-knowing Creator of the universe? Is communication as we know it even possible with God?

When God Fails to Meet Our Expectations

A woman named Patty faked one smile after another for friends at her thirty-fifth birthday party. She blew out the candles on her cake at the appropriate moment, groaned as expected while opening gag gifts such as a cane and bottle of Geritol, and laughed at everyone's jokes. On the outside, she gave the appearance of having a good time. On the inside, she was dying.

Only when she was alone in the kitchen with her best friend, Lynn, did Patty reveal her true feelings. For eight years, she and her husband had attempted to conceive. They'd tried a fertility procedure. Nothing had worked. Now she feared that time was running out—and that God had abandoned her.

"Why don't I get pregnant?" Patty asked. "Where's my assurance that God loves me?...God can't say no forever, can He? After all, the psalms say to 'delight yourself in the Lord, and He will give you the desires of your heart.' And I desire a baby of my own more than anything else. It's okay if God doesn't choose to give me other blessings. He doesn't need to give me a fancy home, a new car, fame, or fortune. I just want a baby! Is that too much to ask?"[4]

How do we answer Patty? How do we answer the teenager who prays to heaven for healing from leukemia, the battered wife who asks God for an escape route, the unemployed and destitute father who seeks guidance in finding that elusive job, the spiritual seeker who longs simply for some evidence that the Lord is listening and that He cares?

What do we say to the man, woman, or child who feels entirely cut off, unable to connect in even the remotest manner with a supposedly loving God?

Perhaps part of the answer begins with an exploration of the expectations we bring to the relationship. As Anne and I discovered early in our marriage, expectations influence every aspect of communication between two parties, for better and worse.

So what do we humans expect of God?

History shows that many of us have looked (and are still looking) for a conqueror, a political and military leader who will subdue evil people and nations and raise up the just in what might be called a benevolent dictatorship here on earth.

Some of us today imagine God as a kind of heavenly genie whose purpose is to grant us wishes. Depending on your religion or philosophy, those wishes can be earned through good works, through sincerity (think of Charles Shultz's Linus in the pumpkin patch), via bartering ("If You'll do this for me, Lord, here's what I'll do for You..."), or by the absence of evil actions.

Others see God as a source and product of energy, present in all things, including ourselves. According to this philosophy, there is no separation between people and deity; we are all connected to the same energy, and have a responsibility to send positive energy into the world.

Many people who consider themselves Christians also adhere to one or more of these beliefs. Those who follow the traditional interpretation of the Bible, however, recognize the scriptural flaws in each. The orthodox Christian perceives God not as a conqueror, genie, or cosmic energy, but as a spiritual being who possesses the characteristics of a distinct person, complete with decision-making intellect, emotions, and an ability to relate to others. For me it is at once comforting and frightening, a mind-bending concept—the all-powerful creator of heaven and earth shares many of the same qualities that make us who we are.

Many, but not all. And there, perhaps, lies the problem. So often, recognizing God's relational tendencies, we want to fill in the rest of the picture by making Him entirely human. We desire a physical being, someone we can see, hear, and touch, even smell and taste. We prefer a deity we can relate to in a manner that's comfortable for us.

We want to communicate with God on our terms.

Outer Limits

Author Philip Yancey speaks to our yearning to connect with a physical manifestation of God in this story about a trip to the Philippines and a church that housed an ebony statue of Jesus.

> Pilgrims, some of whom crawl on their knees for miles to approach the statue, line up to touch its

> toes. They used to kiss the toes, but wear and tear on the statue prompted the church to cover it in Plexiglas, with only a cutout for the toes. Unfortunately for the undersized Filipino pilgrims, authorities also elevated the statue, so the faithful must jump high to touch the sacred toes. Now long lines of short people shuffle up to a certain point, then leap like basketball dunkers to reach the statue's toes, which are again showing signs of wear. Once a year the church allows the Black Nazarene to come outside in a public procession, and most years people get trampled to death in the frenzy.[5]

Our desire to see and touch a physical representation of holy power is strong. It was so when the Israelites constructed a golden calf. It is so today when hundreds of people flock to an office building window, a soybean oil tank, a living room shrine built around a tortilla, or any place that purportedly reveals an image of Christ.

This may help us understand the second commandment: "You shall not make for yourself an idol in the form of anything in heaven above or on the earth beneath or in the waters below" (Exodus 20:4). The text notes for the New International Version of the Bible explain further: "Because God has no visible form, any idol intended to resemble him would be a sinful misrepresentation of him."[6] It appears the Lord knows us well enough to recognize that we will struggle in this area.

We've already seen that we have little trouble accepting the idea that there are limits to our ability to communicate with animals. My old friend Lox was a faithful companion for nine years, yet never once did I ask for his help with my graduate studies. I understood without question that it was beyond his ability to articulate or comprehend. It's silly to even suggest it. Yet we often struggle with the concept that there are limits on our ability to connect and communicate with God.

No matter how much we resist the notion, sooner or later we must confront the unavoidable truth: "God is spirit" (John 4:24). He is like the air. We know the air is there, and that we depend on it for life itself, yet we cannot register it through our five senses. They are no help to us, just as they appear to be no help in detecting spirit. God's presence cannot be identified in the same manner as that of a human being. This leaves us with a formidable barrier to our efforts to forge a relationship with Him.

There is another barrier to communicating with the Lord: God is...well, God. He is bigger, more powerful, more awesome, more *everything* than our words can describe or our minds can accept. There is a reason why God said to Moses, "I will cause all my goodness to pass in front of you, and I will proclaim my name, the Lord, in your presence. I will have mercy on whom I will have mercy, and I will have compassion on whom I will have compassion. But you cannot see my face, for no one may see my face and live" (Exodus 33:19-20). To see God is to be overwhelmed to the point of death.

Life in the twenty-first century includes many marvels. For years, NASA has sent so many shuttles and probes into outer space that scientific exploration of the solar system is considered routine. Companies are developing edible chips that can track when and if patients take their pills and can monitor heart rate, body temperature, state of wakefulness, and more. Plant products such as soybean, corn, canola, and cotton seed oil are genetically modified to make them more resistant to herbicides and improve nutritional content.

Yet through these advances we have grown arrogant. We believe that science and technology have allowed us to remove mystery from our lives and our religion. We have forgotten the incredible and awful wonder of God. The Lord will not be defined by scientists nor confined by minds too closed to even sense the breathtaking power of "I Am": "For the LORD your God is God of gods and Lord of lords, the great God, mighty and awesome" (Deuteronomy 10:17).

Job also forgot for a time. When this faithful servant was afflicted with the loss of his family, property, and health, he pleaded with the Lord for an explanation: "Tell me what charges you have against me. Does it please you to oppress me, to spurn the work of your hands, while you smile on the schemes of the wicked?" (Job 10:2-3).

God reached across the great chasm separating heaven from humanity to respond with what so many of us yearn for—a tangible answer, in the form of a recognizable voice. It is a privilege granted to precious few throughout human history. Yet the Lord's words and tone were not the empathetic, encouraging reply many of us would hope for:

> Who is this that darkens my counsel with words
> without knowledge?
>
> Brace yourself like a man; I will question you,
> and you shall answer me. (Job 38:2-3)

In the words of Frederick Buechner, "God doesn't explain. He explodes. He asks Job who he thinks he is anyway. He says that to try to explain the kind of things Job wants explained would be like trying to explain Einstein to a little-neck clam…God doesn't reveal his grand design. He reveals himself."[7]

I suspect that to hear the answers that Job and everyone who suffers and doubts seeks—to know all as God knows all—would be just as overwhelming as seeing His face. It would mean our death. We must accept that just as there are limits on meaningful communication between people and canines and just as there are limits on interactions between deaf and hearing people, there are limits on communication between human beings and God.

What, then, are we to say to Patty, the woman who desperately wanted a baby—or at least a sign that God was aware of her pain? Are we doomed to stony silence every time we petition the Lord? Is God indifferent to our pleas?

I believe the answer is no. The reason I believe this is that God has so clearly demonstrated His desire to overcome the limits on our communication and reach out to us on our terms.

God Reaching Out

The author Dorothy Sayers writes that we will most easily comprehend God if we imagine Him as a creative artist. Our existence and purpose, according to Sayers, can be seen as the result of three stages: idea, expression, and recognition.[8] Every artist—writer, painter, composer, sculptor—begins with a concept. He then chooses a medium that best matches his abilities with the idea he plans to express and goes to work. But merely completing the project does not bring the process to an end. The artist's aim is not simply to create, but also to communicate. This is the final stage that Sayers described as recognition.

Every artist seeks a response to his work. He hopes that his idea will be understood and even enhanced by an exchange with the person viewing or hearing his work. It is another way, in a manner of speaking, of releasing a balloon into the world. The reward, once again, is seeing that balloon come back, with new balloons attached. Arthur Miller used to sit in the audience during performances of his new plays and watch the eyes of those around him. When he observed that glint of understanding—"My God, that's me!"—he knew his effort had succeeded. For Miller, recognition completed the creative cycle.[9]

I believe Sayers is on to something. Put simply, God had an idea that He expressed in the form of mountains, seas, animals, and human beings. But creating all this was not the end of the process. God desires *recognition*—a meaningful response to His artistry. Within the unavoidable limits that reside between Creator and created, He seeks to communicate not only to us, but *with* us.

We know from the Old Testament that on a few occasions, God spoke in a manner audible to human ears. Adam, Eve, Noah, Abraham, various prophets, and of course, Job, all heard God's voice, or at least a version of it they could understand. So did Moses, who also viewed a representation of God within a flaming bush.

I can't explain why these "conversations" aren't more common throughout history, particularly modern history. I know of a number of people who have claimed to hear the audible voice of God, but I can't help meeting this information with a healthy dose of skepticism. None of the people I count as close friends report this experience. As a deaf person, I have never heard anyone's audible voice, let alone God's. I cannot imagine what it would be like.

Perhaps in rare and extreme moments, these audible intrusions by God onto the turf of men and women are necessary, but unsatisfying from a heavenly perspective. Something more is required to bridge the vast gap between deity and humanity. Perhaps this helps explain the turning point in our existence—the birth of a holy child.

Jesus of Nazareth was God's ultimate effort to reach out on human terms. He made Himself flesh and blood, vulnerable to injury, pain, fatigue, and hunger like the rest of us. He was God on earth, a living and breathing physical being that we could converse with as easily and meaningfully as we do with our families.

Yet Jesus was not the Messiah that people of His time anticipated. Most assumed that if God made a physical appearance on earth, He would take the form of a mighty warrior or king. The trappings of such power, however, create distance, and God already knew what that was like. Imagine being suddenly ushered into the Oval Office for a meeting with the president of the United States. You'd probably have some difficulty relating to him. You might be nervous. You might manage some small talk, but it's unlikely you'd feel comfortable burdening him with your innermost struggles. You would not expect to begin and maintain an ongoing relationship with the most powerful leader on earth.

In Jesus, however, God achieved the opposite effect. Jesus was a common carpenter from a backwater town, someone who at first glance would not intimidate anyone. This was a guy that men and women could relate to. He was someone they could communicate with on their terms.

Once people found out that Jesus claimed to be more than a common man, however, they longed again for the powerful and intimidating version of God, perhaps one accompanied by fire, smoke, and thunderbolts. This usually soft-spoken Jewish Nazarene did not look or act like the God they imagined. One of His own disciples, Philip, said as much: "Lord, show us the Father and that will be enough for us" (John 14:8).

One can sense Jesus' exasperation in His reply: "Don't you know me, Philip, even after I have been among you such a long time? Anyone who has seen me has seen the Father. How can you say, 'Show us the Father?' Don't you believe that I am in the Father, and that the Father is in me?" (vv. 9-10).

Look at the progression from God's perspective. He breathes life into His children. He offers guidance by means of His audible voice, the Ten Commandments, and the wisdom of the prophets. Yet throughout the chronicles of the Old Testament, His children frequently reject and ignore the love and instruction of their mighty and holy Father. The relationship appears strained, perhaps because it is so distant. So God reaches out in the most radical way imaginable—He turns Himself into flesh and walks among us. Yet once again, His children reject Him. Now they find Him too ordinary, too like themselves, and so they crucify Him.

Yet God is not through. His desire to enter into relationship with His children is so strong that He establishes a new way to communicate. He gives us not only each other, but also the Holy Spirit.

God Within Us

After the resurrection, just before ascending into heaven, Jesus describes in His final words to the disciples the amazing new plan for linking God and humanity: "You will receive power when the Holy Spirit comes on you; and you will be my witnesses in Jerusalem, and in all Judea and Samaria, and to the ends of the earth" (Acts 1:8).

Ten days later, on Pentecost, the disciples receive the power Jesus spoke of: "Suddenly a sound like the blowing of a violent wind came from heaven and filled the whole house where they were sitting. They saw what seemed to be tongues of fire that separated and came to rest on each of them. All of them were filled with the Holy Spirit and began to speak in other tongues as the Spirit enabled them" (Acts 2:2-4).

How do we explain this strange and incredible gift? God is so enamored with us, so intent on connecting with us in an intimate manner, that He moves inside of us. In a mysterious way, the Holy Spirit works within us, providing power that enables us to fulfill our purpose—spiritual gifts which may include prophesying, teaching, encouraging, giving to others, governing, and showing mercy.

The Holy Spirit does more. He allows us to more effectively take the message of the gospel to the nations of the world. We see this evidence in the first moments of the Holy Spirit's arrival within the hearts and minds of the disciples, when they begin speaking fluently in languages they did not understand only moments before.

Perhaps most significant of all, the Holy Spirit enables us to more effectively communicate with our Creator. What could be more personal, more intimate, than relating with another from the inside out? Even when we cannot find the words, the Holy Spirit steps in on our behalf and presents our pleas to heaven: "The Spirit helps us in our weakness. We do not know what we ought to pray for, but the Spirit himself intercedes for us with groans that words cannot express. And he who searches our hearts knows the mind of the Spirit, because the Spirit intercedes for the saints in accordance with God's will" (Romans 8:26-27).

This is a God of mystery, but also a God of infinite compassion. Even when we continue to attempt to encounter God in ways that are comfortable for us yet do not work, He gives us new opportunities to connect. He is relentless in His efforts to establish a relationship with us.

Our efforts are often clumsy and misguided—at least mine frequently are—but I believe we too are desperately seeking this link between Creator and created. Frederick Buechner has described it this way:

> For what we need to know, of course, is not just that God exists, not just that beyond the steely brightness of the stars there is a cosmic intelligence of some kind that keeps the whole show going, but that there is a God right here in the thick of our day-to-day lives who may not be writing messages about himself in the stars but in one way or another is trying to get messages through our blindness as we move around down here knee-deep in the fragrant muck and misery and marvel of the world. It is not objective proof of God's existence that we want but the experience of God's presence. That is the miracle we are really after.[10]

If Buechner is right, perhaps we will be willing to give up the expectations that block us from God and trade them in for a new strategy, one that involves reaching out on His terms. My journey has shown me that meaningful communication with God *is* possible, and more rewarding and joyful than I'd ever imagined—if only we can learn to combine a fresh attitude with a different approach.

Allow me to share what I mean.

3

Made For Intimacy

No man is an island.

John Donne

We don't like to be alone.

I'm not talking about those welcome moments of relief after a challenging day at the office...after being trapped in a traffic jam with seven noisy elementary school soccer players...or after talking on the phone all morning with an uncooperative accountant to resolve a billing error. We certainly need and look forward to respites from responsibilities and relating with the mass of humanity. Even the most outgoing among us will savor a period of solitude after too much stimulation.

What I am referring to is prolonged isolation, whether physical or emotional. We are social beings, designed to connect and interact with a larger body than ourselves, just as the organs in our bodies are designed to function as part of a larger whole. From experience with organ transplants, we know that a heart can be preserved in ice for four to six hours outside of its former body and still be resuscitated in a new host, bringing life from death. Anything longer than those few hours, however, and the heart will not function. It must connect with a compatible set of organs in a new body or it will wither and die. It is much the same with human beings.

In the movie *Cast Away*, Tom Hanks plays a character, Chuck Noland, stranded on a deserted island in the South Pacific for four years. His need for companionship is so strong that he draws a face on a volleyball and names it "Wilson." Chuck has regular conversations and arguments with Wilson. Chuck builds a raft and sails away from the island, but after a storm, Wilson falls into the ocean and drifts irretrievably away. Chuck is so distraught over the loss of his "friend" that he drops his oars into the water and gives up. He's overcome many obstacles during his ordeal, but separation from Wilson is more than he can bear. Chuck is ready to die (though he's soon saved by a passing cargo ship).

Former presidential candidate John McCain faced a similar, real-life ordeal after his A-4 jet was shot down during a bombing run over Hanoi, North Vietnam. McCain parachuted out of the jet, was captured by North Vietnamese soldiers, and was taken to the infamous "Hanoi Hilton" prison camp. Badly injured during the ejection, McCain survived neglect, torture, and near starvation over the next five and a half years. For more than two of those years, McCain was confined alone to a tiny cell.

"It's an awful thing, solitary," McCain wrote in his biography. "It crushes your spirit and weakens your resistance more effectively than any other form of mistreatment. Having no one else to rely on, to share confidences with, to seek counsel from, you begin to doubt your judgment and your courage...The first few weeks are the hardest. The onset of despair is immediate, and it is a formidable foe."

McCain fought back with memory games, attempts at creating books and plays in his mind, and intense prayer. Yet it was human contact he valued most. Prisoners had invented a coded tapping system that allowed contact between cells when guards weren't around.

"Of all the activities I devised to survive solitary confinement with my wits and strength intact, nothing was more beneficial than communicating with other prisoners," McCain wrote. "It was, simply, a matter of life and death." Through these covert messages, McCain and his fellow captives kept track of the prisoners in camp. They treated it as a solemn responsibility.

"We would fall asleep at night while silently chanting the names on the list," McCain said. "Knowing the men in my prison and being known by them was my best assurance of returning home. Communicating not only affirmed our humanity. It kept us alive."[1]

John Donne, the seventeenth-century poet, once wrote that "No man is an island, entire of itself; every man is a piece of the continent, a part of the main." For humans, the state of being truly alone, cut off from meaningful contact with others, is devastating. The reason is that we've been designed to enter into, maintain, and enjoy relationships. Not just any relationship, either—the kind of communication we seek is most satisfying when it is heart to heart and soul to soul. We long, as John McCain wrote, to know and be known. We yearn to love and be loved. To fulfill one of our basic needs and purposes in life, we seek to experience *intimacy*.

We are easily confused by this purpose, however. The phenomenon of social media allows people to create a massive list of online "friends" without actually meeting any of them in person. It can become a superficial substitute for genuine, close relationships.

"At one point I realized I had a friend whose child I had seen, via photos on Flickr [a photo-sharing website], grow from birth to one year old," said Caterina Fake, one of the founders of Flickr. "But it was weird; I also felt that Flickr had satisfied that getting-to-know you satisfaction, so I didn't feel the urgency. But then I was like, 'Oh, that's not sufficient! I should go in person!' These technologies allow you to be much more broadly friendly, but you just spread yourself much more thinly over many more people."[2]

The increasing quantity of our relationships may be replacing their quality. If so, the shift is not in our favor.

Psychologist Lori H. Gordon has written that research and her personal observations of patients show that a lack of connection with other human beings leads to anger, depression, addiction, and illness. "Intimacy, I have come to believe, is not just a psychological fad, a rallying cry of contemporary couples," she wrote. "It is based on a deep biological need."[3]

I didn't appreciate all this as a young boy growing up in Staunton, Virginia. But it wasn't long before I discovered how vital such close and loving relationships were to me as well.

The Family Teddy Bear

From the beginning of my life, my entire family shared in the responsibility of caring for, protecting, and guiding me. My three brothers, especially, joined my mother in picking me up, talking to me, carrying me, changing my diaper, feeding me, burping me, and changing my sheets. My father was often away because of his duties as a pastor, but he too participated when he was available.

My affectionate and protective brothers called me "the Teddy Bear," no doubt because I was chubby with a round face. Their affection and my deafness certainly did not lead them to coddle me, however. One of my earliest childhood memories is of wanting to get on top of the garage at the back of our home when I was probably two years old. I remember gesturing to my family and pointing to the top of the garage. My parents didn't think it a good idea.

Finally, however, my brother Dunbar told me I could do it with his help. The fact that I had no sense of balance certainly must have entered his mind, but it didn't stop him. He encouraged me to climb up the ladder, so I went up with him climbing right behind me. He formed a sort of cage against the ladder, surrounding me with his arms in case I fell. When we got to the top, we crawled along the ridge, Dunbar still surrounding me on all fours. We kept crawling all the way to the roof peak, where we finally sat down. As I looked around at the yard below, I must have been very proud of myself, thinking, *Wow, I am high up here, aren't I!*

My brothers also showed me no mercy when it came to the teasing, games, and tricks they routinely played with and on each other. One favorite performed at the dining room table was for one of them to point with animation behind me, and while I turned to look for the source of the excitement, they hid my dessert. When I turned back, they pretended to be astonished at the disappearance of my cake or ice cream and began a search.

Another early memory is also from the dining room. We were eating green peas for supper. My father was away and Mother went into the kitchen for something. Dunbar and David each put a pea on his fork and flipped it across the table at me. To get revenge, I dug my spoon into my bowl and fired a salvo back at them—just as Mother reentered the dining room. They had heard her coming and timed it perfectly. Much to my brothers' delight, I was the one punished for throwing food!

My parents were naturally inclined to include their children in their discussions, even when these focused on the political, social, and moral issues of the day. Because Jonathan and I were deaf, they made even more of an effort to be sure we understood what was being said. My mother, especially, patiently mouthed without voice, repeating to me what each person in the room was saying.

Mother worked continually with me to develop my communication abilities. She brought out jigsaw puzzles, which helped me understand spatial relationships. As I put the pieces together, Mother spoke to me, encouraging me to lipread and imitate her. I formed many words on my lips and eventually burst out with my own voice.

My family also worked with me on pronunciation. I particularly recall struggling with Dunbar to master the word *potato*. Dunbar said the word and I repeated it, only I pronounced it "pay pay toe." Then he repeated the word with my hand held in front of his mouth, hoping that I would feel the breath and vibrations and be able to imitate this with my voice. Eventually I got it.

I learned much more in those early years, however, than how to fling peas and how to begin communicating as a deaf child in a hearing world. I also recognized that I was important to my family, that I belonged to them and they to me. Through the lessons and games and adventures and conversations, I developed a close and distinct relationship with both parents and each of my brothers. I understood at a deep level that they loved me.

This knowledge was essential for my survival in the years ahead.

Alone in St. Louis

After Jonathan's birth, my parents both felt it was important to prepare him for living successfully in a hearing society. My father graduated as valedictorian of his class from Davidson College in North Carolina. My mother graduated with high honors from the Conservatory School of Music, affiliated with the University of Cincinnati, at a time (the early 1930s) when it was unusual for a woman to even attend college. When an ear specialist recommended they provide Jonathan with the best possible education, it reinforced my parents' strong feelings about the value of education. Though we were a family of meager financial means, they began to visit schools for the deaf across the country.

In most cases, they were not impressed with what they observed. They found instructors who often lacked the specialized skills needed to work with deaf children. They also noticed that some teachers had little respect for their pupils. Once, for example, my mother saw a seven-year-old girl ask her teacher how old the teacher was. The teacher immediately slapped the girl's face and told her not to ask adults their age. The poor girl didn't understand the teacher, and my mother was shocked by the harshness of the punishment.

My parents' most consistent reaction to these visits was dismay at how little language the deaf children seemed to have and how poor their reading was. Both my parents came from families where everyone loved to read, and they wanted Jonathan to love reading as much they, Dunbar, and David did. My mother had always enjoyed reading to the boys at bedtime. My father even read to them during breakfast. My parents wondered how the deaf children they saw would acquire the incentive to read if they were not learning any vocabulary in the classroom.

Through advice and correspondence with friends and knowledgeable people, my parents finally decided that the best place for Jonathan was Central Institute for the Deaf (CID) in St. Louis, a residential school and one of the most renowned institutions for the deaf in the country. At CID, students seemed to use spoken language and read more than at other schools. The teachers seemed to know how to correct language errors and how to guide students in their reading.

The problem with CID was that it was a thousand miles away from home. It was always wrenching for Jonathan and my mother and father to say goodbye to each other, knowing they would not see each other again for months.

By the time I came along and approached school age, it was natural for my parents to decide to also send me to CID. Once again, however, they—and I—would have to deal with the painful trauma of separation.

I was just five years old when my parents drove me for the first time from our new home in Arkansas to the four-story brick school building in St. Louis. It was a special day, so I wore my favorite footwear: black cowboy boots with red spots. I understood that I would be going to school there. What I did not fully understand was that I would be left there alone.

The first few days at CID were an adventure for me, but it wasn't long before I grew homesick. I flew home for the Thanksgiving and Christmas holidays, which was exciting not only because I was returning to my family but also because they were my first airplane trips. Going back to Central Institute for the Deaf, however, was another matter.

The process was nearly always the same. As the day neared for me to return to school, I cried and said I didn't want to go back. Mother explained why I had to go. We looked at a calendar and counted the number of "sleeps" until I could come home again. I said I understood and stopped crying. But the next morning, knowing I had only one more "sleep" with my family, I cried again.

After going to bed that evening, I awoke in the middle of the night, walked around, talked to my parents, and cried some more. In the morning, I tried without success to convince my parents to let me stay.

At the airport I hugged Mother, Father, and my three brothers. My mother and I both cried. My brothers tried to make jokes. "Do you have your ticket?" Father asked.

"Yes," I said.

"Go on then."

There was nothing more for me to do but go. As I walked from the gate to the ramp, I cried yet again. On the plane, a stewardess read the note with my name and destination on it, and led me to my seat by the window. I always picked the window so I could see my family. They waved, bringing out more of my tears. Eventually I felt the doors being closed tight, the change in pressure, and the engines starting. I watched baggage handlers pull the ramp away from the plane. I waved frantically at my family.

At takeoff, I felt the wheels speed over lines on the concrete—thump, thump, thump. Then we lifted into the air. I looked back at the airport where I knew my family stood and watched it grow smaller and smaller. Finally, exhausted and resigned to my fate, I fell asleep.

At CID, I learned much and made new friends, but the sense of missing the most important people in my life was overwhelming. Anything to do with airplanes often brought back the intense emotions I associated with leaving my family. I recall a time when I was about eight and playing with toy planes in the CID dormitory. The other boys moved their planes around the table toward the "runway" and talked about taking off. Before I knew it, I was bawling.

It was around this time that I had one of the worst teachers I encountered at CID, Mrs. Larsen. She was not a natural teacher and was sometimes so impatient when we didn't obey or understand a lesson that she picked up the offender and shook him, as if the problem might fall out of his pocket like a marble.

Every Monday, students at CID wrote a letter in class to their parents. On one of these Mondays I was so homesick while writing my letter that I decided to add to the last line, "I love you very, very, very, very, very, very..." all the way to the bottom of the back page, with just enough room for me to add, "much. Paul." When Mrs. Larsen saw the letter, she gave it back it to me with one of her terrifying facial expression and said I had to erase all the extra "very verys." Why hadn't she simply asked me to rewrite the letter on another paper? The erasing took a long time. I was so unhappy at the thought that my parents would never see how much I cared for them (years later, I learned that my mother was able to read those faded words after all, which warmed her heart).

As much as I missed my parents and brothers, however, I did not blame any of them for sending me away. I understood that my parents believed it was important and would benefit me. More significantly, I understood that they loved me and that I was still a vital member of the family.

My parents communicated this message in a variety of ways. At Christmas vacation during that year of "terror" with Mrs. Larsen, Mother gave me her special scarf, which she wore often. It was just the right thing to carry back to school. The smell of my mother and her perfume was still in the scarf. Wearing and smelling it made me feel secure. It gave me a sense of her presence and helped me through some rough times.

Mother wrote me frequent letters, which was also a great comfort. They often contained pictures, drawings, or images cut out from newspapers and magazines, which further stimulated my education and communication skills.

It is possible that my years at CID actually helped foster a closer relationship between me and my parents. When I was home for the holidays or the summer, my parents and brothers gave me extra and focused attention. For example, Mother brought me along when she went grocery shopping or on other errands. She didn't want to miss any opportunity to spend time with me while I was home.

My father found different methods to show his love. One was during a trip I took with my parents to the Civil War battlegrounds in the large area around Gettysburg, Pennsylvania. We visited several memorials, but it was hard for me to visualize the scope of what had happened where. When we discovered a helicopter available for tours, I grew excited about the idea of viewing the battle scenes from above.

Mother was hesitant about the tour. She feared it was too expensive, and perhaps was leery of sending the rest of her family skyward in this metal contraption. My father, however, overruled her concerns. He convinced the tour guide to give us a thorough explanation of what we would see before we took off, because he knew if I watched the tour guide's speech while in the helicopter I'd miss everything else.

The flight delivered a vivid perspective. This historic war suddenly became real to me. I started to understand that battles are not always the well-organized affairs I'd seen on television and in movies.

Our tour also revealed how much my father cared about me and my education. He wanted to show me what the world was like and how I might interpret it. He placed importance on knowledge. The trip with him left me feeling not just more knowledgeable, but also valued and loved.

Without realizing it, I was discovering a deep truth: loving, intimate relationships give us the strength to overcome the most challenging of circumstances. I cherished the closeness and abiding sense of belonging I felt with my family, even when we were separated by hundreds of miles. I was learning about the value of human-to-human relationships.

What I did not understand then was that I had also been designed for another kind of close relationship, this one forged between human and Spirit.

Breaking Bread, Forging Bonds

A mealtime is a golden opportunity to make and maintain friendships. There is something in the shared experience of replenishing ourselves with a sandwich, a salad, a bowl of soup, or even a cup of coffee that breaks down barriers and encourages relaxed and heartfelt communication. One of my favorite pastimes is to invite someone over for a meal and talk about each other's interests and ideas about life.

I also fondly recall, starting when I was in graduate school, visiting my extended family in Berkeley and taking my nephew Christopher or niece Stephanie—teenagers—out to lunch or dinner, just the two of us, a tradition we continued until they got married. At these meals we talked for hours about people and events in their lives. In the years since, both have indicated how much they appreciated our talks. They say they try to imitate our individual lunches with their own children, especially now that their kids are becoming teenagers.

The phenomenon of forging bonds over a meal has been known and practiced since the beginnings of the human community. It is part of every culture. In some areas people embrace mealtime as a sacred moment or act, one that promotes goodwill between strangers, acceptance between friends, bonding of families, and connection among all. At every mealtime in these cultures, there is acknowledgement of God.

Jesus certainly understood this when He spotted a wealthy and unpopular tax collector named Zacchaeus in a sycamore tree and called, "Zacchaeus, come down immediately. I must stay at your house today" (Luke 19:5). It was an astonishing invitation. Jesus was a man of the people attracting crowds for His wise teaching and miraculous deeds. Zacchaeus was a man shunned by Jewish society, in part because he probably cheated his constituents. The invitation clearly implied that the Jewish Nazarene and the tax collector would dine together as friends, and Zacchaeus gladly accepted.

The people on the street saw everything that happened and muttered about Jesus to themselves, "He has gone to be the guest of a 'sinner'" (v. 7).

That is the point. Jesus seeks to dine with and establish a relationship with cheats, drunks, gossips, liars, addicts, and thieves. Sinners. That includes me, and I suspect it also includes you.

"Here I am!" Jesus announces in some of his last recorded words in the Bible. "I stand at the door and knock. If anyone hears my voice and opens the door, I will come in and eat with him, and he with me" (Revelation 3:20).

Eat with him, and he with me. Jesus is expressing more here than a wish to share a few words over a burger. He is speaking within the context of a culture that views meals as a central connection point. He is expressing His desire for intimate friendship, one that brings understanding and pleasure to both sides.

When I imagine Jesus extending this invitation that is also a promise, I see that His eyes and face are warm and expressive. His lips are easy to read. He gestures with His hands, demonstrating how He will "come in." He is careful and patient with His communication, making sure that everyone comprehends His message.

"We know also that the Son of God has come and has given us understanding, so that we may know him who is true" writes the apostle John (1 John 5:20). God took on the frailties of human flesh, died, and rose from His dark and damp tomb so that we might *know him*. I don't believe He went to all that trouble just to achieve a passing acquaintanceship. He created us so that we might know and love Him in a personal, intimate way, and vice versa.

Brennan Manning comments on the nature of this human-to-heaven relationship:

> In essence, there is only one thing God asks of us—that we be men and women of prayer, people who live close to God, people for whom God is everything and for whom God is enough. That is the root of peace. We have that peace

> when the gracious God is all we seek. When we start seeking something besides Him, we lose it. As [Thomas] Merton said in the last public address before his death, "That is his call to us—simply to be people who are content to live close to Him and to renew the kind of life in which the closeness is felt and experienced."[4]

Succinctly put, that is intimacy to me, and it leads us to the next secret for our journey:

We were made for deep relationship—with each other and with God.

When we fully understand and embrace this truth, it changes everything about how we approach our relationships with fellow humans and with the Lord. Facebook friendships simply are not enough. We want more. We desire something real. We seek an exchange that touches us at the core.

The apostle John expressed this same desire in his letter to a Christian woman and her children: "I have much to write to you, but I do not want to use paper and ink. Instead, I hope to visit you and talk with you face to face, so that our joy may be complete" (2 John 12).

So that our joy may be made complete is nearly the same phrase John uses in a previous letter (1 John 1:4), where he talks about sharing fellowship with God and Christ. I believe John is referring to both kinds of relationship in his letter to the lady—the human kind which is most rewarding when conducted face to face, and the fellowship-with-the-Father-and-Son kind that is central to our existence. Only when these are both realized do we discover the result we were created to experience—a joy that is fully satisfying and complete.

Ten-month-old Paul with his family (L to R: thirteen-year-old David, Mother, Father, eleven-year old Jonathan, fourteen-year old Dunbar) in 1949.

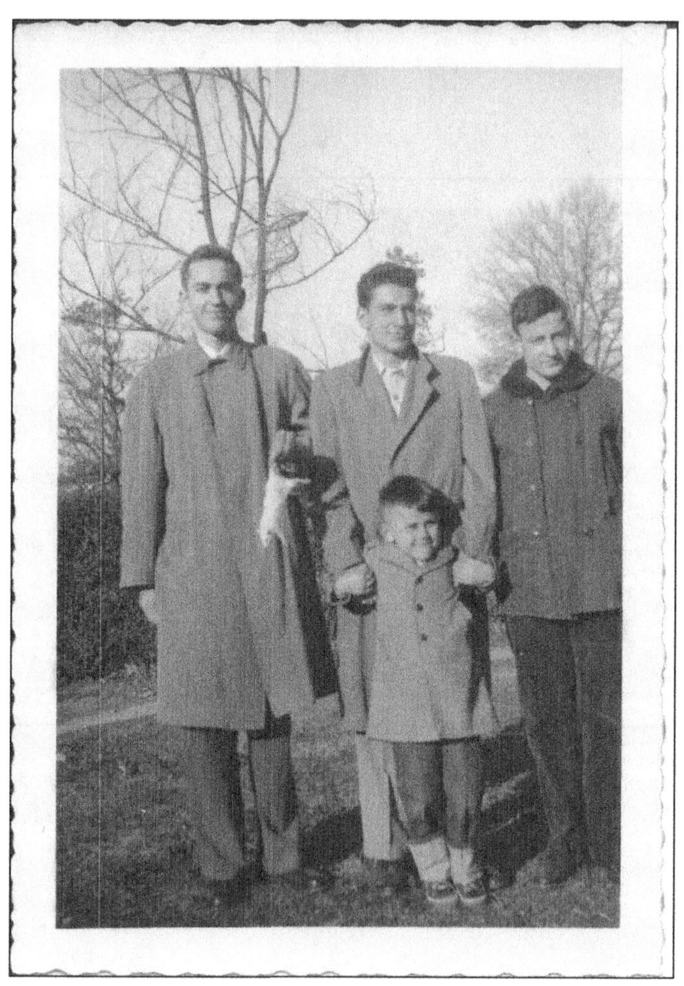

Paul with his three brothers: David holding George the rat by the tail, Dunbar clutching Paul's arms, and Jonathan.

Paul with his parents at the Central Institute for the Deaf graduation in St. Louis, Missouri in 1964, ending his many battles with homesickness. He had attended the private boarding school for ten years.

4

All People, All Nations

I have a dream that one day on the red hills of Georgia, the sons of former slaves and the sons of former slave owners will be able to sit together at the table of brotherhood.

Martin Luther King Jr.

Gail and Steven love rock music, and when their two daughters were old enough to appreciate it, the couple decided to take Anastasia and Annemarie along to concerts. Both daughters enjoyed the performances, but they experienced them in different ways. Anastasia was deaf, while Annemarie was hearing. Though Anastasia couldn't hear the music, she could absorb the excitement and visual stimulation. She felt the resonant beat and loved the crowds and colorful atmosphere.

Sometimes, though, Anastasia grew bored and irritable at the concerts, and her parents wondered if they expected too much of her. It seemed the only alternatives were giving up on these family events or leaving Anastasia out of the experience.

Steven thought long and hard until he hit upon a solution. He decided to show Anastasia how to discriminate among the various vibrations she heard through hearing aids and felt with her body, and how to relate them visually to individual instruments. At concerts, he acted out the sounds generated by one of the musicians, duplicating their rhythms with his hands. Then, moving as close to the stage as possible, he showed Anastasia which musician's hand movements matched his own. Once she caught on, Anastasia loved to stand up close and watch the performers. She was able to enjoy not only the crowds and atmosphere but, visually, the music as well. Steven's idea was a creative method of including Anastasia in a fun family activity.

I've already explained how hard my own family worked to communicate with me and make me feel part of everything going on. I was treated as one of the gang by my brothers and as an intelligent, contributing member of the team by my father and mother.

Unlike many parents, mine did not shield me from or gloss over most of the "grownup" issues they dealt with daily. I can remember, for instance, when they discussed a man named Gary who wanted seventy-five dollars from my father to buy a new mattress for his bad back. Mother explained to me that Gary was an alcoholic and strongly suggested to my dad that he buy the mattress himself, rather than give the money to Gary, so Gary wouldn't spend it on drinks.

As we talked about it over dinner, the telephone mounted on the wall in the kitchen rang. My father answered. It was Gary calling about wanting the money. Mother enunciated for me: "Your father says that it's better for him to go to the store and buy the right mattress instead of giving the money to Gary." Then Gary began yelling so loud that my mother could translate both sides of the conversation (I found it interesting to learn that hearing people could be heard through the phone from so far away).

"Gary says he wants the money now so he can buy the mattress himself," she said. "Gary's upset. He wants the money now, but we're not going to give it to him. It's a bad idea." Suddenly, while my father was talking, Gary hung up.

My father sat back down with us. "Well," he said. We returned to our dinners.

A few minutes later, the phone rang again. "Don't answer it," Mother said. She told me it rang twenty times. "That was Gary," she said. "Anyone else would have hung up after five or six rings." This was also interesting new information for me. Since I had no experience with telephones, I didn't know that most people stopped calling after five or six rings.

Another adult issue surfaced during a visit to our home by my Aunt Elizabeth, sister of my father. She, my father and mother, and I sat at our dining room table. During our conversation, Father spoke slowly for my benefit, so I could read his lips. But I had trouble lipreading Aunt Elizabeth, so Mother translated, silently mouthing the words to me. We were talking about my grandparents, Father and Elizabeth's parents.

"They had a bit of a rocky relationship, didn't they?" my father said.

"No," my aunt said, with a quick glance at me. "Their marriage was fine. It was perfect."

"They had different personalities," my dad said. "I think they had a difficult marriage."

Suddenly, I felt the floor vibrate. I realized something was happening under the table—my aunt was kicking my father!

I turned to my mother. We could communicate entire sentences to each other just through facial expressions. Mine now said, "What is this about?"

She mouthed her answer: "Your aunt doesn't want us to say anything bad about your grandmother and grandfather."

Elizabeth continued maintaining that my grandparents had a wonderful relationship. My father interrupted.

"They weren't perfect, though," he said. "They were like any married couple."

The floor beneath us vibrated again.

"Stop kicking me!" my father said to Elizabeth. "I'm just telling Paul the truth. You can't hide that. He has to know the truth."

This was my father's philosophy on parenting in a nutshell. He wanted his children, hearing and deaf, to know and understand the world as it was. He treated us as maturing individuals who were able and deserved to participate in any conversation.

It wasn't until I was older that I discovered this was not how many other parents raised their children.

Feeling Left Out

When a woman named Rebecca received an invitation from her older brother, Moses, to his wedding, she couldn't help a feeling of dismay. She was happy for Moses, wished him well, and did want to attend the ceremony. She wasn't *that* concerned about traveling eight hundred miles with her husband and two sons. The issue was something else entirely.

At the first party on the weekend of the wedding, a gathering of the bride and groom's families, Rebecca's fears were confirmed. Moses greeted his sister and her family, but then returned to the party without introducing them to anyone. Rebecca was not surprised.

Rebecca was born deaf. For her parents, this was an embarrassment, one they didn't deal with in a straightforward way. They never explained deafness and its related issues to Rebecca's brothers. It was an unspoken rule that when Rebecca was at home, her brothers were responsible for watching out for her, which they both resented. Moses coped with Rebecca's deafness by ignoring it—which usually meant ignoring Rebecca.

When she married a deaf husband and their two children were born deaf, Moses' habit of excluding his sister from whatever was going on extended to her family as well.

As his wedding approached, Moses and his brother, Aaron, worked out every detail and communicated closely with the bride's family about the ceremony. They forgot, however, to hire a professional sign language interpreter. For Rebecca and her family, this was a serious oversight. Though Rebecca and Ken, her husband, were skilled lipreaders with people they knew, they were not nearly as proficient with strangers. They had to arrange for their own interpreter so they could understand what was being said at the wedding. The experience left Rebecca feeling, once again, like an outsider.

A few years later, however, the tables were turned.

Before the bar mitzvah of one of their sons, Rebecca and Ken invited Moses and Aaron and their families to attend. The weekend began with a crowded, high-spirited barbecue at Rebecca and Ken's home. Most of the guests were deaf and communicated in sign language. Because neither of Rebecca's brothers signed, they were left out of the animated conversations. The only exception was when someone remembered to shift into spoken English and interpret for them. Even then, the brothers often found it difficult to understand the speakers. They felt disconnected from the good time everyone seemed to be having. For Moses and Aaron, the event was a revelation.

On the day of the bar mitzvah, when Moses and Aaron were about to leave for the synagogue, Ken said, "Uh-oh! I forgot to get an interpreter. Oh, well. You don't need one, right? You'll be able to follow."

"What!" Moses sputtered. "You mean the bar mitzvah is going to be in sign language? How are we supposed to follow that?"

Ken and Rebecca burst out laughing. "Only kidding," Ken said. "We've already got somebody lined up."

Rebecca hugged her brothers. She'd forgiven them long before this. But she wasn't sure she would ever forget the loneliness and hurt she'd endured for so many years.

As I grew up and made more deaf friends, I learned how common Rebecca's experience was. Some parents were embarrassed to have a deaf child and tried to pretend the hearing loss didn't exist. Some insisted that their son or daughter learn spoken English and never use sign language. For some children this was the best approach. For others, however, it isolated the deaf or hard of hearing child from other deaf people who did use sign language. For the deaf child who struggled with learning to communicate through speech and speechreading, this restriction was doubly daunting.

Other deaf friends told me about how their parents or siblings simply didn't include them in conversations. Even when it was a subject my friends were interested in, their inquiries about what was happening were met with comments such as "Oh, it's nothing," or even, "Please don't interrupt! You're being rude." My friends couldn't help feeling rejected and insignificant.

Communication begins with a choice: *Whom should I include or exclude from what I'm about to say or write?* The decision we make about our intended audience communicates as much, if not more, than the actual message. When we include, we're essentially saying, "You are important to me. You are worth the time and effort it takes for me to pass this message to you. I believe you are intelligent and wise enough to process the information I'm about to share and may have something to contribute. I want to know what you think."

When we exclude, on the other hand, we can be interpreted as saying, "I don't value you enough to give you this message. I'm not sure I trust you with it. You probably wouldn't understand, I don't have time to explain it, and you probably wouldn't add anything important to the conversation anyway."

There are times, of course, when it is not appropriate to share information with a child, a coworker, or even a spouse. Yet when we are as open and inclusive as reasonably possible with our communications, our professional and personal relationships thrive. The mother or father who takes the time to explain to their kids why the family is moving to another state will find the transition much smoother than the parent who says, "Start packing. We're moving tomorrow." The staff member who keeps everyone in the department up to date by email on her project is understood, viewed more favorably, and more likely to garner support for her ideas than the employee who rarely emails or talks to anyone.

My experience as a college professor has certainly shown this to be true. I've found that when I sponsor a major proposal, the better my colleagues understand its purpose, the more likely they are to pass it if I take the time to meet with them individually before the vote to explain details and answer questions.

Inclusion forges bonds and communicates understanding, caring, and love. Exclusion fosters isolation, misunderstanding, bitterness, and fear. I saw this principle expressed dramatically during my childhood when my family found itself at ground zero for one of the great social and political movements of our time.

Big Changes in Little Rock

In 1954, my father accepted a position as pastor of a Presbyterian church in a town in the Deep South: Little Rock, Arkansas. I was five years old when we moved into our new home at 1863 Chester Street.

In many ways, the South was a wonderful area in which to grow up. The people were proud of their heritage and traditions. Most we knew were well-mannered and polite, and frequently warm and friendly. But in the 1950s, the American South also had an ugly side.

On the morning of September 4, 1957, our family—minus brother Dunbar, who was overseas attending university in Munich, Germany—sat around our breakfast table in Little Rock. I was eight years old and hadn't yet left to start my new year of schooling at Central Institute for the Deaf. As always, we ate oatmeal. As always, my father, wearing pajamas and a bathrobe, pulled out his Bible. He read to us each day, straight through the Bible over the days and weeks and months.

On this morning, however, my father altered the sequence. He turned to the Psalms and read aloud: "The Lord is my shepherd, I shall not want." His voice cracked. "Even though I walk through the valley of the shadow of death, I fear no evil; for thou art with me."

The night before, my father had received a momentous phone call from Daisy Bates, co-owner of the local black newspaper and head of the Arkansas chapter of the National Association for the Advancement of Colored People (NAACP). A federal court order required that Little Rock's Central High School be integrated that year. For the first time, black students would legally walk the halls with whites at the school. Nine students who'd earned excellent grades in their black-only schools had been selected to take this historic step.

A lot of citizens and many governing leaders of Arkansas had other ideas, however. Governor Orval Faubus, citing "evidence of disorder and threats of disorder," had instructed the Arkansas National Guard to prevent black students from entering school on September 4. Fearing harm, the "Little Rock Nine," as they later became known, didn't even try.

Later that day, a federal judge ordered integration to begin the next day. But the word from angry whites was that if the teenagers attempted to enroll, they would be murdered. The

Ku Klux Klan promised "bloodshed if necessary." The school superintendent told the students' parents to stay away to prevent a riot. There would be no police protection. Only two years earlier, a black fourteen-year-old visiting his family in neighboring Mississippi had been kidnapped, beaten, shot to death, and dumped in a river. The situation in Little Rock felt like a powder keg awaiting a match.

When Daisy Bates called on the evening of September 3, she had a simple yet profound request: Would my father gather a group of white ministers to accompany the black students to Central High in the morning? My father agreed to make calls and meet the students in the morning, but said he didn't know if he would go with them. He phoned a dozen church leaders. Only one local minister said he would join my father.

After our breakfast, my father drove to meet the students. My brother David, twenty-one years old and six foot one, went with him. David wanted to protect my father. My dad didn't argue.

Seven of the eventual "Nine" students, along with another girl who thought she wanted to join them in the attempt to enroll at Central (she later changed her mind), were gathered at a street corner a few blocks from the school. My father spoke to the teens, praising them for their faith and courage. They planned to begin walking to the school at 8:10 a.m. At 8:09, a black man asked if my father was going to walk with them.

"I don't know," my father said.

"Reverend Ogden, isn't it about time you made up your mind?"

At that moment, a strange feeling came over my father. He later recalled, "I felt: This is right; this is what I should do. There was not the slightest doubt but that I should do it. I ought to do it. And I felt this was the will of God for me. Every bit of fear just drained out."

"All right," my father said. "We will go with you."

My father began walking toward the mob gathered at the school, followed by the students, David, two visiting white pastors, and two black pastors. The local minister faded into the crowd.

My brother Dunbar describes the reaction of the mob in his book *My Father Said Yes*:

> People down the street spotted the little group. They surged forward. They picked up their pace: heavy-necked burly men in short-sleeved shirts and hats; some younger with crew cuts and polo shirts; and hard-jawed, hair-sprayed, thick-armed women in dresses. Some of the guys laughed, smoked a cigarette, on a rowdy late-summer morning's adventure. Some pointed. "Look, there are the niggers. Get 'em."[1]

The mob did not attack, however. It may have been the presence of my father in his light summer suit, leading the tiny band. It may have been the presence of the National Guard soldiers in uniforms and helmets and carrying rifles.

My father led the students up the steps at the front of the school, where a horizontal line of soldiers blocked their path. The mob closed in around my father and the students. Two soldiers parted a space, and Lt. Col. Marion Johnson, commander of the Guard troops, stepped forward.

My father spoke first, in a loud voice so all could hear: "Are you here to see to it that these children enter this school or to prevent them from entering?"

"The school is off-limits to these people," Johnson said, pointing with a nightstick at the closest of the teens.

"Does that mean that these children cannot be admitted to school?"

"Yes. That is what it means."

One of the two black pastors spoke up. "We understood from Governor Faubus that the soldiers are here to keep the peace, for law and order."

"During the night my orders were changed by the governor," Johnson said.[2]

And that was that. Faubus had decided to defy the federal courts a second time. Though tense and worried, my father led the children away from the mob without incident.

As an eight-year-old, I understood very little of this. Hatred based on race was a foreign concept to me. But when I saw my father on TV that evening, I knew something big was happening. I wanted to be on TV too, so I asked my father if he would take me to the school. The next day, a Thursday, he did. White students sat in their classrooms; the Nine stayed home. Soldiers lined the periphery of the grounds. We walked on the school grounds and examined the jeeps, half-tracks, and stacked rifles. My father explained some of what had happened the day before, pointing to this spot and that, repeating what was said.

A few days after the confrontation at the school, my parents hosted a group of black people in our home. I remember meeting and shaking hands with each of them, though I don't recall much about their faces now. One was a man named Martin Luther King Jr. To me, he was just another of the many visitors that spent time at our home over the years. I would see him again in Little Rock nine months later when he and my father sat together to witness the graduation of the first black student from Central High.

On September 23, 1957, thanks to a diversion and a police escort, the small group of black students successfully entered Central High through a rear door. By late in the morning, however, police could no longer keep the angry crowd away from the school, and they drove the Nine home. That same morning, a black journalist from Memphis was attacked by the mob. He died three years later from his injuries. It wasn't until the end of September 1957, when President Eisenhower issued an executive order placing the National Guard under federal command and ordered a thousand U.S. troops to Little Rock, that the Little Rock Nine were allowed to attend classes at Central.

Most people in Little Rock opposed my father's role in this watershed moment of the Civil Rights movement. Our phone lines were tapped. We received hate mail, obscene phone calls, and even bomb and acid-throwing threats. Friends advised us not to sleep in the front rooms of our house in case a bomb was thrown through a street window, so we all slept in the back of the house.

Most of this went over my head. I did not begin to recognize the danger or intense feelings people had on the issue until my return to classes at CID. While at school one day, I saw an article about my father and the Little Rock Crisis in *TIME* magazine. I was so proud that I began showing it to others at the school. But a teacher suddenly snatched it away and told me not to discuss it, that it was a closed subject. I was learning that not everyone regarded my father as a hero.

That spring, on a sunny and humid afternoon, I was at Busch Stadium watching a St. Louis Cardinals baseball game with the boys from my dormitory. The teenaged sister of one of the boys at our school was visiting from Alabama. She was at the game too, sitting in the row behind me. Someone must have pointed me out to her. She'd read about my father and what he'd done to support the Little Rock Nine.

I turned around and noticed her looking at me. Her face was twisted, her brows furrowed, her lips turned down. "You're a nigger lover. You should be sitting over there with the colored people," she said to me, pointing to the outfield bleachers. "Those people smell. You belong over there, not with us."

I was shocked and puzzled. Why was she angry? What did she have against black people? Avoiding, separating, fearing, and hating people because of their skin color made no sense to me then. It still makes no sense to me today.

How does one explain the existence of racism to a nine-year-old, or to anyone? Part of it must be the fear of the unknown. Part of it is surely insecurity, a desire to feel superior to someone or something. Unquestionably, it is a mindset that is learned at home and passed down through generations. It is an attitude of exclusion. And once we exclude, communication breaks down, planting the seeds for suspicion, misunderstanding, and ignorance.

Over the years, I've come to embrace a philosophy that forms our next secret:

Good communicators adopt an attitude of inclusion.

The more we reach out to others and seek to involve them in our lives, the more we understand and enrich each other. Not every message should be shared with everyone, and not every message will be heard even when it is shared. But if we are open to expanding both the breadth and depth of our communication, we'll usually find the benefits are worth the extra effort.

Our model in this practice, as usual, is Christ. The concept of inclusion is one that begins with God.

Come One, Come All

In the last chapter, we read about Jesus' desire to dine with us and thereby enter into a significant relationship: "I stand at the door and knock. If anyone hears my voice and opens the door, I will come in and eat with him, and he with me" (Revelation 3:20). Notice that He does not say, "If the do-gooders…the wealthy…the well-mannered…the educated…the upright…the rule followers hear my voice and open the door, I will come in." Instead, Jesus uses the word *anyone*. His invitation is to you and me. His intention is to include everyone.

This does not mean He condones our sinful behavior. Every sin we commit distances us from the Lord. You probably know the New Testament story of the woman caught in adultery. The Pharisees try to use the situation to trap Jesus. They bring the woman before Him, saying, "In the Law Moses commanded us to stone such women. Now what do you say?" (John 8:5).

Jesus does not answer at first, instead choosing to draw in the dirt with his finger. But the Pharisees persist, so Jesus stands and says, "If any one of you is without sin, let him be the first to throw a stone at her." The crowd slowly and wordlessly disperses, and Jesus says to the woman, "Has no one condemned you?"

"No one, sir," she says.

"Then neither do I condemn you. Go now and leave your life of sin."

Jesus does not merely rescue the woman and send her on her way. His message to her is to "Leave your life of sin." He intervenes in order to establish a turning point in her life—away from sin and toward Him.

We've already discussed the moment when Jesus and Zacchaeus meet at the sycamore tree. Zacchaeus is so moved by the invitation to begin a relationship with Jesus that he announces, "Look, Lord! Here and now I give half my possessions to the poor, and if I have cheated anybody out of anything, I will pay back four times the amount" (Luke 19:8).

Jesus responds, "Today salvation has come to this house, because this man, too, is a son of Abraham. For the Son of Man came to seek and to save what was lost."

Again, Jesus shows His intent. It isn't to snatch away the "real" believers to heaven and leave the rest to fend for themselves. Instead, it is to search out and bring salvation to everyone, sinner as well as virtuous, if they will acknowledge Him and repent of their sin. Eternity in heaven is not automatic, but the invitation is extended to all.

In His great charge to the disciples, Jesus once more makes no distinctions: "Therefore go and make disciples of all nations, baptizing them in the name of the Father and of the Son and of the Holy Spirit" (Matthew 28:19). Not just the holy nations, not just the most deserving and obedient people groups. *All* nations. Jesus means to include everyone in His kingdom.

From my perspective, what this implies for our faith is that just as Jesus seeks to include us, we also must strive to include Him in every aspect of our lives. It is so easy to compartmentalize God, to mentally set Him aside when life demands our attention. I have often struggled with this, especially in the early years of my faith. When I tackled a big project such as my dissertation, I tended to narrow my focus and shut out all "distractions"—including the people I loved, and including God. My attitude was that this was a problem I needed to work through on my own. By excluding Anne and the Lord, however, I cut myself off from the caring and guidance I needed more than ever.

Some of my favorite seventeenth-century authors—Teresa of Avila, Brother Lawrence, Madame Jeanne Guyon—sought to incorporate God in every aspect of their thinking and lives. Brother Lawrence said, "We must know before we can love. In order to know God, we must often think of Him; and when we come to love Him, we shall then also think of Him often, for our heart will be with our treasure."

Their quest to "be with our treasure" is also ours today. Exclusion does not protect us, elevate us, or serve our communication goals. It is an attitude of inclusion that leads us to a better understanding of and faith in each other and the Lord.

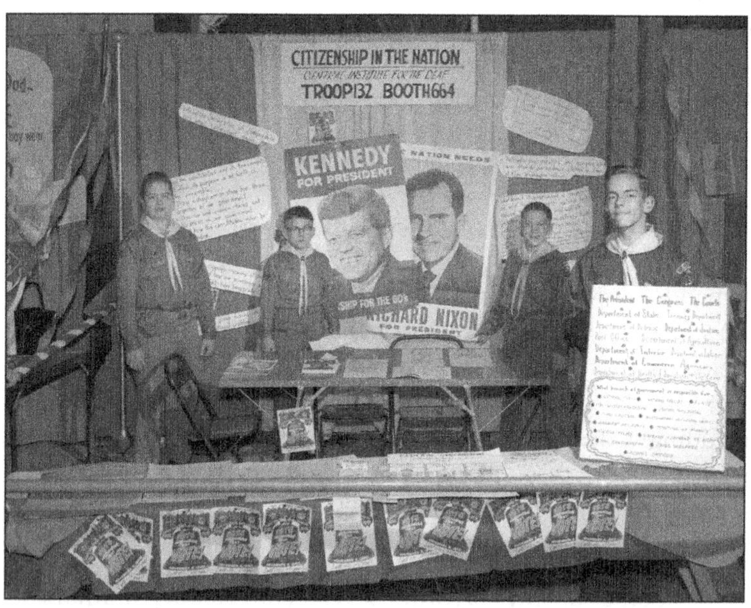

In 1960, during the Kennedy-Nixon election, eleven-year- old Paul (2nd from L) volunteered as a Boy Scout to educate the general public about the importance of voting, his first passion in national politics.

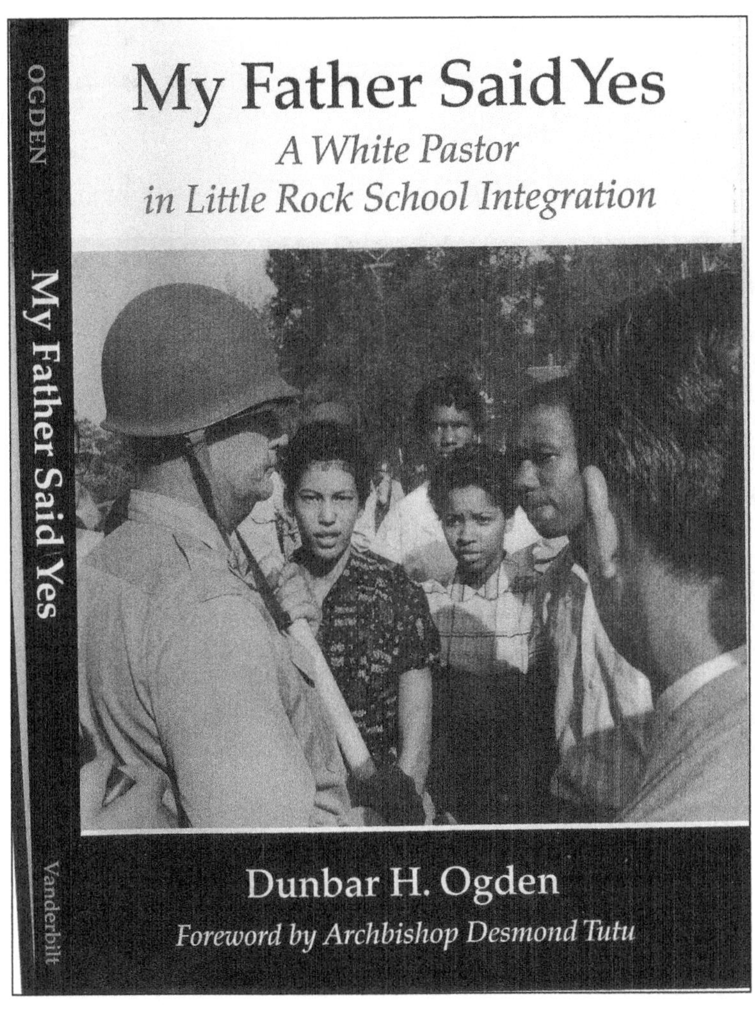

The book cover showing the back of my father as he faced the Arkansas National Guard. The guardsmen stopped the Little Rock Nine from entering Central High, fall 1957.

Thirteen- year- old Paul shaking hands with his father before Paul and his brother, Dunbar, travelled across the U.S. in 1962. It was a most interesting drive, as many lively discussions ensued between the two brothers.

5

Christians And Communication

Apart from me you can do nothing.

Jesus Christ

As a person growing up deaf in a hearing world, I was always sensitive to differences in communication. I observed many examples of people who knew how to connect easily and successfully with others, and I saw other people who seemed unable to relate well to those around them. The difference, as we've just discussed, usually had everything to do with their attitude and approach. In the case of a relationship between a man and a woman, does the man demonstrate a sincere desire to include the woman in his world and see life from her perspective? And vice versa?

By my observation, many of the housemothers at Central Institute for the Deaf struggled with effective communication. The position paid minimum wage, so most of these women had little if any training on how to handle a group of rambunctious boys—deaf or otherwise—living together in a dormitory and away from their families. The housemothers were uneducated, so were usually unable to answer our questions about school and life or to stimulate us intellectually in conversation. I don't mean to sound as if I'm putting them down. The housemothers tried their best. It's just that often, it wasn't enough. They weren't sufficiently prepared.

One of these was a woman named Sara Cays, my housemother when I was fifteen and nearing the end of my time at CID. Miss Cays was in her late fifties, about five-and-a-half feet tall, with black-rimmed glasses and dark hair wrapped almost like a wreath on top of her head. She had no knowledge of how to communicate with deaf children and little inclination to learn. She attempted to rule by force rather than reason, which only brought out the rebellious side in an increasingly independent gang of teenaged boys.

I remember receiving a note in the dining room from Nancy, a girl at CID I had a tremendous crush on. Miss Cays saw the transaction and followed me back to the dormitory. She asked to see the note. I laughed and said, "It's none of your business."

Miss Cays's face turned red. "I'll send for Mr. Maltse [the dormitory supervisor] and have him take the note from you!" she said.

"Fine with me," I said. She stormed off.

I didn't know what to do next. At the suggestion of my friend Erik, I tore the note into tiny pieces, put them in a box, and added a note saying, "Here are the pieces in this box. If you really want to read the note, you'll have to put the pieces together first!"

Miss Cays was furious when I presented her with the box. She called Mr. Maltse, who showed up in my room with the evidence. He told me I had to spend Saturday working on the pieces until the note was glued back together again. I protested that the note was personal and its contents were nobody else's business. Mr. Maltse grabbed me by the arm and said I was to do as he said. He handed me scotch tape and said, "You work on it for as long as it takes to get it back together."

Now what was I going to do? To the "rescue" came Dave, another boy in my dorm. Dave brushed the pieces off the table into his hand, opened the window, and threw them into the wind. An hour later, Miss Cays came to my room to check on my progress. I grinned and said the note was gone for good. Once again, she was furious. Once again, I was confronted by Mr. Maltse. I had three Saturdays to ponder Miss Cays's communication deficiencies, and the dubious wisdom of taking advice from my friends in the dorm, while I endlessly filled pages with the phrase, "I will obey Miss Cays."

On Sunday nights, my friends and I always gathered in the dorm to watch the Ed Sullivan variety show on TV. On February 9, 1964, The Beatles made their first television appearance in America on the show. We couldn't hear the music, of course, but we loved them anyway. There was something innocent, fun-loving, and rebellious about them, all at the same time.

Miss Cays couldn't stand them. "Oh, this is a bad group," she said. "Their hair's too long. They're filthy." Her comments made us love them even more.

Miss Cays also made it clear where she stood on civil rights. For a time, we had a black student teacher. One night Miss Cays found out that he'd been using the men's restroom. "Oh, this is awful," she said. "I don't know why we have a colored person here. Now I have to clean the whole bathroom."

Our problems with Miss Cays were more than just the generation gap. True, our rebellion sometimes went too far, and I regret that today. But it is also true that Miss Cays did not have an inclusive attitude. She was closed minded, uninterested in seeing circumstances from the other person's viewpoint. It's not a coincidence, I now believe, that Miss Cays was unable to enlist our cooperation or make any meaningful connection with me and the other boys in our dorm. Her attitude affected her ability to communicate.

Our housemothers contrasted dramatically with three people who became role models for me at CID. When I was twelve, a graduate named Rich returned to volunteer at the school after graduating from college with a degree in biology. For most of us, it was the first time we could communicate on a personal level with an adult—a bright, interested, deaf adult. Rich understood the problems of being deaf and knew the kind of interaction we needed. He asked us about our lives and feelings and listened attentively to our answers. We talked with him for hours about everything from dating and the responsibilities of marriage to the quality of American cars, politics, and world events. It was exhilarating.

One day Miss Cays overheard some of us asking Rich questions about sex and reported it to the principal. Shortly thereafter, the principal decided it was time for us to have a sex education class. Our principal employed an audiologist named Mr. McBette for the task. Mr. McBette was nice enough but another example of a person who didn't have the skills to communicate properly with us—and this was a subject that required more than the normal amount of skill and tact! Mr. McBette said we were growing up into men and that it was time we learned about the birds and the bees. He was off on the wrong foot. Our bodies had already told us we were becoming men and we had definitely progressed beyond the birds and bees stage.

Mr. McBette brought a movie to do the difficult part for him. The movie didn't have captions and we didn't understand a word of it. We couldn't figure out any of the vague drawings the movie used as explanations. After the movie, Mr. McBette nervously stumbled around for words. When he asked if we had any questions, we replied, "No, no, none at all," to which he showed a great deal of relief. He finally said, "I am very glad you enjoyed the film so much," and left. That was the extent of our sex education from the CID administration. But it definitely was not the extent of our sex education at CID. The next time we saw Rich, we pumped him for information. What a relief it was to have someone who listened and responded to our questions—not with unintelligible movies or embarrassed platitudes but straightforward answers!

The next year, another alumnus of CID entered our lives. Lee was hired part-time as an assistant to Miss Cays in exchange for room and board at our new residence hall. Lee had just graduated from Georgia Institute of Technology with a B.S. degree in chemical engineering and was starting his M.S. degree studies at Washington University in St. Louis. He was intelligent, outgoing, and fun. CID also hired a third alumnus, Sally, to teach physical education and home economics. She had also earned a bachelor's degree. She was one of the best lipreaders I've ever met and was direct and frank in our conversations, always speaking at our level—a relief to deaf children who often sensed that hearing people were condescending.

The difference between Miss Cays and some of the CID administrators and Rich, Lee, and Sally was in their attitude and approach to us. We rarely had the sense that Miss Cays saw or even understood our point of view. Rich, Lee, and Sally, however, showed a genuine interest in our lives, and sought to include us in theirs by sharing the information we needed most. Good communicators, people who combine proper training with a sincere desire to reach out to others, will always make a larger, more lasting, and more positive impact on the people around them. In turn, they'll find satisfaction in their own personal and professional relationships.

But what about, for those of us who are believers, the most important relationship of all? Does our ability to communicate really make a difference in how we relate to God? Do good communicators find it easier to develop their faith? Are poor communication skills a stumbling block to a growing spiritual life?

I submit that the answer to these questions is yes. My theories on the matter began to develop in my father's church.

So-Called Christians

The people of Little Rock—including members of the congregation of Central Presbyterian Church—did not welcome my father's entry into the desegregation movement. He did not stop with that first march to the high school. Instead, at the request of Daisy Bates, he organized what became known as the Thursday Group, a weekly interracial gathering in support of the parents of the Little Rock Nine and others who favored the drive toward desegregation. My father also accepted invitations to preach and speak across the country. Depending on his audience, he was sometimes outspoken about his belief that any follower of Christ should support racial harmony. In addition, he wrote articles that appeared in the local newspapers and he continued his regular visits with impoverished members of the community, which included many blacks.

It was all too much for most of the conservative citizens of Little Rock. People wrote letters to the editor and called our home constantly to complain about my father's actions. Sometimes it was an objection based (supposedly) on biblical grounds. Other times, it was blind hatred and name calling. The fear of someone throwing a brick or bomb through the front window was real.

A few of the telephone callers were from my father's own congregation. One, a Mr. Jones, rang weekly to rail about the incursion of blacks into white life.

By the following spring, attendance at Central Presbyterian had dropped from close to two hundred per Sunday to about eighty. Gifts to the church fell to similarly low levels. That summer, after a series of secret meetings, a group of deacons proposed cutting my father's annual salary from $6,200 to $4,000. It was an attempt to force him out. The proposal failed in a vote of elders and deacons, but my father knew the end was near. A few days later, a group of supportive elders and deacons visited my father at our home on Chester Street and said they could not hold off the opposition for long. They asked my father to find a position at another church.

Father could have fought the backstage maneuvering, which violated Presbyterian Church bylaws, but he chose instead to move on. In October, he announced that he was leaving Central Presbyterian to accept a position as a pastor in West Virginia.

I missed large parts of these events while attending school in St. Louis. But I was around enough and old enough to sense the injustice. What the people in my father's congregation professed to believe and how they behaved did not match up. I began to view people who called themselves Christians with suspicion.

My skepticism was further aroused at Bream Presbyterian Church in Charleston, West Virginia. It started with a man about forty named George. He was in church every Sunday and always sat in the same front-row pew. George was different than most of the worshipers. He wore jeans rather than a jacket and tie. Based on his mannerisms and facial expressions, my guess is that he had a mental impairment. After each service, George hung around, waiting to talk with my father. No one else spoke to him. He never interrupted when my father was greeting others, but simply waited patiently until my father noticed him and said, "George, how are you? I'm so glad you came today."

Because George was different, it made others in the congregation uncomfortable. They went to my father and asked him to tell George to not come to our church anymore. My father refused. These people retaliated by talking behind my father's back, saying things like "There's Pastor Ogden's shadow again" when they saw George.

I couldn't believe it. I was very upset. I thought, *These people are supposed to be Christians?* I talked with my mother about it. "Why are they complaining?" I said. "George is quiet and never bothers anyone. What's he done wrong?" My mother tried to explain that some people are ignorant.

Sometimes the church held meetings after Sunday services. My father participated, while I mostly bided my time and waited for them to end. I vividly recall one of these occasions, a budget meeting on a proposed remodeling project. The committee was trying to set priorities and choose between recommendations. I didn't understand all of what was said, but from the frowns and angry expressions around the table I easily picked up on the feelings of conflict and disappointment. Some of the committee members were the same people who had complained about George.

To me, the arguing seemed petty. Where was God in these debates? Wasn't He the priority? Everyone wanted his own way and had no interest in hearing another point of view. They didn't *listen*.

I was just as disgusted with some of my new Christian classmates at my new school, Stonewall Jackson High School. After ten years of preparation at Central Institute for the Deaf, at age fifteen I'd joined the hearing world. It was both exciting and tremendously challenging. Some students adjusted more easily than others to having a deaf student and classmate in their midst, but most grew accustomed to my presence and treated me as just another member of the student body.

What disappointed me, however, were the attitudes of some of the Christian students. I was particularly infuriated during my senior year, following the stunning assassination of Martin Luther King Jr. in Memphis on April 4, 1968. Two days after Dr. King's death, Fred, one of my teammates on the tennis team, said as we were getting ready for practice, "It's a good thing Martin Luther King was killed."

I thought I'd read his lips wrong. "What?" I said. "I didn't understand what you just said."

"Martin Luther King was a bad influence, a bad guy just causing trouble," Fred said, emphasizing each word by stabbing the air with his index finger. "Now we can have peace. It's good he's dead."

I was so astonished that I barely protested. Fred was from a prominent Christian family in our church. His words made no sense to me. Other families in our church also opposed the civil rights movement and the role my father had played. As I think back on that time, I'm reminded of the words of Mahatma Gandhi: "I like your Christ. I do not like your Christians. Your Christians are so unlike your Christ."

I was further disillusioned when I found out that one of my best friends in school, Scott Gordon, wasn't allowed to play tennis at the local country club. It was because Scott was Jewish. The club directors included members of my father's church. It didn't matter to them that Scott was the best high school tennis player in the state, or that he was one of the nicest guys around. To me, it seemed ridiculous.

During my adolescent years, I observed a sharp division between the actions of my father and the behavior of many of the so-called Christians around me. My father stood beside the oppressed even to the point of putting his life in danger. He visited and encouraged the poor and downtrodden almost daily, handing over food and a few dollars when he could. In so many ways, he lived the life I imagined Jesus living if He were still among us in the flesh. I could sense my father's joy when he did these things. It brought him closer to God.

Yet other men and women in his congregation seemed selfish, petty, and vindictive. They appeared more concerned with their own comfort than with reaching out to people in need or people who were in any way different.

How was this possible? Did these people truly believe in God? Were they imposters masquerading as Christians? Was there a breakdown in their faith?

Once again, it seemed that inclusion and communication were at the core of the problem.

Spiritual Communication

Author Brennan Manning tells the story of a public sinner who is excommunicated and forbidden entry to his church. He takes his woes to God. "They won't let me in, Lord," he prays, "because I am a sinner."

"What are you complaining about?" God answers. "They won't let Me in either."[1]

To excommunicate someone means to exclude them from the rites of the church. It is a way to cut off communication. Yet what sinners—and that's all of us—need most is to include God in our spiritual and everyday lives. Some of us practice "self excommunication." Either consciously or not, we cut ourselves off from the source of successful living. We must communicate on a regular basis with Him in order to fill up with His power and love.

Jesus said, "No branch can bear fruit by itself; it must remain in the vine. Neither can you bear fruit unless you remain in me. I am the vine; you are the branches. If a man remains in me and I in him, he will bear much fruit; apart from me you can do nothing" (John 15:4-5).

I don't think Jesus is saying that an atheist or a Christian who is distant from God is incapable of producing anything good. A person who gives to the poor or who comforts an AIDS patient *does* deliver help and compassion—but that help is limited. The "fruit" that Jesus talks about is the joy of salvation and relationship with God. How compassionate, really, is a brief injection of cash or comfort? Though beneficial to the recipient in the short term, these temporary measures fall short of God's plan. They are "nothing" unless combined with the love and knowledge that lasts for eternity.

Our connection to the Lord is vital for another reason. Whether atheist or Christian, when we fail to maintain consistent communication with God, we eventually stumble. We turn our focus away from Christ and onto ourselves. And when this happens, we are perfectly positioned for the forces of darkness to take us down.

Tracy was a young woman who lived in darkness. She'd grown up going to church, and at the age of nine gave her heart to God. For several months afterward, she enjoyed a close relationship with the Lord. But problems between her parents, along with other issues, pulled her apart from God. Her faith fell away and she dropped into a deep depression.

During her junior year of high school, Tracy decided she didn't want to live anymore and sliced her wrist with a box cutter. Doctors repaired her tendons but not her soul. She was diagnosed with bipolar disorder and put on medications that numbed her. She took drugs. She got pregnant and had an abortion. She experimented with cutting, using a knife on herself in places no one could see—her shoulders, her inner thighs. The pain gave her a perverse pleasure. It was a way to express the darkness she felt inside. At a friend's house one night, she started cutting and couldn't stop. By the end of the evening, she'd cut her arms more than two hundred times.

Tracy moved with her parents to Atlanta, where she discovered S&M (sadomasochism) clubs. The intricate costumes and exotic setting appealed to her creative nature. She'd discovered the "art of darkness." Steadily, like a spider weaving a web around its victim, it drew her in.

At age twenty-three, Tracy discovered she was pregnant again. She locked herself in her car and screamed through tears. *I can't have a baby,* she thought. *I'm not capable of raising a child. But I can't have another abortion—I won't! What am I going to do?*

Tracy was down to her last hope.

God, she prayed, *if You are there, if You are real and can hear this, I need help here. I can't have another abortion. I don't see how I can raise a child, either, but if that's what You want...Your will be done.*

Three weeks later, Tracy had an abortion. It was as awful as she had feared, but also a relief.

In the following weeks, Tracy continued visiting clubs and doing drugs. But the prayer she'd uttered in desperation was the beginning of a conversation with God. The more she prayed, the more it awakened a hunger for a spiritual presence in her life. Tracy found herself going to church and reading her Bible. She heard about Wellspring Living, a local recovery program for women, and felt God telling her she needed to be there. When a staff member asked if she was willing to come, Tracy answered "Yes."

Tracy's passion for God grew at Wellspring, but her dark past also continued to call her. One Saturday night, Tracy drove through Atlanta toward a familiar warehouse. Before she knew it, she was in a large room crowded with dancers dressed in fanciful costumes. The dominant color was black. It was a celebration of evil.

"Tracy!" a woman dressed in black leather screamed. "You're back!" Old friends greeted her enthusiastically. Yet Tracy felt awkward and empty. She didn't belong here anymore.

Later that night, Tracy cried while reading and rereading a Bible passage that seemed written only for her: "Listen, O daughter, consider and give ear: Forget your people and your father's house. The king is enthralled with your beauty; honor him, for he is your lord" (Psalm 45:10-11).

Tracy made her decision. God would be the central relationship in her life, the one she would listen to above all others. She would exclude darkness, not her Lord.

I believe we all face this choice daily. Will we listen to God or the forces of darkness? Who will we worship, our heavenly Father or ourselves? Will we seek to include other people—and God—in our lives, building bridges to meaningful relationships? It doesn't matter if we call ourselves Christian or not. If we don't communicate consistently with God—pouring out our joys and frustrations, our triumphs and sorrows—we reject or misinterpret His will and fall prey to evil. Darkness comes in many forms: fear, arrogance, self-loathing, pride, and racism are only a few examples. When spiritual communication is blocked, our behavior reveals the truth behind our next secret:

> *Lousy communicators usually make lousy Christians.*

The antidote is to develop a thriving relationship with God. But what does this mean on a practical level? How, exactly, do we light the fuse that leads to lasting and rewarding exchange with our creator?

When I graduated from high school, a relationship with God was one of the furthest things from my mind. I didn't rebel outwardly while at home, but my observations of people who called themselves Christians pushed me away from anything to do with the Christian church and Christian religion. Maybe you've had a similar experience.

What I began to discover as I entered my college years, however, is that the path I thought would lead me toward a new and enlightened outlook on life would actually bring me back to the God I did not yet know or understand.

6

Love In Action

Dare to love and to be a real friend. The love you give and receive is a reality that will lead you closer and closer to God as well as those whom God has given you to love.

Henri Nouwen

I inherited a great deal from my father. My inheritance did not come in the form of monetary wealth or possessions, but in a legacy. He gave me a framework for viewing and encountering life. This legacy enriches and sustains me to this day.

One of the foundational aspects of my father's approach to life was an empathy for anyone in need—an empathy, or compassion, that he consistently transferred into action. I saw it almost daily when I was around him, enough to know that it was deeply ingrained in his philosophy.

One demonstration of this philosophy occurred when I was about six years old. My parents and I were on a cross-country car trip. We were in Colorado, traveling down a highway, when ahead of us we saw a car and an overturned boat in a ditch. Clothes and camping equipment littered so much of the road that my father had to swerve to avoid the debris.

Two men in their twenties stood beside the vehicle, staring at the scene with dazed expressions.

Other cars continued to speed past, but my father immediately pulled over. I watched from our car as he walked up to the men. One of the pair was crying. Later, I learned that the driver had fallen asleep at the wheel.

I couldn't see what my father said, but I knew he was offering comfort and probably advice. Then I saw him reach into his wallet and hand over a few dollars. It was a typical scene—someone, even a stranger, in trouble and my father doing what he could to help. Almost daily, he visited hospitals, shut-ins, and people struggling to make ends meet. He worked to arrange jobs for people new to the area or others out of work. His kinship with blacks and involvement in the Civil Rights movement was simply an extension of his strong belief that part of being a Christian was to help those in need.

In his final year in Little Rock, my father preached these words to his congregation:

> Surely we ought to be in the vanguard as to the matter of concern and ministry for others. Are we really stirred in heart as we think of the underprivileged, the disinherited, and the disenfranchised? More than half the people in the world go to bed hungry every night and more than half the babies of this world sleep restlessly and fitfully because their mothers cannot provide them with sufficient milk, being themselves undernourished. We need to have a very sensitive social conscience, and to lead instead of to lag in ministering to others.[1]

My father passed his sensitive social conscience on to me. At Central Institute for the Deaf, I felt compassion for the boys and girls who struggled with their studies or with fitting in. Unlike some of the boys, I talked with these students and treated them with respect. I wanted them to know I was an ally.

Later, during my sophomore year of high school in Charleston, I heard about and volunteered for a low-income housing project in the Appalachian Mountains. It was similar to today's Habitat for Humanity program. For several months, I drove an hour each way on Saturdays to haul lumber, pound nails, and rub shoulders with people very different from the members of my parents' church. They were Quakers, and they demonstrated a gentleness and genuine respect for others and for God that I'd rarely encountered anywhere else. Each morning we gathered for a quiet time of prayer, followed by hours of hard work, a well-earned lunch and social time, and then more labor before we parted ways at the end of the day.

At various times I brought a friend with me to these Saturday work parties. Several complained about it; none but one seemed to appreciate what we were doing. I, however, always enjoyed these trips into the mountains. Something about laboring to benefit families who needed help, working side by side with people sharing the same goal, produced in me a powerful sense of achievement and satisfaction. Although my feelings about faith at the time were ambiguous at best, I was surprised to even discover occasional moments where I felt connected with God.

I recall one afternoon break where I sat on a pile of lumber along with more than fifteen men and a few women. We were dirty and tired. A few feet away stood the wood frame of a new home. Piles of bricks and boards littered our worksite. The background, however, was picturesque—miles of green trees amidst Appalachia's rolling hills.

Our work break was more than a pause for rest. My comrades used this time to pray. Few spoke aloud. Many closed their eyes for a time of silent conversation with the Lord. A handful of others let their eyes wander over the countryside as they quietly expressed thanks and concerns to heaven.

I didn't understand it and couldn't explain it, but it was uplifting to be with these people at such moments. Despite my skepticism, I sensed a spiritual presence.

Another satisfying experience during my high school years began when a classmate invited me to visit her sister. Nancy Morgan had spina bifida, the condition where the backbone and spinal canal fail to close before birth. She used a wheelchair to get around. In those days, students with such a disability were not welcomed into classrooms with the rest of the students. Instead, a few teachers were assigned to visit Nancy at home and work with her at various times during the week.

The result was that Nancy was isolated. When I visited, I was able to read her lips and she understood my speaking, so we communicated easily. She asked many questions about other students and what was happening at school. I thought, *Wow, it must be tough to always be stuck doing homework at home, all alone.* For the rest of my time in high school, I stopped to chat with Nancy at least once every two weeks.

I didn't see myself as a particularly selfless person, so I used to wonder where this consideration for others came from. What motivated me to invest afterschool hours and weekends in the welfare of people around me? Why do any of us reach out in this way?

In my case, I believe part of it was a sense of duty, probably combined with an unconscious desire to follow in the footsteps of my father. I admired and respected my dad, and even at an early age intuitively understood that the things he did and stood for were important and good.

There was also a feeling of fulfillment. For example, Nancy's eagerness to learn about what was happening beyond the walls of her home was obvious. By her smile and barrage of questions, I could tell she appreciated my visits. It was gratifying to realize that I was delivering a benefit to someone's life.

At the time, I did not connect this tendency for compassion to faith or a desire to know or please God. It simply felt personal, part of the person I was and wished to become. Only later did I realize it was something more.

Who and what I would be was very much on my mind the summer I graduated from Stonewall Jackson High School. It was an exciting time. All my years of schooling and preparation were about to be tested. So many possibilities awaited. Yet I was full of conflicting ideas and theories about life and faith. I had not figured out my place or purpose. My awareness of the needs and struggles of others was about to intensify, as was my search for meaning in a chaotic world.

Antioch

One of my favorite teachers at Central Institute for the Deaf once loaned me the course catalog for Antioch College in Yellow Springs, Ohio. I remember being impressed with the college's work-study program. Later, during my junior year of high school, my brother Dunbar pointed out that the percentage of Antioch students who completed their doctoral studies was among the highest in the nation. I also learned that Coretta Scott King, wife of Martin Luther King Jr., had attended Antioch. It wasn't long before I made Antioch my choice for pursuing higher education.

In 1968, my freshman year, Antioch was in many ways emblematic of the tumultuous sixties. With the help of a grant, Antioch increased its black student population that year from nearly zero to a tenth of its two thousand students. Most were recruited from the inner city. At about the same time, the college established coeducational residence halls, with no adult supervision. Authority figures were "square" and the hippie lifestyle was "in," including sex, drugs, and rock and roll.

Equally in was a zealous idealism. In our classes, we read about genocide throughout history—in China, in South Africa, in Germany during World War II, and our own country's brutal treatment of Native Americans during the 1800s, when treaties were repeatedly broken and native people either killed or forced to relocate. We read about how the wealthy and powerful manipulated and abused the poor and underprivileged. It was startling to realize the breadth and depth of so much evil.

Many students at Antioch believed they could and should change the world. They wanted to stop the killing and put an end to the Vietnam War. They desired to bring racial equality to the nation. They agitated for a dramatic shift in the political landscape. They wanted to wipe out poverty in America and around the world. They launched protests supporting women's rights, making Antioch one of the forerunners in the feminist movement.

Many of these attitudes resonated with me. I had discovered a group of people who, unlike those I'd observed in my father's church, didn't call themselves Christians while ignoring the needs of others. They were authentic. They didn't complain or brag about their acts of service, but quietly did what needed to be done. They cared about making a difference. I embraced their philosophy wholeheartedly.

When associates of Cesar Chavez spoke on campus and urged us to support their efforts to improve conditions for migrant workers in California, some friends and I volunteered to help. After the manager of a local grocery store refused our request that he stop buying fruit from growers that hired nonunion field laborers, we picketed the store. I doubt we had a major impact on the plight of migrant workers, but we did convince a few shoppers to change their buying habits.

Later, Fidel Castro announced that there was a labor shortage in Cuba and that his people desperately needed help with the sugar harvest to survive. A friend and I, as well as several other students, decided to fly to Cuba. This was illegal at the time, so we planned to fly to Canada, then Mexico, and then Cuba so the U.S. government wouldn't be able to track us. Only when my friend's parents found out about our intentions and threatened to stop funding his studies did we drop the idea. We may have been naïve about Castro's motivations, but our desire to help the people of Cuba was sincere.

In addition, I attended each of the writer and community organizer Saul Alinsky's three visits to campus and listened intently to his views on how to organize, boycott, and take action to change systems and help the poor and oppressed. I also participated in protests against the Vietnam War, including one at the state capital after four students were shot dead by the National Guard at Kent State University.

In these examples and others, my friends and I hoped to change lives for the better. We attempted to bring meaning to an era often filled with confusion, conflict, and indifference. We tried to demonstrate our concern for humanity itself.

My studies at Antioch began just a year after the "Summer of Love," when thousands of young people from across the country flocked to San Francisco to celebrate music, free love, and an alternative lifestyle. That same year, 1967, the Beatles released their international hit "All You Need Is Love." Although the tensions of the times would soon explode into confrontations and violence, *love* was the underlying theme that spoke to me and thousands of other people. We were searching for new and lasting solutions to the problems all around us, methods that were rooted in respect and compassion. Put another way, we wanted to communicate our love for others to the world.

I believe we were on the right track all those years ago. What I didn't realize at the time was how little I understood love, and that no matter how hard I tried to push God away, my desire to bring compassion to the world was leading me right back to Him.

Authentic Love

Love has been defined in many ways. Webster's dictionary describes love as "strong affection for another," "attraction based on sexual desire," and "affection based on admiration, benevolence, or common interests," among other definitions. Literature is filled with examples of every kind of expression of love. As a species, we are fascinated with the subject.

Everyone has heard of the concept of "love at first sight." You may have experienced just such a feeling before. Yet the kind of love I want to talk about—genuine, sincere, lasting—cannot be formed in an instant. I don't believe we can truly love someone we've just met. We can be attracted by the packaging and our idea of what's inside, and we call it love because we like the way it makes us feel. But it's all based on assumption and emotion.

Even when we start to get to know someone, we're still operating mostly on feelings. Couples at the beginning of romantic relationships are often so infatuated with each other that they're certain they're deeply in love. Yet the sense of bliss is temporary and still based almost entirely on how *we* feel about the relationship.

Wholehearted, authentic love is something else entirely. It is founded not on emotion but on the choice we make to love. The evidence for our love isn't based on our feelings, but on our actions.

Years ago, a father and son named Phil and Mark Littleford and two other men flew a sea plane into a secluded

Alaskan bay for a day of fishing. The next morning, when the group tried to take off, the plane managed only a low, circular pattern. They realized one of the pontoons had been punctured and was filled with water. It was dragging the plane down.

The plane crashed into the bay and capsized. Everyone survived the crash, but they couldn't find any safety equipment. After a hurried prayer, the three men and twelve-year-old Mark jumped into the bay to swim to shore. The water was icy cold and the riptide strong. Two of the men finally reached the Alaskan shore, exhausted. When they looked back, they saw Phil and Mark on the horizon, arm-in-arm; they were being swept out to sea.

The men knew Phil was a strong swimmer and could have made it to shore. They surmised that Mark wasn't as strong a swimmer. Phil wasn't going to leave his son behind. Phil chose to die with his boy rather than live without him.[2]

That is sincere, authentic love—powerful affection backed up by action. It is a love so strong that we would rather give up our life than let it go.

I believe we were designed to experience and display this kind of love by the source and author of love, our Father in heaven. Scripture spells it out: "Dear friends, let us love one another, for love comes from God. Everyone who loves has been born of God and knows God. Whoever does not love does not know God, because God is love" (1 John 4:7-8).

What exactly does this verse mean? That our caring and compassion for each other are a gift from the Lord. Love and our knowledge of and closeness with God are intertwined. Our relationship with Him stands on love. It is the connector, the means of communication between heaven and earth. No matter how much we pray, worship, and profess to be Christian, if we do not love, we don't have a genuine relationship with God.

Jesus Christ showed that the kind of love God looks for is not temporary or based on feelings or our assumptions about what He'll do for us. The kind of love He displays and desires to see in us is bold, committed, and complete. It is so strong that, much like Phil Littleford, Jesus gave up His life on the cross so that we would not have to die in sin, alone.

> This is how we know what love is: Jesus Christ laid down his life for us. And we ought to lay down our lives for our brothers. If anyone has material possessions and sees his brother in need but has no pity on him, how can the love of God be in him? Dear children, let us not love with words or tongue but with actions and in truth. (1 John 3:16-18)

This is the kind of love—with actions and in truth—that my father demonstrated so often during his lifetime. It's the love and lifestyle that I instinctively pursued and responded to during my early school and college years. I did not then see the central link between love and God, but I sensed its presence. The answer to everything I sought was God all along.

As a seminary student, author Jim Wallis and other fellow students examined the Bible and found thousands of verses on the poor and God's response to injustice. One member of the group took a Bible and a pair of scissors and began cutting out every line of text that related to the poor. Throughout the Old Testament and New, the cuts were massive. When he was finally done, that Bible barely held together. The students had created a Bible full of holes.

"We still have that old Bible full of holes," Wallis has written. "It serves as a constant reminder to me of how you can miss so much, even when it is right in front of your eyes. I learned in my little home church that people can really love the Bible, believe they are basing their lives upon it, and yet completely miss some of its most central themes. We don't see what would most challenge us and perhaps change our lives."[3]

This, I believe, is what happened with many members of my father's churches in Little Rock and Charleston. They believed in God, yet they had missed one of the central themes of the Christian faith. In a different way, I too missed an important message of the Bible. I didn't yet see that what I believed and felt in my heart matched the very essence of God and what He wishes for all His children. In both cases, we missed the message because we did not have an open channel of communication with the Lord. We did not yet see that authentic love is more than a feeling—it is a choice backed up by commitment and action.

The Least of These

What, then, does all this mean for those of us who would seek greater meaning for our lives and, if we believe in Him, a deeper relationship with God? Perhaps that the ball is in our court—that we must *act* in love if we expect to cultivate a genuine faith and truly know and understand our Lord.

Jesus, when He related the parable of the sheep and the goats to a crowd that included His disciples, said that the Son of Man would sit on a throne and separate people one from another as a shepherd separates his sheep from his goats. He continued:

> "Then the King will say to those on his right, 'Come, you who are blessed by my Father; take your inheritance, the kingdom prepared for you since the creation of the world. For I was hungry and you gave me something to eat, I was thirsty and you gave me something to drink, I was a stranger and you invited me in, I needed clothes and you clothed me, I was sick and you looked after me, I was in prison and you came to visit me.'

> "Then the righteous will answer him, 'Lord, when did we see you hungry and feed you, or thirsty and give you something to drink? When did we see you a stranger and invite you in, or needing clothes and clothe you? When did we see you sick or in prison and go to visit you?'
>
> "The King will reply, 'I tell you the truth, whatever you did for one of the least of these brothers of mine, you did for me.'" (Matthew 25:34-40)

This is our calling—to feed the hungry, provide water for the thirsty, house those with nowhere to stay, clothe those who have no clothes, care for the sick, and personally encourage criminals and the incarcerated. This is authentic, powerful love in action. It is performed not only for the benefit of those who receive it, but also for those who give it. It is the kind of love that brings us into contact with our Creator.

This, then, is our next secret:

When we love the "least of these," we link our hearts to God's.

I don't believe this is only for Christians on the "front lines" of ministry, those who feel they have a special calling or gift to bring compassion to people in need. All of us can care in some way for the men, women, and children we come into contact with daily, whether they are familiar or people we've never met. It's not so hard to offer a kind word to the homeless man on the street corner, or even better, to buy him a meal or offer to take him to the local shelter or job center. When we imagine that person not as a bum but as God in human form, it can change our perspective in a hurry.

The same call to love in action applies to public figures. I think of C. Everett Koop, an evangelical Christian and America's surgeon general from 1982 to 1989. In the midst of the AIDS crisis, Koop released a report recommending more research and sex education at the lowest grade possible. The report prescribed abstinence and sex within monogamous marriage as the safest method for avoiding the disease but recommended condoms for anyone who had multiple sex partners or engaged in homosexual acts. Many political and religious conservatives were outraged.

After the report's release, Koop spoke to several religious groups. He told his audiences, "I am the surgeon general of the heterosexuals and the homosexuals, of the young and old, of the moral and immoral" and "You may hate the sin, but you are to love the sinner."[4] Philip Yancey, in his book *Soul Survivor*, wrote that Koop "had vowed to look out for the weak and disenfranchised, and clearly there was no more weak or disenfranchised group in the nation."[5]

Koop's approach to the AIDS crisis not only showed how to move closer to God's heart, but also how to communicate God's love to a non-believing population. As Yancey wrote, "It does no good to quote Bible verses to people who do not revere the Bible, or threaten God's judgment on people who do not believe in God…After valiantly conquering most infectious diseases, we have now substituted new health problems for old, many of which stem from moral choices. Christians believe that the commands God gave were not arbitrary, but for our own good, and the health results in modern society bear out that principle. If we can communicate more of the spirit of a concerned family doctor, and less of the spirit of a nagging moralist, we may catch the attention of a society headed down a path of self-destruction."[6]

Love in action takes us into God's company and communicates better than any words we can express who He is. I sensed this during my often-confusing years at Antioch. Though I was skeptical about God at the time, I remembered the peace and connection I'd felt when I was with the Quakers in the Appalachian Mountains. There was a Quaker house near the

Antioch campus, and I felt the need to go there from time to time. During meetings, all of us—a few faculty, several students, and townspeople—sat in chairs facing each other in a square. Different people got up to speak, sometimes about the war. Yet even when the subject was contentious, the tone of the conversation was always polite and humble.

Like the Quakers I knew in the Appalachians, these people did more than talk. Several were involved in nonprofit organizations or other efforts to care for people from abusive backgrounds or to promote recycling and environmentalism. Some left campus to work in refugee camps in Africa. Some, after graduating, would volunteer for the Peace Corps. Once again, I was impressed by both their attitudes and their actions. When three Quaker friends asked me if I'd like to serve as a bookkeeper for a cooperative food store, I agreed. It was another positive experience.

Through the Quakers, I discovered compassion and a sense of peace. I encountered a way of life that resonated with my own beliefs about love in action and how relationships between people could function if love was at the core. Yet I was confounded by the spiritual foundation that seemed to sustain my friends. It was one of the factors that challenged me to explore my own skepticism and my own feelings about faith in a deeper way.

I had to figure out what I was going to do about God.

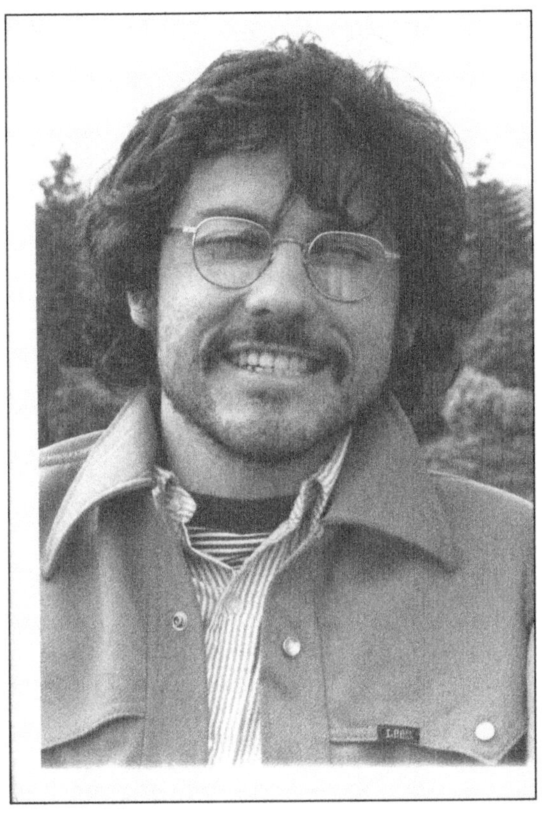

Paul at a political protest rally against the war in Vietnam during his years at Antioch College, Yellow Springs, Ohio in the early 1970s.

7

DARING TO DOUBT

Any belief worth having must survive.

Author unknown

I remember vividly the moment I found out about the death of Martin Luther King Jr. It was a Friday morning during my senior year of high school—April 5, 1968—and I'd been up early doing homework in my bedroom. I walked downstairs and saw my father sitting at the dining room table in his pajamas and bathrobe. For the first time in years, I saw that he was crying.

"What's wrong?" I asked.

"I am so upset," my father said. "Martin Luther King has been assassinated."

I knew this was a terrible blow to my father, who had hosted Dr. King in our home, escorted him to the graduation of the first black student from Little Rock's Central High School, and visited him in a New York hospital after a deranged woman had stabbed him. I, meanwhile, was simply shocked. I sat at the table with my dad, where we prayed and discussed what a terrible time it was for America.

Two months later, this scene played out a second time in eerily similar fashion. On Wednesday morning, June 6, I again walked downstairs and found my father sitting at the dining room table, tears in his eyes. He told me that U.S. presidential candidate Robert Kennedy had been shot early that morning after winning the California Democratic primary.

This time, my first response was anger. "That's crazy!" I said. "What is going on? What is wrong with America? America is going to hell." The next morning, Robert Kennedy died at Good Samaritan Hospital in Los Angeles.

These events coincided with the start of a trip I was to take to England for a summer work-study experience before starting classes at Antioch. I'd already arranged to stay with a friend in New York City before flying on to England. I cancelled my plans to spend time with my friends in New York and instead went to St. Patrick's Cathedral, where Robert Kennedy's body lay in repose. I sat for hours near his closed casket in one of the front-row pews. For much of that time, I was alone.

I was not only angry, but also overwhelmingly sad. Just a few days earlier, I'd watched this energetic man on TV speaking about the importance of civil rights and the changes he hoped to make as president. Tom, a good friend, was a volunteer for Kennedy's campaign and had recruited me to help on occasion. I looked up to Kennedy and felt he was the best hope for our country's future. Now, suddenly, he was gone.

God seemed absent as well. For years my faith had wavered between belief and doubt, plagued by fears and questions and damaged by the inconsistencies I saw in the attitudes and actions of members of my father's congregations. During my years at Central Institute for the Deaf, I viewed God as a stern authority figure, as someone who waited to catch me breaking the rules. When I did something wrong I felt terribly guilty. I've talked with many people who also grew up with or still maintain the idea that God is only concerned with punishment and justice.

As I grew older, I drifted away from my faith. I met an atheist friend who influenced me. I did not rebel openly against religion or my parents' views about God—my father was a pastor, after all—but I quietly pushed Him out of my life. For a long time, I felt no link to the Lord, no sense of communication or presence.

As I sat in front of Robert Kennedy's lifeless body, the spiritual void in my own life had never felt more pronounced.

God, where are You? I prayed. *What's wrong with You? How could You allow this to happen?* I thought, *Maybe people are right. Maybe there is no God.* It was a bleak time for the nation and for me personally.

Yet I was not ready to give up on the Lord. I could not discount the love my father demonstrated and the joy he seemed to experience when helping and standing up for others. Nor could I ignore the peace and strength my mother seemed to draw from her faith, as well as the commitment, fulfillment, and quiet faith I observed among the Quakers.

I entered my college years with far more questions than answers. I was on a quest not just for knowledge but for spiritual truth.

A Time of Searching

I've already mentioned my interest and involvement in the words and work of Cesar Chavez and Saul Alinsky, as well as my participation in Vietnam War protests. Our intention to help the people of Cuba with their sugar harvest was inspired in part by our interest in observing firsthand the attributes of communism. Like many young people, I explored new ideas and philosophies with gusto, searching for the connection between what made sense in my head and what I felt in my heart.

That search took me in other directions as well. I had many friends at Antioch who practiced Buddhism, which led me to write a research paper about it and study it further. I was attracted to Buddhism's moral foundation and its contrast with what seemed our nation's obsession with materialism. The more I studied it, however, the more I understood that it was a philosophy rather than a religion. Though it offered many admirable qualities, it did not resolve the spiritual yearning I felt.

I also investigated socialism and communism. I met and talked three times with the activist and Communist Party leader, Angela Davis, when she visited and spoke on the Antioch campus. One of these meetings was a dinner with a group of fellow students. I found Angela Davis to be warm and easy to talk with, quite adept at communicating with deaf people. Her presentations interested me as well. I was particularly concerned about the exploitation of underrepresented people and found the idea of equal treatment and fair distribution of wealth appealing. I took an independent college course about the Russian revolution that focused on the Bolsheviks and Karl Marx.

I was so intrigued with these philosophies that some friends and I spent nearly three weeks traveling in Russia. What I saw and heard there did not match up with my idealistic vision of communism, however. Our Russian tour guide, for instance, seemed brainwashed. She said that Russia's agricultural system was much stronger than America's and described a nonexistent crop failure and famine in the 1960s that supposedly caused thousands of Americans to starve to death. When we told her this had never happened, she thought we must have been too young to remember it. She refused to believe us.

I was taken aback by other experiences in Russia as well. I observed long lines of people waiting to buy limited and inferior food and supplies. I met people who wanted to buy our things so they could sell them on the black market. The people were not as open and friendly as in other nations; many drank heavily. Police were everywhere. The flourishing country I had expected to see did not exist. Instead, the atmosphere was oppressive. I eventually realized that neither of the Russian brands of socialism and communism provided the answers I sought.

I investigated Islam and spoke with Black Muslims on campus. I also read about and was inspired by Viktor Frankl's concentration camp experiences in his book *Man's Search for Meaning,* in which he described love as the ultimate and highest goal to which man can aspire. Yet in these cases, again, something seemed missing.

It was a frustrating period for me, exacerbated by the confusion and heated tone of the times. Many of my friends and fellow students were angry about the Vietnam War, about the prevailing political establishment, about authority in almost any form. During my senior year, students and faculty upset about a variety of issues launched a strike that effectively shut down the campus and created ill will among students, faculty, the administration, and the community for years to come.

It was fortunate that my "preceptorial" group at Antioch, a team of students that met regularly throughout my college years, was filled with students who seemed more mature and level-headed than most. Our academic advisor, a man named Howard Swann, provided an amazing sounding board for us to vent frustrations and explore ideas. The friendships I made among this group saved my sanity during these tumultuous times.

Surprisingly enough, it was an existentialism class that finally put me on the road to spiritual discovery. In that class, I read and was fascinated by the works of Fyodor Dostoyevsky, Franz Kafka, and Jean-Paul Sartre, among others. But it was a work of Scripture—the Bible's book of Ecclesiastes—that resonated most deeply with me.

The author of Ecclesiastes might be described as the first existentialist. Written about or by King Solomon himself, one of the wealthiest men who ever lived, the book details a search for meaning in a meaningless world. The resigned, cynical tone matched the feeling on the Antioch campus and in America at the time. Beneath the frustration and rage we all felt toward the injustices around us lurked a nagging sense of futility.

Some of the first lines of the book captured this succinctly:

> "Meaningless! Meaningless!"
> says the Teacher.
> "Utterly meaningless!
> Everything is meaningless."
> (Ecclesiastes 1:2)

I had encountered Ecclesiastes before, but while reading it in class at Antioch the verses suddenly seemed to describe everything I saw and felt. The book states that wisdom, pleasure, toil, advancement, and riches are all meaningless. I wanted to stand on a table and shout to my classmates, "Yes, that's right! World, do you see this? We're wasting our time and energy."

The words "What has been will be again, what has been done will be done again; there is nothing new under the sun (v. 9)" also made a powerful impression on me. I walked between classes on campus and saw the people, buildings, trees, and birds in a new light. I thought, *The sun comes up every day and has seen everything on this planet. Its rays stretch to every corner of the earth, revealing all. If only the sun could tell us about what it has seen and experienced, we'd be amazed to hear the stories of what men have done.*

It was astonishing to find these messages in a book of the Bible, tucked between advice on how to live wisely—the book of Proverbs—and a treatise on love—the book Song of Songs. I'd found an author that understood and spoke to my heart. But where and how, I still wondered, did God fit into all this?

The Back Door of Doubt

Many Christians treat spiritual doubt as a deadly plague, and believe that all who suffer from it must be cured quickly or quarantined so they will not infect the rest of the faithful population. In most of our churches, we are not encouraged to express our doubts, but rather to work our way through them as quickly and quietly as possible. All too often, one could say, doubt is like the elephant in the sanctuary—obvious yet unacknowledged.

My journey to faith has allowed me to view wavering belief differently. I think of doubt as a normal, most-often healthy, and perhaps even necessary stage in a growing faith. Novelist Flannery O'Connor wrote to a friend, "I don't know how the kind of faith required of a Christian living in the twentieth century can be at all if it is not grounded on the experience of unbelief."[1] Philip Yancey, meanwhile, has written, "When I wish to explore how faith works, I usually sneak in by the back door of doubt, for I best learn about my own need for faith during its absence."[2]

Doubt and testing are, perhaps, something like the searing heat of a fire sweeping through a forest. The results appear devastating at first, but the aftereffects can be just the opposite. The fire cleanses the landscape, allowing for a new ecosystem of plants, insects, and animals to thrive. Abundant life, stronger and more widespread than before, can grow out of death.

Doubt and testing have their place in our personal relationships as well. They protect us from people who might wish to deceive us. They also help us grow confidence in our friendships. We may have a friend we think we can count on in a crisis. But how deep is that friendship really? When the crisis arrives—say, your home is burned down and you need a place to live for a few months—you may wonder if your friend will actually come through. Some would become so consumed by these doubts that they would not even ask for help. But others, when they ask despite their doubts and receive a positive response, would find faith in their friend taken to a new level. They would have confronted their doubts.

After years of buildup, I confronted my spiritual doubts during my college years. To my disappointment, my explorations of atheism and other philosophies and religions did not lead to a credible alternative to faith in God. The more I sought answers, the less I seemed to uncover. Feelings of frustration, futility, and despair were never far from my mind. This is why I identified so well with the searching and the "meaningless" outbursts expressed in the book of Ecclesiastes. Yet my period of seeking and doubt was not a waste of time. Instead it prepared me to accept the discovery that would change my life.

I began to realize that faith has little to do with gathering knowledge. Our faith in facts and intellect alone, in actuality, can hinder our faith in matters of the spirit. God does not ask us to put our brains on the shelf. I believe He expects us to use them to question, seek answers, and discover the meaning of faith in our lives. Yet as in all things, there must be a balance. To rely on intellect without spiritual faith is simply dangerous. It can easily lead to an empty existence.

Perhaps this is why Jesus chose disciples who were for the most part ordinary, uneducated men. Perhaps it helps explain why many church denominations are in crisis or have already disappeared from the "sophisticated" populations of the United States and Europe, yet the Christian church is growing exponentially among the less educated peoples of Africa and China. It surely is related to the statement by Jesus, "I tell you the truth, anyone who will not receive the kingdom of God like a little child will never enter it" (Mark 10:15). We can be too sophisticated for our own good.

Maintaining this balance between intellect and simple faith, between doubt and conviction, is rarely easy. But perhaps it is not supposed to be easy. Our God is not a dictator, forcing us to bend to His whims. He remains mysterious, often hidden in shadow, revealing just enough of Himself to inspire a continuing sense of wonder. We are like the French mathematician and philosopher Blaise Pascal, "seeing too much to deny and too little to be sure."[3]

It is when we choose to overcome this hidden nature of God that we bring meaning to our faith. Despite our doubts, we make the leap and believe. It is not an empty act, but a decision that involves risk, commitment, and trust. I agree with Philip Yancey's statement that "the opposite of faith is not doubt, but fear."[4] To give life to our faith, we gather our courage and step fully into the spiritual unknown.

Peter took just such a step centuries ago. On a windy night, he and the other disciples were on a boat in the Sea of Galilee. Jesus, starting from the shore, walked on the water out to the boat. Peter and the rest shrank back in fear until Jesus called out, "Take courage! It is I. Don't be afraid."

Peter still wasn't sure. "Lord, if it's You," he said, "tell me to come to You on the water."

"Come" was the reply. So Peter got out of the boat and actually walked on the water toward Jesus—until he saw the wind whipping the waves, was overcome with fear, and began to sink.

"Lord, save me!" he cried.

Jesus quickly reached out with His hand and grabbed Peter. I imagine the tone of His response did not convey exasperation, but compassion. "You of little faith," Jesus said to his wavering disciple, "why did you doubt?" (Matthew 14:22-31).

I think Jesus knew the answer to His question, but asked for Peter's benefit—and ours. In the span of a few seconds, Peter demonstrated amazing courage and faith, followed immediately by fear and doubt. He walked the journey we all walk when we step out of the boat toward Christ, an undertaking both glorious and perilous. Like all of us, Peter stumbled. Yet the experience helped solidify his faith. It was part of the process that turned him into the great rock of the early church.

To move toward God—to communicate with Him—we must regularly test and strengthen our faith. This is the next secret in our journey:

Doubt is often the path to deeper faith.

A father once brought his son to Jesus, hoping for healing. The son was possessed by an evil spirit that caused him to fall to the ground, foam at the mouth, and gnash his teeth. When the father asked if Jesus could do anything, Jesus replied, "Everything is possible for him who believes."

The father's response mirrored what we all experience when we seek God: "I do believe; help me overcome my unbelief!" (Mark 9:14-24). We believe and disbelieve at the same time. Our doubt, however, can be the fuel for igniting a more intense and closely held faith, one that will burn longer and brighter with each spark of renewal.

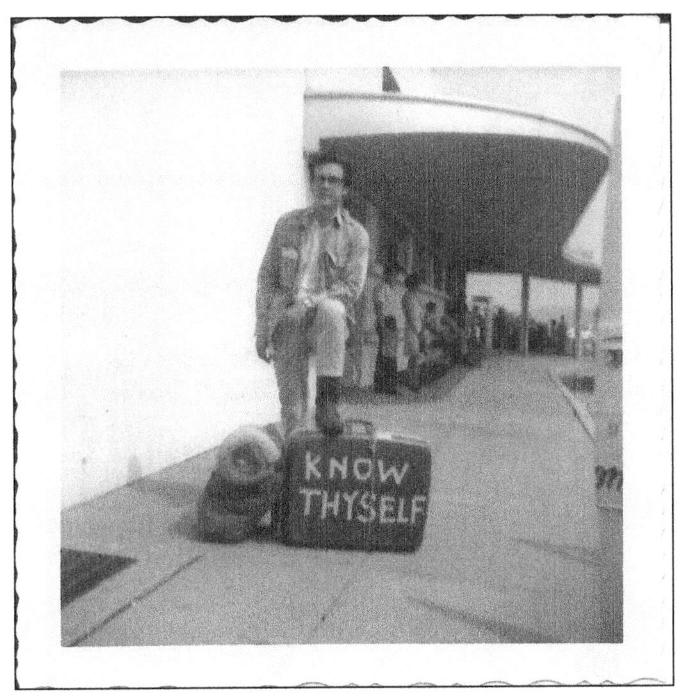

Paul on his way to England for a year of study abroad, 1970-1971

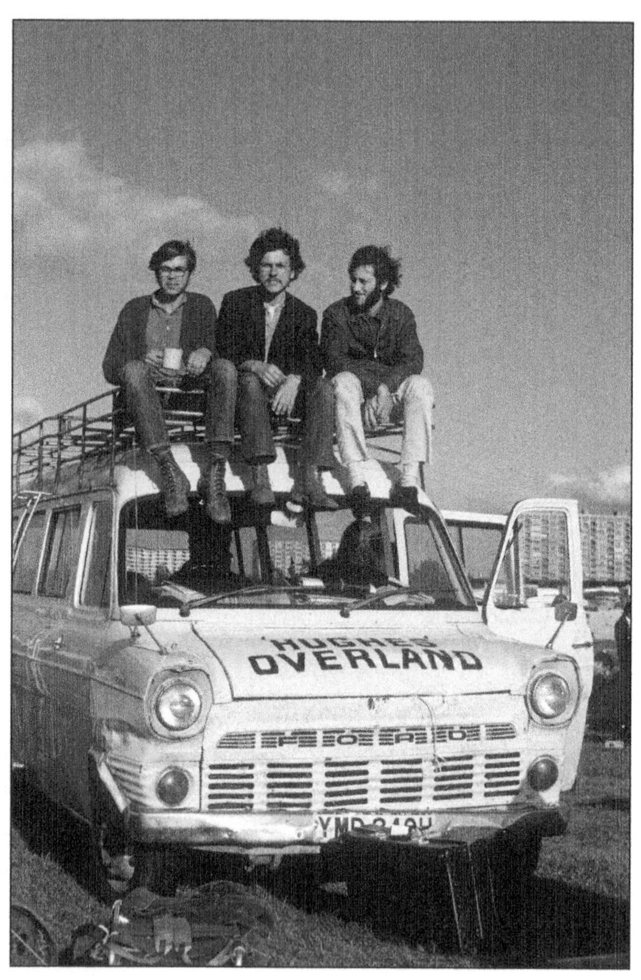

Paul and his college friends toured Eastern Europe and the USSR in 1971.

8

FINDING FAITH

God does not demand of me that I accomplish great things. He does demand of me that I strive for excellence in my relationships.

Ted W. Engstrom

The strike during my senior year at Antioch College effectively shut down the campus for nearly two months. Though some professors continued to hold classes in their homes, most normal college business was suspended. The strike destroyed the respectful, supportive spirit that had been so prevalent at Antioch. For me, it was depressing and demoralizing.

At the end of that academic year, the administration announced that all seniors would graduate and plans for a ceremony were thrown together. I decided to add some levity to this difficult time.

A couple of years earlier, Antioch President James Dixon had come to my apartment for dinner with my roommates and friends. Everyone in our group admired President Dixon, and of course my parents were impressed that he would take the time to meet with us.

They were impressed again when, early during my graduation week, I told them "the president of the college wants to have a private graduation ceremony with just me and my family and friends early in the morning before the official ceremony." My parents, other family, and friends—everyone who was coming to help me celebrate—was excited about this news.

That morning, we all drove to the thousand-acre Glen Ellen nature preserve adjoined to the campus. I led them to a life-size statue of Horace Mann, which towered several feet above us. President Mann was the first Antioch president, known as an education reformer, for being among the first college presidents to hire female faculty paid on an equal basis with their male colleagues, as well as to admit black students. My family and friends were surprised to see that the statue clutched a real, paper diploma, complete with a ribbon, in his right hand.

"Oh, there's the president," I said. "And he has my diploma."

Everyone burst out laughing. Our family often played jokes on each other, and they realized I'd just played a big one. I then climbed up to "accept" my diploma and announced that "Horace has just given me some valuable advice: Be ashamed to die until you have won some victory for humanity." This was the college motto.

Whether or not my joke was a sign of increased cleverness, my years of study at Antioch certainly added to my intellectual knowledge and experience. The college at the time had no grades (only pass/fail), no fraternities, no sports. The educational philosophy was "the world is our classroom." As students, our focus was on experience and politics. Despite or perhaps because of this unorthodox approach, I felt I'd received an excellent education. I earned a bachelor of arts degree in mathematics and computers with a minor in psychology and felt prepared to further my studies in graduate school.

Yet much of my time at Antioch was also deeply frustrating. Though I'd repeatedly explored avenues that initially promised to offer answers, I had not resolved my questions about a life philosophy, religion, or God.

I was also frustrated with my personal relationships. Though I had a few friends in my campus academic group, I felt this little band was too small to satisfy me. So much was happening on campus. So many ideas were being discussed and tested. I wanted to meet and interact with more people, but it was difficult to make these connections. When I did get around a new crowd, I usually couldn't follow their lively discussion by lipreading. Though I dated several girls, I didn't enjoy much success in the area of romance either. I was always searching for better communication and a better companion.

Looking back, I realize that I was surrounded by lively, caring people. I missed out on the opportunity to enjoy them because I was never satisfied. Today, many of these people are dear friends. At the time, though, I did not appreciate them nearly enough. Because of this, I often felt isolated.

In the middle of my undergraduate experience, I studied for more than a year at the University of Manchester in England. I originally viewed the idea as an adventure. After I arrived, however, my perspective soon changed. I found the British people reserved and hard to communicate with. They had their own culture and seemed unfriendly.

My loneliness intensified when the nation's postal workers went on strike. Suddenly, I had no way to communicate with family or friends. Both the university and my "flat" offered no telephone options for a deaf person. This was long before email and Facebook. For seven weeks, I was cut off from everyone I was close to.

Even after I left England and returned to Antioch, I was depressed. Most of my college friends were in a different sequence of classes or had dropped out. Howard Swann, my former academic advisor and, for me, a voice of reason, logic, and common sense, had left for a new teaching position at San Jose State University in California. He felt the faculty, students, and administrators on campus were no longer communicating and working together. Without my friends and Howard, I felt lost.

We've already talked about our deep-seated need for intimate relationships, both human and spiritual. During significant periods of my Antioch years, I lacked both. I was to discover that I was missing a key ingredient for achieving the kind of close relationship I sought.

Living in the Twilight Zone

The old TV series *The Twilight Zone* included an episode called "The Parallel." In it, an astronaut named Robert Gaines is orbiting the earth when he blacks out. He wakes up back on earth, seems to be fine, and is released into the custody of his family. The only problem is that certain details from his life no longer seem to line up—and Gaines's own daughter does not recognize him. He eventually concludes that the people he's living with aren't his family at all. He's entered a parallel universe.

Our existence depends on assumptions we make every minute. We assume that when our alarm goes off in the morning, the clock is keeping the correct time. We assume that our office job will still be waiting for us when we leave home in the morning. We assume that the cars moving toward us on the highway will stay in their lanes. And when we get home from work, we assume that the man or woman waiting for us, who certainly *looks* like our husband or wife, is indeed the same person we left that morning.

We'd go crazy if we tried to establish the veracity of every assumption we make via our senses each day. Our sanity wouldn't survive it. We accept these daily assumptions as an act of faith.

Our reliance on such faith extends to our relationships. After observing and interacting with a person for a period of time, we believe we've begun to understand them. If it's someone we've experienced on a deeper level over years—a father or mother, brother or sister, or spouse—we believe we *know* them. These have the potential to be the most fulfilling relationships of all.

Yet lurking in our minds, usually at the subconscious level, is the knowledge that it's all based on assumptions. Television shows from *The Twilight Zone* and *Star Trek* to the more recent *V* series, as well as hundreds of movies over decades, have tapped into this tension by featuring aliens guised as humans. Is the person standing before us *really* who we think it is—or have we been fooled by a potentially malevolent stranger?

The question goes far deeper than mere entertainment in the form of science fiction stories, as anyone with a spouse who's cheated on them knows from painful experience. Hidden in our psyche is the fear that the person we love and believe we know intimately will suddenly turn into someone frighteningly foreign. There is a measure of mystery about even those closest to us.

We can try to protect ourselves from these potential strangers. A relationship based on fear, however, will never become intimate. If we hold back, always suspicious of those around us, never venturing to reveal our vulnerabilities, we'll never achieve the intimacy that marks the best of human interaction.

I know of a couple named Ray and Lois that confronted this problem. Though they'd been married for more than thirty years, theirs was not an intimate union. Yet their marriage appeared solid, at least from the outside.

Then Ray changed. He began spending significant blocks of time with a group of new friends. When Lois asked what they did together, Ray became angry. Lois finally discovered that her husband and his buddies were visiting topless bars and strip clubs. She asked him to move out.

That was the blow that shook Ray out of his self-centered preoccupations. He realized he wanted to save his marriage, and believed it was still possible. He met with his pastor, who made a casual suggestion: "Why don't you and Lois spend some time praying together?" Ray was desperate enough to give it a try.

Lois was surprised by and suspicious of the idea. But she too believed there was a chance of restoring their relationship, so she also agreed to try it. Ray had moved out at this point, but after each of his visits with Lois, they ended their time by pouring out their feelings to God. The impact was dramatic.

"Our prayer times often led to long conversations in which Ray was very open and honest with me," Lois said. "I felt like I finally got to really know my husband…I was able to learn more about his fears, his inadequacies, and generally what was on his mind. It helped a lot in my learning to trust him again."[1]

Ray and Lois got back together. But it was only possible because they both believed their marriage could be renewed. In other words, it takes *faith* for a relationship to thrive—faith in our instincts and conclusions about the other person, faith in our mutual desire and ability to form and sustain a relationship, faith that such a relationship will be rewarding.

Faith, then, is a risk. Without it, no intimacy will grow.

Falling in Love

I wasn't thinking about the role of faith in relationships when I graduated from Antioch in 1973, but I'd always been fascinated by communication. A few months before, I'd been at Stanford University, completing my final work-study program.

One day I struck up a conversation with a marriage and family counselor who was visiting the campus.

After a few minutes, the woman said, "Paul, you are so easy to talk with (she was hearing), and you're obviously a passionate person. Have you ever thought of working in deaf education, working with parents and helping them communicate better with their children?"

Wow, I thought. For me, it was a life-altering question. I'd always focused on math, statistics, and computers, and never considered a career in education. But suddenly the idea made perfect sense. When I got back to my office, I used my arm to sweep the graduate school applications on my desk into a trash can. I ended up enrolling at the University of Illinois to seek a master's degree in educational psychology and deafness.

In Champaign, Illinois, my progress in the area of relationships took a dramatic turn for the better. I fell in love. Her name was Naomi. She was a beautiful girl with long black hair from Morton Grove, Illinois, studying deaf education. Her Jewish grandparents had come to America from Germany.

Naomi and I seemed to be a perfect match. We talked about and agreed on everything. We always enjoyed each other's company. I found her one of the easiest people to communicate with I'd ever met. The fact that she was hearing and I was deaf didn't bother either of us. Nor did the fact that she was Jewish and I was still seeking to define my beliefs. We both said that if we got married and had children, it didn't matter what religion we'd choose to raise them by.

I discovered, however, that religion mattered very much to Naomi's family. They were completely against our relationship because I was not Jewish, and deaf besides. Once, when we were at Naomi's parents' house and she was calling for me to reserve a rental car, her parents began saying things to Naomi, literally behind my back. "You see, the boy can't even make phone calls for himself," one said. "You'd have to be his interpreter for life!" Though I didn't understand why at the time, Naomi burst into tears. Naomi's grandparents, meanwhile, threatened to disown her if she married me.

After we dated for more than a year, the pressure from her family became too much for Naomi. She broke up with me.

I was devastated. I had a hard time accepting that a relationship that seemed so perfect could collapse just because of family disapproval. Because of her family, Naomi could no longer picture herself as happy being with me. She lost faith in the idea that we could have a future together.

The following year was extremely difficult for me. I confessed some of my troubles to friends but kept most of my feelings inside. During this time, I could have used a spiritual "friend" to confide in, but my faith was too undeveloped.

I did believe that God existed, but I didn't see or think about Jesus Christ as His Son. To me, Jesus was a religious and moral figure, someone to be admired as a role model the way I admired Gandhi, Martin Luther King Jr., and Robert Kennedy—but nothing more.

What I could not reconcile was the image of a compassionate Jesus—the one that my father mirrored and my mother trusted—with the stern, rule-making, "religious" God I'd learned about at Central Institute for the Deaf and heard about elsewhere. The church seemed to "own" this strict and judging God, and after what I'd seen of my father's congregations, I wanted little to do with church. This God seemed distant and unapproachable to me. I didn't know how to communicate with Him or if I even wanted to.

Early in my time at Antioch, I began to participate in the work-study program. Through the college, I secured a position to work at Wayne State University in Detroit for six months. I rented an apartment in Detroit, packed my things, and prepared to leave Antioch. My parents drove up to help me make the transition.

Two days before I was to leave, however, my work-study adviser at Antioch called me into his office and told me that things hadn't "worked out" after all and that I would have to look for a new position (I later found out that Wayne State rescinded its offer because officials found out I was deaf).

I was extremely upset. I'd already signed a six-month lease for an apartment adjacent to the Wayne State campus. Suddenly my academic program was in limbo and I had nowhere to live.

My parents did their best to calm me down. They told me that God has a plan for our lives and that everything happens for a reason. "Something even better will come along," my mother said. "I'm going to pray about this for you."

My response reflected my feelings about God and prayer at the time. I was indifferent. Though I didn't say it aloud, my reaction to my mother's words was *Okay, fine, whatever you want to do.*

The next day, the adviser again called me in and told me about an opportunity that had just opened up at Beloit College in Wisconsin. An economics professor was seeking an innovative student to set up mathematical models for his statistics students and researchers. The position was above my skill level, but when I inquired, they said they wanted me to come. It turned out to be the best job I'd ever had and enabled me to follow it with a work study opportunity at Stanford. I heard from other students at Wayne State, meanwhile, that my work there would have been mostly mindless, minimum wage duties.

Yet I didn't attribute my change in fortunes to God or my mother's prayers. I felt it was just luck—or coincidence.

Years later, not much had changed in my attitude toward God. I'd mostly put Him and my searching aside to focus on my studies. Though my career was progressing nicely—I earned my master's degree at Illinois in 1975 and began work on my doctorate—the rest of my life was confused. I still didn't know why I was there or what life was really about.

What I didn't realize was that a virus would soon lead me to an epiphany that would change everything.

It's About Relationship

In November 1976, I was still living in Illinois and pursuing my Ph.D. The arrival of winter weather brought with it an unwanted gift in the form of the flu. Feeling miserable and looking for relief, I decided to visit the university student health clinic.

At the clinic, I asked for a nurse named Coy. She was petite, with salt and pepper hair, probably in her late forties. Coy was my favorite nurse because she was friendly, expressive, and easy to lipread. When she entered the waiting room, she greeted me with a big smile.

"How are you? she asked.

I sighed. "Oh, I'm just not feeling well," I said. "I have the flu. I've got stress at work. I feel terrible."

We discussed my illness for a bit. Then, wondering at Coy's consistently upbeat attitude—and in my frazzled state, even feeling irritated by it—I asked about the source of her joy.

"Why are you so happy all the time?" I said. "People are always complaining to you. Don't you ever get sad?"

"No, not really," she said, "It's because Jesus is in my heart."

I rolled my eyes. This wasn't what I wanted to hear.

"I don't want to talk about religion," I said. "I'm not interested in religion."

Coy leaned a little closer and locked eyes with mine. "It's not *about* religion," she said. "It's about having a relationship with Jesus. You know, I can talk with Him. He's my best friend. I have a great relationship with Him."

Somewhere deep down, it was as if all the tumblers in my inner mechanisms clicked into place. I uttered a silent, *Ohhhh.*

Coy still looked at me intently. "Paul, do you have that relationship with Jesus? You know, like a close friend, someone you can talk to?"

My mind processed at breakneck speed. It fit. It felt right. Why hadn't I seen this before? My mother talked about Jesus this way, but she never used the word *relationship.*

"I...I've been way off on another path," I said. "I think it's too late for me to have a relationship like that."

Now it was Coy's turn to shake her head. "No, no," she said. "You can start right now. You can ask Him to be your friend. Ask Him into your heart. Ask Him to be your savior."

I must have looked surprised.

"If you don't like it, you can ask Him to get out," she said. "Just try it for two or three months."

I left the clinic that afternoon feeling strangely hopeful. *Wow.* I thought. *I have a lot to reflect on here.*

A few days later, I mentioned this idea of relationship with Jesus to a fellow graduate student. He was only a casual friend, but I knew he was a Christian. "Yes, yes, you can have a relationship with Jesus," he said. He seemed to have understood this all along, but it was a new concept to me.

The student reached into his backpack. "Here," he said, "you should read this." It was a copy of the C. S. Lewis book *Mere Christianity.*

I soon started reading and couldn't put the book down. I was impressed from the opening pages. It all seemed so logical. It made sense.

Something in those words connected with me not only intellectually, but also emotionally. I found myself crying as I contemplated a God who was real and someone I could communicate with. Incredible as it would have seemed to me only days earlier, I began to believe in the possibility that there could be a genuine, lasting relationship between God and me.

End of the Search

My renewed enthusiasm over my spiritual search caused me to look closer at the Bible. I examined the psalms and was struck by the words of Psalm 139:

> O LORD, you have searched me and you know me.
>
> You know when I sit and when I rise; you perceive my thoughts from afar.
>
> You discern my going out and my lying down; you are familiar with all my ways. Before a word is on my tongue you know it completely, O LORD…(vv. 1-4)
>
> For you created my innermost being; you knit me together in my mother's womb.
>
> I praise you because I am fearfully and wonderfully made; your works are wonderful, I know that full well. (vv. 13-14)

As I read, I thought, *He is the reason we're here. My personality was planted in me by God. My ego, my passion, the way I'm restless and driven, all of it is from God. He created me the way I am and sent me on this journey of searching for Him.*

I also reevaluated my thinking about Jesus. As I looked closer at the Bible, I realized that I agreed with so much of what He did and stood for. He was a rebel who challenged unjust authority. He was a champion of the poor and underprivileged, often healing them of illness and disease. He treated women with respect. He chose rough, uneducated "nobodies" to be His disciples. He mingled with common people and "sinners" even as He encouraged them to leave their sins behind and turn to God.

I finally confronted the account of the greatest miracle of them all—the crucifixion and resurrection of Jesus—and found it plausible. The distant Jesus so often distorted by the church wasn't the one I was looking for. But there was another Jesus. The *real* Jesus of the Bible, the one Coy knew personally, was more than a prophet or religious figure. He truly was the Son of God.

Soon after, I made my decision. It was a cool and cloudy afternoon a few days before Thanksgiving. I sat in an easy chair in my studio apartment, the one with the huge window and view of sycamore trees. I was still recovering from the virus that had bothered me a couple weeks before, but my thoughts were on something else entirely.

I stirred from my chair and dropped to my knees. I was crying. I knew what I wanted to accomplish but wasn't sure how to say it.

"Hi, God," I said. "Hey, how's it going? I'm sorry I didn't do this before. I'd like to ask You to forgive everything I've said and thought about You. I'm sorry for the bad things I said about You, for taking your name in vain. Please just reject all of that. I didn't have a high opinion of You, and I'm really sorry.

"Please forgive me also for all the people I haven't been nice to. Thank You for taking my bad behavior onto Yourself…for dying for all of us."

I took a deep breath. "Lord, would You come into my heart now? I'm ready to give my life to You."

To my amazement, I distinctly felt the Lord's presence in those moments. There were no flashing lights or booming voices, but I *knew* that He was real and that He was with me. The sense of love and relief was overwhelming. After all these years, I'd found what I sought.

My search was over.

The Value of Faith

Philip Yancey talks about the parallels between getting to know another human being and forging a relationship with God.

> I first learn a person's name. Something in his personality attracts me to him. I spend time with my new friend, learning what activities we have in common. I give gifts and make small sacrifices for that friend. I do things to please my friend that I wouldn't do otherwise. I share happy times and sad times; we laugh together and weep together. I reveal my deepest secrets. I take risks of relationship. I make commitments. I fight and argue, then reconcile. All these stages of relationship apply to God as well.[2]

Now I too was in the process of getting to know and establishing a relationship with God. I'd found someone I could share my innermost thoughts and concerns with, things I'd never revealed to anyone. I told Him that I often felt so insignificant, like a "nothing." I talked about being restless, about always searching for a purpose, that I desperately wanted to be useful. It felt both exhilarating and a little frightening to share these feelings for the first time.

The key that opened the door for me was faith—not only faith in the reality of God, but also in His love for me and my ability to connect with Him in a personal, meaningful way. I saw for the first time that we could indeed have a future together.

Peter and the other disciples went through an experience like this. Remember when Jesus walked on the waters of the Sea of Galilee and saved Peter, and when Peter tried to join Him, he grew afraid, and began to sink? The disciples already knew about Jesus' divinity, but seeing His power and compassion so vividly deepened their faith: "Then those who were in the boat worshipped him, saying, 'Truly you are the Son of God'" (Matthew 14:33).

I had no such miracles to base my faith on, however. I suspect that you rarely encounter them either. Unlike faith in our relationships with humans (or God in human form), it seems that our faith in spiritual matters must rest on less physical or tangible evidence.

The Lord has said as much. It seems, in fact, that He prefers it this way. After His death and resurrection, He appeared to some of the disciples. But Thomas, who had not viewed the resurrected Christ himself, doubted their story.

> "Unless I see the nail marks in his hands and put my finger where the nails were, and put my hand into his side, I will not believe it."
>
> A week later his disciples were in the house again, and Thomas was with them. Though the doors were locked, Jesus came and stood among them and said, "Peace be with you!" Then he said to Thomas, "Put your finger here; see my

> hands. Reach out your hand and put it into my side. Stop doubting and believe."
>
> Thomas said to him, "My Lord and my God!"
>
> Then Jesus told him, "Because you have seen me, you have believed; blessed are those who have not seen and yet have believed." (John 20:25-29)

We can infer from this passage of Scripture that we are most blessed and honored by God when we develop faith without the benefit of obvious signs and miracles. In some way, it pleases Him when we overcome our doubts and choose to believe based on the limited evidence at hand. We may not fully understand or comprehend our Lord, yet we place our trust in Him anyway.

Faith alone in God and the potential of our connection to Him is not enough for a thriving relationship, however. It also requires the practical ability to communicate. Remember Ray and Lois? After years of distance and Ray's indiscretions, they each took the first step toward each other by believing their marriage could be saved. Yet it was when they combined this faith with openhearted prayer that they began to revitalize their bond.

My relationship with Anne traveled a similar road. We both loved each other. We had faith in that love and what could be. Yet we also struggled mightily in the early years of our marriage. It wasn't until we met with counselors and wise Christian friends that we discovered communication techniques that allowed us to nurture and develop our union.

This, then, is our newest secret:

Faith combined with effective communication leads to strong relationship.

It is true for our friendships and marriages. It is also true for our relationship with God. One without the other is valuable and offers hope, but ultimately leaves us realizing that we are missing out. When we fuse both faith and an ability to connect, however, we find our lives abundantly blessed.

9

The Truth Of The Matter

Honesty is such a lonely word.

Billy Joel

One dictionary definition of communication is "a process by which information is exchanged between individuals through a common system of symbols, signs, or behavior."[1] The information we exchange must be complete and reliable, however, or the whole system falls apart. If we hold back or misrepresent what we know, the result can be more than a communication breakdown—it can be devastating.

My personal witness to a communication breakdown began to take place during a family tragedy. My brother David, thirteen years older than me, was sensitive, imaginative, and mischievous. He indulged in all kinds of creative and sometimes even dangerous antics, especially when Jonathan and I were around to serve as his audience.

David was a fantastic storyteller. I loved to sit in front of him, reading his lips and gestures and savoring every detail. He told wild tales of monsters and horrors. The storytelling often took place at night. David would turn down the lights to make the room spooky. He used many facial expressions and hand gestures. From time to time, he acted out how a character in the story walked, ate, and behaved. I loved every minute of it—yet I was also petrified.

One night when I was about eight, my parents told me to answer the doorbell. At the door stood a tall, ugly man whose face was badly disfigured. He gestured that I was to come with him. I refused but froze in panic. I couldn't move and couldn't take my eyes off him. Just as I was working up the courage to bolt and run, I realized it was David standing there with a stocking over his face, dressed in shabby clothing.

Another prank occurred when I was eleven and on a break from Central Institute for the Deaf. David took me to the city zoo at Hot Springs, Arkansas. When no one was looking, he snuck over a barrier, grabbed a crocodile by its tail, swung it over his head, and tossed it into the pond.

Shortly after the zoo incident, David left our home in Huntington, West Virginia, telling my parents that he was driving to visit his girlfriend in Tennessee. Three days later a pair of police officers came to our door. They spoke to my parents, who started to cry.

"What's going on?" I asked my mother.

"David's happy now," she said through tears. "He's in heaven."

"You mean he's dead?" I said. I was numb. I couldn't believe it.

I wanted to know what had happened. I kept asking my parents about it, but the answer was always the same: "We don't know."

Later, I found out that David had been killed by a shotgun. On our way to Rogersville, Tennessee, to claim David's body, we visited a rest stop. In the restroom, I again asked my father about what had happened to my brother. "We don't know," he said. "Maybe he was cleaning his gun and the gun went off."

"Did somebody kill him? Did somebody come in and shoot him?"

"We don't know. Maybe."

With no definitive answers, I got more and more frantic. My mind filled with wild possibilities. "If someone shot him, we should all get the police and catch the bad person," I said. "We should put him in jail."

My father did not want to talk about it. "We'll have to wait and see," he said. Later, I asked to read the obituary. "We haven't received one yet," was my father's reply.

The funeral was to be in Springfield, Ohio, home of my grandmother. Dunbar and his wife drove in from Connecticut. At my grandmother's house the night before the service, I woke up in the bedroom I was sharing with Jonathan and saw that he was gone. I went to my parents' bedroom and found my entire family there, talking. I felt excluded and sensed that everyone was withholding information from me.

At breakfast the next morning, I finally erupted. In an angry and loud voice, I said, "Where is the obituary? I know it's in the newspaper. I want to read it!"

At last, my mother produced the paper and handed it to me. The article said that David had taken his own life. *Oh, now I understand,* I thought. *This explains everything.* I knew David had suffered from terrible headaches after he'd hit his head in a car accident years before. He also, like my father, dealt with depression. He committed suicide because he was in great physical and emotional pain.

My parents and I were also in pain. In their grief, they could not bring themselves to tell me what David had done. I'm sure they felt that hiding the truth would protect me somehow.

The result, however, was additional anguish and confusion for me. My grief was intensified because I didn't understand, and because I sensed others knew what had happened yet would not tell me.

I Think I'm Going to Die

Two years later, when I was thirteen, I went through another incident made worse by incomplete information. I was home on a vacation from my studies at Central Institute for the Deaf. My father took me to our family doctor for my annual checkup. I'd already been told that I had a heart murmur. During this exam, the doctor placed a stethoscope on my chest. He frowned and listened for a very long time. I saw the growing concern in my father's eyes. Finally, I was told to put my clothes back on and sit in the waiting room.

Through an open door to the doctor's study near the examination room, I watched the doctor talk with my father. Both had serious expressions. Intermittently, my father clenched his fists. This went on for more than fifteen minutes. I was so nervous that my own hands shook. I said to my friend who'd come with us, "The doctor kept listening to my heart. I think I'm going to die." I'd learned from David that dying was a nasty business that upset everyone.

Eventually my father came out. "There's nothing to worry about," he said. "Everything is fine."

I didn't believe him.

Later, I asked my mother about it. She said that it was just the heart murmur, and that I would be fine. I didn't believe her either. My doubts intensified during the following months and years when my father sometimes pulled me aside to say, "Paul, please be careful. You don't want to overdo things. You need to have a long life."

Though my parents were wonderful communicators in so many ways, the experience with David's suicide, and now this, led me to mistrust them on certain issues. It wasn't until many years later that I discovered my parents and the doctors knew there was a problem with my heart but didn't understand what it was or what to do about it. The technology to explain it didn't exist. Today, I know that I have a bicuspid aortic valve—one of the three parts to one of my heart valves is missing. It's not as serious a condition as I had feared it was back then.

Though my parents and the doctors didn't understand my heart issue, I wish they'd been up front with me about it. Instead, I grew up suspicious of doctors, doubting what my parents were telling me about my health, and expecting to die at a young age.

These suspicions intensified during my year of college study in England. I wanted new glasses, so I went in for an eye exam. After a series of tests, the doctors handed me a piece of paper that said I had a rare condition called retinitis pigmentosa (RP). The doctors seemed in a hurry and told me nothing more. I thought I must have acquired RP during my recent spring break trip to Africa. Research at the Manchester library revealed, however, that the disease is genetic. That made sense, since I knew my brother Jonathan had it also.

The prognosis was troubling. For most people, the disorder gradually gets worse. Many people with RP go blind by the age of forty or even thirty. There is no cure. I was twenty-two at the time and terrified by the idea of losing my sight. I depended on it for everything.

I was also disturbed by the thought that my parents might already know. I'd had regular vision exams while growing up. A family member or someone who knew me well had always accompanied me. Had the doctors discovered my condition and informed my parents while keeping me in the dark?

Soon after, my year of study in England ended and I flew back to America. My parents were at the airport to pick me up. When I walked down the ramp and saw them, I didn't offer a cheery greeting or give them a hug. Instead, the first words out of my mouth were, "Did you know I have RP?"

My mother burst into tears. It was true. They'd known all along.

"Why didn't you tell me?" I said.

My parents explained that since I was deaf and had a heart issue, they felt I already had enough life challenges to worry about. They didn't want to burden me with another serious medical concern.

I was still upset, but at the same time, I understood. *My poor parents. They've gone through so much. I'm not going to blame them. I'll do them a favor and say nothing more about it.*

In the years since, my vision has deteriorated a little, but it has been stable for some time. I've learned that my particular strain of RP is an unusual one and less damaging than the more common version. Nevertheless, I would have much preferred learning about it from my parents and having the chance to investigate the issue at a younger age. Their decision to again keep the truth from me caused enormous stress and inserted another wedge of mistrust into our otherwise trusting relationship.

Destroyed by Duplicity

Human beings have practiced deceit since the days of Adam and Eve. We withhold information or lie outright for a variety of reasons: love, grief, ignorance, fear, to avoid embarrassment, and certainly to manipulate others for our personal gain.

Whatever our motives, our deceit—whether intentional or not—comes at a cost. Sooner or later, someone will experience anger, confusion, mistrust, pain, or sorrow as a result of our duplicity. Frequently, the primary victims are ourselves.

I experienced this firsthand during graduate school. A professor at the University of Illinois was famous for his research on people's attitudes. I found it extremely interesting and desperately wanted to take a class from him, so I enrolled in one. On the first day, forty students showed up. The professor said this was far too many. He asked how many of us had taken a particular course. "This course is a prerequisite for my class," he said. "If you didn't take it, leave right now." A few students got up and left.

The professor repeated this process, mentioning other courses. More students got up and left. Eventually, we were down to ten students.

"This is perfect," the professor said. "Now we can go to work."

I was still in the class—but I shouldn't have been. I hadn't taken three of the courses the professor listed. I was so stubborn and so focused on taking the class that I lied by my silence.

And what did my deception accomplish? I had a terrible experience in that class. The professor essentially treated us as guinea pigs for a book he was working on. He tested out his theories by proposing them in class and then monitored our responses during discussions. I didn't understand half of what he said and didn't enjoy the class at all. I ended up earning my first C in graduate school, a big disappointment. I would have been much better off taking another course.

Scripture tells us that "the unfaithful are destroyed by their duplicity" (Proverbs 11:3). Sometimes, however, we have a hard time remembering this truth. Our lies lead us into trouble. And when we lie to the people we're closest to, it's as if we build a wall of mistrust between us. Each half-truth or dishonest statement, no matter how minor, adds another brick, making it harder to create the kind of connection we desire.

I practiced a different kind of dishonesty as a boy growing up deaf. For my friends and me at Central Institute for the Deaf, interacting with hearing people was a challenge. We often did not understand what they were saying to us. If the situation promised to be volatile or embarrassing, however, we pretended that we did understand. At these moments, I knew it was wrong to pretend, but I felt like such a failure for not comprehending hearing people that I did it anyway. Most of the time, this only made matters worse.

When I was thirteen, however, I observed a new example of how to handle these kinds of situations. Lee, the part-time assistant and alumnus of CID, took several of us boys to a theater to see the movie *Lawrence of Arabia*. The movie was long and complex, of course with no subtitles, and we simply couldn't follow it. Lee often explained a movie before we saw it and talked with us again afterwards to answer further questions. This time, however, he too was at a loss.

With the group of us in tow, Lee went to the manager and tried to persuade him to refund our money since we hadn't gotten much out of it. The manager refused, but did give us a handbook that summarized the plot.

For me, it was revolutionary to see an adult deaf person admit to a hearing person that he didn't understand something. Lee was not embarrassed in the least. Instead, he assertively addressed the manager and politely requested the refund. We didn't get our money back, but through the handbook we did end up with a better appreciation of the movie. I'm sure that Lee also earned the respect of the manager.

I began to realize that being open and honest about my limitations or lack of understanding was the best way to approach such situations. Honesty clears away the obstacles, allowing for complete and satisfying communication.

This was an important lesson for me, one I remembered during one of the most critical conversations of my life.

Out in the Open

In December 1976, I was at a Christmas party with more than forty people in an upscale, four-bedroom home high in the hills of Pasadena, California. The box-like structure, definitely art deco, was built into the hillside. The interior was both classy and homey. Rows of books and contemporary art—Picasso and Matisse reproductions, as well as several original paintings by an Israeli artist—lined the walls, along with photographs of our host with the actor Spencer Tracy and other celebrities. A Porsche was parked in the garage. To someone who'd lived the last few years as a financially strapped college student, it was an impressive environment. I felt honored to be included.

The party included a mix of deaf, hard-of-hearing, and hearing guests. Our host, Dr. James Marsters, was well-known to everyone in the deaf community. He'd earned a bachelor's degree in chemistry and then graduated from New York University's dental school, which led to a successful career as an orthodontist. He was a licensed pilot at a time when only a handful of deaf people had been approved to fly.

What Dr. Marsters was most famous for, however, was inventing the text telephone system known as the TTY. In 1964, he and two colleagues converted a Teletype machine into a device that could relay a typewritten conversation through a telephone line. For the first time, deaf people could communicate over the telephone like everyone else. It was a breakthrough that opened up many new possibilities for the deaf and hard of hearing.

Dr. Marsters wasn't the only distinguished party reveler that night. Other deaf pilots had also joined us, as well as an accountant, social worker, and occupational therapist. Another guest was a computer analyst, one of the first deaf graduates (and without any support services) from Harvard. I was also singled out for pursing my doctorate from the University of Illinois.

And then there was a young woman named Anne Keenan, among the first hard-of-hearing registered nurses in the country. While Anne was out of the room, Dr. Marsters passed around an article featuring her that had appeared in a hospital trade magazine. She had applied to twenty colleges. All turned her down because of her hearing loss save one, the Saint Anthony School of Nursing in Rockford, Illinois. "She's tough," our host said, obviously admiring her persistence.

I, however, was more impressed by the picture of Anne that accompanied the article. It showed a portrait of Anne in her nurse's uniform, an inviting smile on her face. Even in black and white ink on a flat magazine page, something about her expression conveyed both softness and unusual depth. I felt I could see into her soul.

I had good reason for my interest in Anne that evening—we were on our first date together. We'd met two years before at a youth leadership conference in Atlanta. We were both dating someone else at the time. Anne lived in California while I went to school in Illinois. There was little reason to think about pursuing a relationship, but since we were both officers elected to two-year terms with the organization that sponsored the leadership conference, we were expected to stay in touch as we conducted business.

For me, remaining in contact with Anne was a pleasure. I found myself occasionally sending her short notes that had little to do with our duties as leadership officers. I was delighted when she responded. I told her how disappointed I was that I couldn't join the leadership officers during their next meeting in Boston. I was scheduled to take my Ph.D. qualifying exam, a comprehensive, three-day written test that covered everything we'd learned in the last few years. She wrote back after the conference, telling me who was there and how it went. There was a familiarity in the way we talked and wrote to each other that made it seem as if we'd known each other for years.

By the time of the Christmas party, my life had begun to change. I'd broken up with Naomi was nearing the end of my doctoral studies at Illinois. I wanted to start my teaching career somewhere near my parents and my brother's family in Berkeley, so I applied for positions at colleges on the West Coast. My pursuit of a job was also an opportunity to visit old friends. Anne and I made plans to see each other after one of my job interviews, and when she invited me to the Christmas party, I quickly accepted. I hadn't seen Anne for two years, but when we drove up to the party from Long Beach, it was as if we were continuing where we left off in Atlanta. The conversation flowed easily.

That comfortable communication continued at the party, both between Anne and me and with the other guests. Everyone seemed to be enjoying each other's company, and Dr. Marsters and his wife, Alice, went out of their way to make sure everyone was having a good time.

There was just one problem with the evening: Anne seemed to be avoiding me. Anne and I would chat and laugh together for a few minutes, and all seemed to be well, but then she'd find something to eat or someone to talk to and drift away from me. The first couple of times it happened, I tracked her down and tried to resume our conversation. But after she disappeared for the third time, I changed my strategy.

I'm not sure what's going on here, but I'm not going to follow her anymore, I thought. *I don't want to scare her away.*

For someone who prided himself on communication and thought he'd found a kindred spirit, it was a puzzling situation. Only later did I learn the explanation for Anne's behavior: nerves. She'd decided she liked me and thought I might even be someone she could fall in love with, but she'd promised herself she would never fall for a deaf person.

After the party, at Anne's apartment, the two of us sat at her kitchen table drinking coffee. I was about to learn that when

Anne has something on her mind, it doesn't take her long to express it.

She wrapped her hands around her mug and locked her blue eyes on mine. "So, Paul," she said, "what do you want out of this relationship?"

I leaned back a few inches. *Wow, I can't believe she just asked me that,* I thought. *She's very straightforward.*

I'd thought a great deal about communication in relationships by this point in my life. We both had gone through difficult experiences with relationships, so I appreciated Anne's desire to start ours in an open and honest manner. Yet I also felt it was important to establish some connections between us before we launched into deep conversation. We needed to find out if we had similar interests, backgrounds, and passions.

"Well," I said, "I think if we're going to date again, we should get to know each other better to see if we might be right for each other. I believe if you want to have a good relationship with someone of the opposite sex, you have to learn to communicate well with that person over a long period of time. That way you become bonded.

"Unfortunately," I continued, "people start too fast. They don't communicate for very long, the companionship isn't there yet, and then they have sex. That complicates everything. They miss the opportunity to get to know the other person well and enjoy them for who they are. Too many people jump into sex. It messes things up and leaves them with hurt feelings."

Anne just looked at me, absorbing my words. "That's true," she said. "I'm not interested in games. I agree with you."

I added that I had believed Anne had a strong ability to communicate. Then I told her that just the month before, I'd invited Jesus Christ into my heart. I knew Anne was Catholic, and wasn't sure how she'd respond.

Anne's eyes widened. "Really?" she said. "I just did the same thing in August."

It seemed that we did have much in common. We were talking openly and easily. My interest in this young woman was soaring higher than the hills above Pasadena.

Now, more than thirty years later, I can say that the "ground rules" we established that night—avoiding games and simply being frank and truthful with each other—are among the foundations of our marriage. They also help explain our next secret:

Open, honest communication leads to trust and intimacy.

Just the Facts, Ma'am

Conrad Smith, a pastor and author of the book *Best Friends,* describes three levels of human interaction:

> Level One—Facts: "I talked with the boss today."
>
> Level Two—Opinions: "I don't think my boss liked my presentation."
>
> Level Three—Feelings: "I'm worried because my boss was silent after my presentation. I'm discouraged because after all the hours I put into it, I wanted him to tell me that he liked it."[2]

Too many relationships, especially marriages, are centered on the first level of communication. Couples stuck at "level one" talk only about surface issues and fail to get to know each other in a deep way. They avoid expressing true feelings because they're afraid their partner will belittle them or somehow use the information against them. When asked a direct question, they even lie to protect themselves.

You may have done it yourself. When your partner says, "What's wrong?" and you answer, "Nothing, I'm fine," is that really what you mean? Chances are you're thinking something closer to *The kids are driving me crazy, I can't keep up with life, and I'm worried that you're losing interest in our marriage and will leave me one of these days*. A little honesty on your part can lead to a heart-to-heart conversation and a renewed relationship.

Anne and I found it easier to open up and express our feelings when we employed the "I have something to say" technique I mentioned earlier. When we knew we had ten minutes to express our feelings and that we wouldn't be interrupted, we both felt more comfortable talking about our deeper concerns, fears, and mistakes. In this way, we learned to listen better to each other. That in turn encouraged us to open up more. You might try it with your close relationships.

Of course, a certain amount of common sense ought to accompany your truth-telling. You probably don't need to tell your spouse how haggard he or she looks the morning after a restless night or how foolish he or she sounded at the party last week. Your aim should be to promote, not injure, with your honesty.

My father once faced this dilemma. While sitting in a hotel restaurant, he struck up a conversation with a blind man. The man took out a picture, showed it to my father, and said, "This is the woman I'm going to marry."

After my father offered his congratulations, the man asked, "Can you do me a favor? Can you tell me something? Be honest with me. Can you look at the picture and tell me how pretty she is? I don't expect her to be beautiful. But can you honestly tell me on a scale of one to five, where five is beautiful?"

My father looked at the picture in his hand. The woman was not especially pretty, probably a one or a two.

"Well, to me," my father said, "I will say she is a three, maybe a four."

The man smiled. "Really? That's not bad! It's better than I expected. Thank you."

Later, when my father told me this story, I was flabbergasted.

"You weren't honest with him," I said. "That's awful."

"What difference does it make?" my father said. "Beauty is relative. It doesn't really matter. But to him, it was very important."

At the time, I questioned my father's words to the blind man. Now, however, I've come to appreciate that beauty is in the eye of the beholder—and that in certain situations, perhaps, so is honesty.

Being Honest with God

We've looked at the value of honesty in our person-to-person relationships. But what about truthfulness in communication between person and spirit? How important is honesty in our relationship with God?

Let's examine God's side of the equation first. We can see from examples throughout Scripture that the word of God is always true. My experience has shown that His commandments and guidance for loving and living with others are the surest road to fulfillment. The wisdom of Jesus' words in the Sermon on the Mount (Matthew 5:3–7:27) is as relevant today as it was two thousand years ago: "Your word is a lamp to my feet and a light for my path" (Psalm 119:105).

The Bible is amazingly consistent, despite the fact that it was written by forty authors over a period of fifteen hundred years. No other religion or philosophy—and I've explored many of them—makes more sense.

We also know from Scripture that God keeps His promises. When He said He would make Abraham the father of a great nation, He did. When He said He would bless Abraham and barren Sarah with a child, He did. When He promised Moses He would deliver the people of Israel, that's exactly what happened. When He told Joshua He would be faithful to him as He was to Moses, He kept that promise too. The word of Jesus was equally sacrosanct—just as He foretold, He died and rose again.

Finally, the Bible makes it clear that God places the highest value on *our* honesty. The ninth of the Ten Commandments is "You shall not give false testimony against your neighbor" (Exodus 20:16). We know from the words of King David that the Lord is "pleased with integrity" (1 Chronicles 29:17). The apostle Paul, in his letter to the Colossians, explains that honesty is one of the tenets of our new life in Christ: "Do not lie to each other, since you have taken off your old self with its practices and have put on the new self, which is being renewed in knowledge in the image of its Creator" (Colossians 3:9-10).

Furthermore, we can be encouraged by the fact that when we are tempted to speak in half-truths or outright falsehoods by the "father of lies" (John 8:44), God always gives us the means to find our way back to the truth: "When you are tempted, he will also provide a way out so that you can stand up under it" (1 Corinthians 10:13).

We can also be encouraged by the example of Peter. The rock of the early church was, in addition, the source of one of the most famous lies in history. When confronted by the crowd in the bitter, confusing hours after the arrest of Jesus, Peter three times denied knowing Him, saying "I don't know what you're talking about" and, with an oath, "I don't know the man!" Peter then wept bitterly after he realized what he'd done (Matthew 26:69-75).

Yet God did not discard the man that turned away from his Lord at a moment of crisis. Nor did Peter allow his lie to destroy his destiny. The same man who out of awful fear refused to admit his link to the Nazarene built upon that failure to become a foundation of the Christian movement. Once a coward, he grew—with the help of the Holy Spirit—into a fearless leader who boldly proclaimed the truth before the powerful and antagonistic Jews who made up the Sanhedrin. After healing a cripple and being thrown in jail for the night, Peter said to the assembly, "Know this, you and all the people of Israel: It is by the name of Jesus Christ, whom you crucified but whom God raised from the dead, that this man stands before you healed" (Acts 4:10).

The Lord expects truthfulness from us in our human interactions. But His plan is bigger than that. He also wants us to be honest with Him. He desires the kind of honest interaction so central to His relationship with King David, a man after God's own heart. Through his psalms, David expressed some of the most bitter complaints, as well as some of the most rapturous joys, in recorded history. Sometimes they even appeared in the same psalm: "How long, O LORD? Will you forget me forever? How long will you hide your face from me? How long must I wrestle with my thoughts and every day have sorrow in my heart?...But I trust in your unfailing love; my heart rejoices in your salvation. I will sing to the LORD, for he has been good to me" (Psalm 13:1-2, 5-6).

Unlike David, some Christians, when they pray, go to church, and worship, pretend that everything in their lives is fine. When they do, however, they miss out on the renewing power of honest communication with the Lord.

God already *knows* how we feel. Our heartfelt praise—or angry or anguished cries—aren't for His benefit, but ours. It's when we openly and genuinely communicate our deepest feelings that our relationship with our Father grows exponentially. By expressing our hearts, we gain intimacy with and trust in Him.

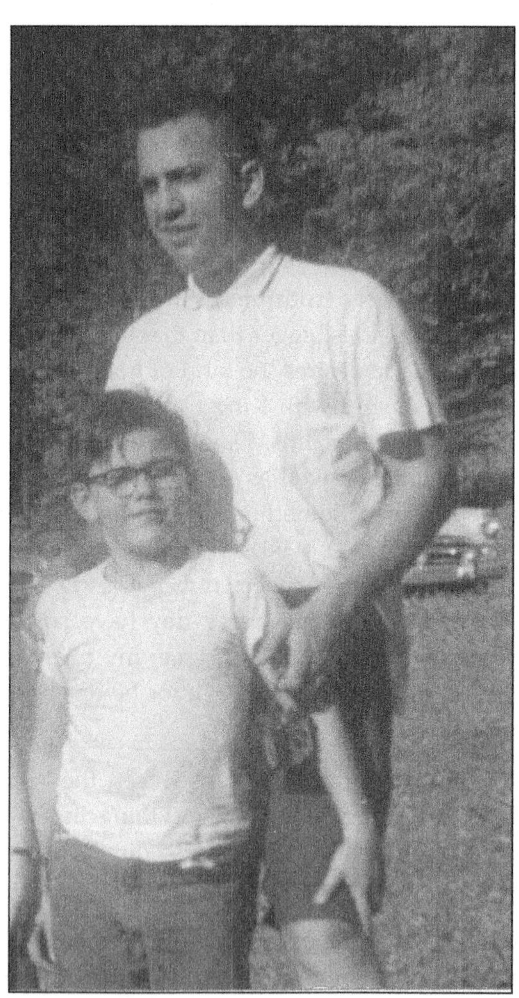

Paul with his 24-year-old brother, David, a few days before David took his own life.

Anne's graduation photo at St. Anthony School of Nursing, Rockford, Illinois, in 1971

Anne on her first date with Paul on December 11, 1976

Paul, after completing his Ph.D. degree at the University of Illinois, Champaign-Urbana, joined the Deaf Education Faculty, Bette J. Baldis and Karen M. Jensen, at Fresno State University in 1979.

10

God's Love Letters

I have hidden your word in my heart.

Psalm 119:11

In this age of email, texting, Facebook, and instant messaging, the hand-written letter seems almost a dying art form. I can't help thinking, however, that we are losing something in the transition to modern and increasingly rapid communication. Unlike email and the rest, letters generally signal a more thoughtful and nuanced approach to imparting information. Most emails, even from friends, are forgotten nearly as quickly as the time it takes to hit the delete button. A letter from a friend, on the other hand, is a treasure to be cherished.

Why is that? Maybe it's the time that we know was invested in putting pen to paper, in inscribing one's thoughts character by character, in finding a stamp and transferring the letter to the postal system. Especially in today's fast-paced world, a personal letter imparts meaning and weight. It suggests friendship and care. It often indicates love.

Emily Dickinson wrote the poem, "A Letter is a Joy of Earth." In that vein, John Donne wrote, "Sir, more than kisses, letters mingle souls; for, thus friends absent speak." Throughout history, letters have revealed the intimate and significant details of our lives.

I have certainly observed this in my own life. During my years at Central Institute for the Deaf, where I was often homesick, I eagerly anticipated every letter from my family. When I was first learning to read, the high point of our classroom days was sharing a newly arrived letter with the class. These letters from my parents often included photographs, drawings, and cut-outs from newspapers and magazines, important stimuli for developing my communication skills.

My mother wrote regularly. Rusty, my best friend during those early years at CID, rarely received correspondence from home, however—perhaps one letter every three or four weeks. Rusty got visibly upset every time mail arrived without a letter from his parents. Even when he did receive mail from them, there wasn't much information about what was happening at home, and that also was a big disappointment.

Our teacher those first two years, Mrs. Olmstead, was a sensitive, caring person. She noticed Rusty's distress and asked my mother to write to him from time to time. I remember my surprise at seeing Rusty reading a letter with handwriting that was none other than my own mother's. I wasn't jealous, though. I knew it cheered him up.

Later at CID, starting when I was about ten and continuing until I was thirteen, I received letters from a different and surprising source -- a cat named Jezebel. The feline belonged to my brother Dunbar, who was working on his doctorate at Yale University. Jezebel's letters—written with considerable "help" from Dunbar—always made me laugh. She told me how she was always trying to get Dunbar's attention by meowing or jumping onto the table when he was working and walking over his papers, and that Dunbar always rudely pushed her off. She also described the time she was accidentally shut inside the closet all day, with no food or water. She was "furious," but the description of her dilemma was hilarious. She always signed with an inked paw print.

After David's death, Dunbar made even more of an effort to communicate with me through letters, which allowed us to grow closer than ever. Many years later, Dunbar wrote another letter that meant a great deal to me. My application for tenure at California State University, Fresno, had just been denied, and I was deeply disappointed. Soon after, I received a fourteen-page, single-spaced letter from Dunbar filled with insights and wisdom about how to survive as a faculty member. By that time Dunbar was a full professor of dramatic arts at the University of California, Berkeley. I've followed much of the advice in that letter in the years since.

All of these letters from family communicated more to me than the details found in the pages themselves. They told me that even though I wasn't around, I was still important to them. They indicated that I was missed and appreciated. They expressed that I was loved.

I also used the form of a letter to communicate my love to Anne when we were dating. We were at a restaurant in Visalia, California, celebrating the end of the first week of my new job at the College of the Sequoias. A waiter approached our table and said to Anne, "Are you Anne Keenan?"

Since she was a nurse, Anne thought the interruption must be about some kind of medical emergency. Yet she was surprised, because she didn't think anyone at the restaurant knew who she was. "Yes, I'm Anne," she said.

The waiter produced an envelope. "Here's a letter for you," he said. "It just came."

Now more puzzled than ever, Anne tore open the envelope and immediately recognized my handwriting. She laughed, finally understanding that I was behind the trick. Inside the envelope was a five-page letter—a proposal for marriage.

Included in the letter was a copy of "The Marriage Creed" by Ginny and Manny Feldman, which captured the attitude I wanted to bring to our marriage:

COMFORT EACH OTHER

Provide a refuge and sanctuary for each other from the chill winds of the world.

Your marriage is a hearth, from whence comes the peace, harmony, and warmth of soul and spirit.

CARESS AS YOU WOULD BE CARESSED

Warm your loved one's body with your healing touch.

Remember that as babies can die with lack of touching, so can marriage wither from lack of closeness.

BE A FRIEND AND PARTNER

Friendship can be a peaceful island, separate and apart, in a world of turmoil and strife.

Reflect upon the tranquility of the many future years you can share with a true friend, and beware of becoming battling enemies under the same roof.

BE OPEN WITH EACH OTHER

Bind not yourselves in the secretness that causes suspicion and doubt.

Trust and reveal yourselves to each other, even as the budding rose opens to reveal its fragrance and beauty.

LISTEN TO EACH OTHER

And hear not only words, but also the non-language of tone, mood, and expression.

Learn to listen to understand rather than listening to argue.

RESPECT EACH OTHER'S RIGHTS

Remember that each is a person of flesh and blood, entitled to his or her own choices and mistakes.

Each owns himself, and has the right to equality.

ALLOW THE OTHER TO BE AN INDIVIDUAL

Seek not to create for each other a new mold that can only fit with much discomfort and pain.

Accept the other as they are, as you would have yourself accepted.

GIVE EACH OTHER APPROVAL

Remember criticism divides, while compliments encourage confidence in the other.

Hasten not to point out the other's mistakes, for each will soon discover his own.

CHERISH YOUR UNION

Let no one come between your togetherness; not child, not friend, nor worldly goods.

Yet maintain enough separateness to allow each other his or her own unique oneness.

LOVE ONE ANOTHER

Love is your river of life—your eternal source of recreating yourselves.

Above all else, love one another.[1]

I watched Anne's face as she read. By the third page, she had tears in her eyes. I knew then she would say yes. Yet I waited patiently, enjoying the moment and admiring her beauty.

When Anne had read every word and tears fell down her face, she stood and gave me a warm embrace—then we both broke into laughter. Our life together was off to a good start.

Never discount the power of a letter!

Letters from History

Letters have also given us an important glimpse into history. Correspondence by lawyer and magistrate Pliny the Younger revealed a fascinating picture of the Roman Empire at its height, including an eyewitness account of the eruption of Mount Vesuvius in 79 A.D. To rally public opinion, John Dickinson began publishing his famous "Letters from a Farmer in Pennsylvania to the Inhabitants of the British Colonies," an explanation of principles claimed by the American colonists, in 1767. Abraham Lincoln penned "A Letter to Mrs. Bixby," an elegant attempt at consolation following her loss of five sons in the Civil War, in 1864.

More recently, Albert Einstein wrote President Franklin Roosevelt in 1939, warning him of Germany's efforts to build an atomic bomb and urging him to finish one first. And in 1963, from a Birmingham jail, Martin Luther King Jr. reminded us that "justice too long delayed is justice denied," which helped spur the momentum of the civil rights movement.

Yet the most significant correspondence of all was recorded earlier than any of these efforts. The Epistles of the Bible's New Testament, composed by Paul, Peter, James, John, and Jude in the first or second century A.D., contain some of the greatest wisdom known to man. They offer inspired and detailed information and instruction on Jesus Christ, the

Christian life, and other practical and spiritual matters, presented in some of the most elegant language ever recorded.

Taken more broadly, all of Scripture can be viewed as a series of letters written for our benefit. The Holy Bible is made up of sixty-six books composed by forty authors and is the best-selling text in history. According to Billy Graham, "The Bible is God's 'love letter' to us, telling us not only that He loves us, but showing us what He has done to demonstrate His love."[2]

This explains our next secret:

God speaks to us through Scripture, His love letters to His children.

I haven't always held this view of the Bible. Thanks to my father's daily Scripture readings over breakfast, I became quite familiar with the Bible while growing up. But my conflicted outlook on God and the church left me feeling disconnected from the words I heard. Like God, they seemed cold and remote.

I also learned that my father had a negative experience with Scripture while growing up. The old saying that it's possible to have too much of a good thing is true. According to my father, his mother quoted Scripture to her children nearly every minute of every day, and used it to justify everything she did and didn't do. My father and his siblings were so overwhelmed by this barrage that after a few years, they no longer heard the words or absorbed their meaning.

For this reason, other than at breakfast, my parents mostly avoided talking about Scripture to their kids throughout the day. They discussed God and their faith with us, but said little about the Bible. They preferred to live and lead by example. I understand their reasoning, but this approach left me with a distant relationship with the Word of God.

After I invited Jesus into my life, however, my perspective began to change. The words and verses of the Bible seemed to come alive. This continued for me after I married Anne. During those difficult first years of our marriage, in fact, it was Scripture—combined with the encouragement of a wonderful Christian couple and practical advice by a counselor—that saved us.

Seeing Scripture with Fresh Eyes

Bill Ward, vice president of a Visalia dairy and food company, was in his early fifties. His wife Ann was about ten years younger. We met Bill and Ann through mutual friends and discovered they were excited about learning sign language. We also learned that they were steadfast Christians. The four of us began spending time together, and it wasn't long before Bill and Ann offered to study the Bible with Anne and me. It was a gracious gift to a struggling young couple, one that helped change the course of our marriage and spiritual lives.

We met weekly at a restaurant or in one of our homes. Someone would serve herbal tea and we'd tell jokes and chat about what was going on in our lives. Then one of us would ask a question and it would lead us into the Bible. Sometimes we stayed together for the evening; at other times, Bill and I broke off for private conversation while Ann and Anne did the same.

There were days when Anne and I went into these meetings furious at one another. Yet Bill and Ann were so easygoing and positive, telling us that we were an "amazing people" and that we could work out our problems. They always made us feel comfortable, as if we were in a safe zone. Our meetings with them were a reprieve from the tension Anne and I often felt when we were alone.

Most encouraging of all was the time we spent with Bill and Ann in the Word. Their enthusiasm and love for God allowed us to see Scripture with fresh eyes. Verses that had seemed flat before grew into a real, breathing presence in our lives. For the first time, we understood the meaning behind the words: "For the word of God is living and active. Sharper than any double-edged sword, it penetrates even to dividing soul and spirit, joints and marrow; it judges the thoughts and attitudes of the heart" (Hebrews 12:4).

These revelations could not have come at a better time. Anne and I had been single for years; we were both fiercely independent. The adjustment to learning to compromise and share life with another person, combined with my grief over the death of my father, my stress over finishing my doctoral dissertation, my health concerns, Anne's frustration with her night shift schedule and job, tensions in her relationship with her mother, and Anne's attempt to quit smoking, left us emotionally and physically exhausted. Our constant bickering added fuel to an already volatile situation. I cannot imagine surviving that time without the inspiration we received from Scripture.

During one of our evenings together, I told Bill that I had so many questions about life. It deeply frustrated me that I couldn't find all the answers. I'd grown up always seeking the best in education and everything else. Now I didn't have the financial means to make this happen. It was difficult to figure out what this meant and where God was leading me.

"Paul, I don't believe our brains were designed to grasp everything," Bill said. "We are finite beings. I think we sweat too much in our attempt to analyze and grasp matters of infinity. Sometimes we are able to understand and sometimes we aren't."

Bill pulled out his Bible and flipped some pages. "This is my favorite passage in Scripture." he said. "It's Proverbs 3:5-6: 'Trust in the Lord with all your heart and lean not on your own understanding; in all your ways acknowledge him, and he will make your paths straight.'"

I reflected on these words as if hearing them for the first time. They suddenly made so much sense. Perhaps I wasn't meant to understand everything in the moment. God knew. I had to trust that He would lead me in the direction I needed to go.

I soon adopted Proverbs 3:5-6 as my favorite Scripture passage as well.

At other times Bill and I talked about the incredible stress and grief I was dealing with. He prayed for me and pointed me to passages that brought relief. He also taught me the value of Scripture memorization, something I hadn't done before. I found that committing a passage to memory allowed it in a mysterious way to work on my heart. It took root inside me in a way I'd never experienced.

One of the first passages I committed to memory was Philippians 4:6-7: "Do not be anxious about anything, but in every situation, by prayer and petition, with thanksgiving, present your requests to God. And the peace of God, which transcends all understanding, will guard your hearts and your minds in Christ Jesus."

I leaned on these words often during those tumultuous months. I sometimes woke up in the middle of the night, worried about my dissertation and thinking, *I've got to write!* I repeated this passage to myself to calm down. I also meditated on the passage at lunchtime. By continually reminding myself to give my burdens to God and let Him handle them, I found comfort and peace.

Messages for Life

The Wards pointed out other verses that came to mean a great deal to Anne and me. I told Bill how much I cherished the book of Ecclesiastes, in particular Ecclesiastes 12:13: "Here is the conclusion of the matter: Fear God and keep his commandments, for this is the whole duty of man."

We talked about my background at Central Institute for the Deaf and how I viewed God as a fierce judge while growing up. I feared Him, but it seemed such a negative feeling.

Bill pointed out that there is more than one way to interpret fear. "Fear is usually united with punishment," he said. "We might fear God because we fear punishment. But fear can also be a way of looking at someone with awe. We might have such love and respect for a person—or for God—that we can be said to fear them." He reminded me that while God is the ultimate judge, He is also the author of and embodiment of love: "Whoever does not love does not know God, because God is love" (1 John 4:8).

Bill used this conversation as a springboard to inform me that Psalm 118:8 is the middle verse of the entire Bible, and therefore the "central message" for life: "It is better to take refuge in the LORD than to trust in man." He was partly joking when he said this, but there was no disputing the wisdom of the passage. So often, I'd been disappointed by the words and actions of humans. God was the one who would not disappoint, whom I could trust.

Other epiphanies followed. My mother had always demonstrated a consistent faith, saying and believing that things would work out. Psalm 112 helped me to better understand and appreciate her attitude: "Surely [the righteous] will never be shaken; a righteous man will be remembered forever. He will have no fear of bad news; his heart is steadfast, trusting in the LORD. His heart is secure, he will have no fear" (vv. 6-8).

I recall getting into a discussion with Bill and Ann about tithing. We challenged them to show us where the Bible said that we had to tithe, that is give 10 percent of our income. Their answer surprised us. They pointed out that God does not say we *have* to tithe, though the Bible indicates people historically did so. The book of Malachi implies that when we *do* tithe, however, we will be blessed: "'Bring the whole tithe into the storehouse, that there may be food in my house. Test me in this,' says the Lord Almighty, 'and see if I will not throw open the floodgates of heaven and pour out so much blessing that you will not have enough room for it'" (Malachi 3:10).

Scripture clearly encourages us to give—not out of obligation, but out of love for God and each other: "Each man should give what he has decided in his heart to give, not reluctantly or under compulsion, for God loves a cheerful giver" (2 Corinthians 9:7).

"Why don't you try it and see what happens?" Bill said to us. His gentle approach, so much like the style of Jesus, made us *want* to tithe. We began giving more than 10 percent of our income and did experience both blessing and a sense of peace. Once again, Scripture proved inspiring, accurate, and beneficial.

Perhaps most inspiring of all were the passages we discovered about God's love. I remember complaining to Bill about Christians who seemed so judgmental. My impression was that after inviting Christ into their lives, these Christians became *more* critical and *less* compassionate. That terrified me. It didn't fit my image of a loving God or who He wanted us to be.

"You're right," Bill said. "That's not what's in Scripture. There is so much in the Bible that shows how much God loves us and wants us to care for each other."

Bill and Ann were the embodiment of this caring attitude. Their manner with us was, naturally, also biblical: "In your hearts revere Christ as Lord. Always be prepared to give an answer to everyone who asks you to give the reason for the hope that you have. But do this with gentleness and respect" (1 Peter 3:15). Bill's faith, style, and love for us in particular reminded me of my old Quaker friends in the Appalachian Mountains. He would have made a great Quaker!

The Wards showered us with verses from the book of Psalms and the New Testament revealing the Lord's love for His children and His extreme desire that we love Him, and those around us, in return. They did not use the approach I have seen in some churches, emphasizing the dangers of sin and hell to coerce us into a deeper faith. Though these dangers are real, by focusing on the negative, the Wards could easily have pushed Anne and me away from God.

Instead, verses like these filled us with a sense of the Lord's profound interest in relationships and lives based on love:

> The only thing that counts is faith expressing itself through love. (Galatians 5:6)
>
> We love because he first loved us. (1 John 4:19)
>
> "'Love the Lord your God with all your heart and with all your soul and with all your mind and with all your strength.' The second is this: 'Love your neighbor as yourself.' There is no commandment greater than these." (Mark 12:30-31)
>
> "Love your enemies, do good to those who hate you, bless those who curse you, pray for those who mistreat you. If someone slaps you on the cheek, turn to them the other also. If someone takes your coat, do not withhold your shirt from them. Give to everyone who asks you, and if anyone takes what belongs to you, do not demand it back. Do to others as you would have them do to you…Be merciful, just as your Father is merciful" (Luke 6:27-36)

The more we explored such passages and illustrations through the centuries, the more we understood the depth of God's love for us and how important it was for us to care for and love each other. It wasn't just a nice, "touchy-feely" philosophy. It was central to God's nature, to our faith, and to lives marked by joy. Once again, Scripture was the key to our understanding.

"New" Ideas, Old Truths

In the years since our early marital days in the Word, I have found more and more examples of the validity of Scripture for faith, relationship with God, and a balanced life. I've also found it thought-provoking to see how often authors, scientists, politicians, and philosophers present "new" ideas that seem based primarily on foundations already laid out in the Bible.

A pair of bestselling books from a few years ago are titled *The Power of Now* and *A New Earth* by Eckhart Tolle. They describe a process of letting go of thoughts to discover inner peace and love. Tolle says that by "being in the now" we can find "The Truth" within ourselves and reach our own heaven.

This contradicts the core message of Christianity, of course, in that it claims we don't need the Lord's intervention to wash our sins away. But it does borrow from Scriptural admonitions such as "Do not worry about tomorrow, for tomorrow will worry about itself" (Matthew 6:34) and "Be still, and know that I am God" (Psalm 46:10). Its appeal rests largely on the extent it relies on biblical values.

The same is true for a scientific endeavor I read about recently in an article titled "The Science of Happiness." It relates the research and conclusions of Barbara Fredrickson, an author and psychologist who has spent more than twenty years studying positive emotions. Today, Fredrickson's field is known as "positive psychology" and is considered groundbreaking in some academic circles.

In the article, Fredrickson talks about data suggesting that "positive emotions have less to do with material resources than we might think; it's really about your attitude and approach to circumstances." She also describes training people in "loving-kindness meditation, which focuses on creating more feelings of warmth and kindness toward others." Her studies showed that the positive emotions generated from such meditation led people to experience more meaning and purpose in their lives, more awareness of the moment, increased positive relations with others, and more ability to savor the good in life. They even slept better.[3]

None of this "new" research sounds new at all to me, however. It mimics the advice Paul gave in his letter to the Philippians two thousand years ago. While under house arrest in Rome, Paul wrote, "I have learned the secret of being content in any and every situation, whether well fed or hungry, whether living in plenty or want. I can do everything through him who gives me strength" (Philippians 4:12). When Christians follow Paul's wisdom, they rely on God, who leads them to the attitude and ultimate resource that will carry them through every circumstance.

In the same letter, Paul also wrote about what today might be called "loving-kindness meditation": "Finally, brothers, whatever is true, whatever is noble, whatever is right, whatever is pure, whatever is lovely, whatever is admirable—if anything is excellent or praiseworthy—think about such things. Whatever you have learned or received or heard from me, or seen in me—put it into practice. And the God of peace will be with you" (Philippians 4:8-9). Paul already knew what some of today's academics are just discovering—that when we consistently focus our minds on what is good and right, we will appreciate life more and know peace.

The Best Advice

I believe the vast majority of good advice we receive from modern "experts" in science, psychology, and spirituality is rooted in Scripture. The Judeo-Christian tradition and the influence of God's Word on our thinking runs far deeper than many realize. Though our society has in so many ways moved away from this tradition and tried to exclude God from daily life—for example, government regulation of separation between church and state, originally established to protect the church—we seem to continually discover "new" truths that are actually repackaged versions of biblical wisdom. A closer examination shows that God knew what He was talking about in the first place.

When I read the Bible, I am repeatedly amazed by its consistency and relevance to my life. It makes so much sense—not just parts of it, part of the time, but all of it, all of the time. It does not strike me as the ramblings of deluded human beings, nor do I experience it only as the recorded counsel of a group of wise men. It goes beyond that. It is too perfect—and too centered on God as the source of its truth.

The only conclusion I can make is that these words are holy and inspired by our Creator. Paul wrote, "Continue in what you have learned and have become convinced of, because you know those from whom you learned it, and how from infancy you have known the Holy Scriptures, which are able to make you wise for salvation through faith in Christ Jesus. All Scripture is God-breathed and is useful for teaching, rebuking, correcting and training in righteousness, so that the servant of God may be thoroughly equipped for every good work" (2 Timothy 3:14-17).

This is the best advice I can imagine. Scripture is one of the greatest gifts we'll ever receive—a guide for life on earth and for eternity. It is a demonstration of God's compassion for His children, a collection of love letters provided for us by the author of love Himself.

11

To Forgive Is Divine

There is no love without forgiveness, and there is no forgiveness without love.

Bryant H. McGill

I still can't believe it. I hate 'em both. I hate 'em!"

The voice belonged to Bob, an overweight man sitting at a round kitchen table. He held a cup of coffee in one hand and a cigarette in the other, and waved both as he spoke. A woman sat across from him at the table with another cup of coffee and nodded in agreement.

"He's a crook, that's what he is," Bob said. "If he'd given us half of what we deserved, things would be different around here."

The woman nodded again. "Mom's just as much to blame," she said. "He was always her favorite. We were the black sheep."

For this brother and sister, the exchange was the beginning of a familiar litany. Their mother had recently passed away. Before she died, their brother, Eldon, had persuaded their mother to sign over all her possessions to him. Eldon was executor of her estate. He'd sold everything—the house, the furniture, the cars, the rental properties, even the organ she'd wanted to leave to her grandson's family. It was all gone, along with the money from the sales. So was Eldon—he'd disappeared.

Now Bob and his sister, left with nothing, were rehashing it all again, just as they did every time they got together. "My own brother. How could he do it?" asked Bob. "What did I do to him to deserve this?"

Bob had been a practical joker most of his life. Lately, however, the jokes had been less frequent, often replaced by angry outbursts. Today, his face was red and taut, his jaw set. The decibels of the words flying back and forth across the kitchen table increased and the gestures grew more animated. Suddenly, Bob pounded the table so hard that the silverware jumped.

"I wish I knew where he was," he said. "I'd like to get my hands on him just once. He's ruined my life. I just want a few minutes to ruin his too."[1]

Like Bob and his sister, all of us confront bad experiences that we don't expect or "deserve." Often, they are little things such as a flat tire or burned dinner. Sometimes, though, they are much more serious and devastating—betrayal, disease, job loss, divorce, rape, or perhaps the death of someone close.

Hard times are inevitable in this life. No one escapes the storms that sweep through. Jesus warned us of as much when He said, "Here on earth you will have many trials and sorrows" (John 16:33 NLT). How we respond to these trials, however, is up to us.

Journey to Bitterness

It's natural to feel hurt, as Bob did, when we're wounded by an offense. It's just as natural to search for a way to deal with the pain. We may ask ourselves questions such as *Why me?* and *Why now?* Like Bob, we say, "What did I do to deserve this?"

Frequently, we also look for someone to blame. Perhaps subconsciously, we figure that we'll feel better if we can assign responsibility for what's happened—especially if we can assign it to someone else! We continually rehearse, either with ourselves or others, the damage done to us in an attempt to justify our desire to blame the offender.

It doesn't take long to move from self-pity and blame into anger. We seethe. We clench our fists. Our blood pressure goes up. Every time we think about what that "so and so" did to us, we want to get back at the person somehow. Sometimes we do just that.

At other times our anger spills over onto just about everyone else. We snap at our spouse and friends and are furious if anyone dares suggest that we calm down or try to move on from our hurt. People begin avoiding us because they don't want to be around an angry person.

If we don't deal with our anger, we reach the final destination on our journey: bitterness and resentment. We become prisoners of our own making. We are outraged, discouraged, depressed, disillusioned, vindictive, and unable to concentrate on our responsibilities. We live with a sickness that infects every aspect of our lives.

What happens when we reach this stage? We become isolated. Our bitterness cuts off our ability to communicate. We put up walls built on volatile emotions that even those closest to us can't penetrate. And when we try to reach out ourselves, the poison inside prevents us from making meaningful contact.

I know of a couple I'll call Sam and Leanne. Their marriage lasted forty-five years, until Leanne's death from cancer, but little of their time together was happy. Sam had an affair during the early years of their marriage. When Leanne found out about the relationship, she was furious and deeply hurt. Sam apologized and broke it off.

Leanne didn't ask for a divorce, but she never got over the affair. She stayed angry at her husband for the rest of her life. When they were together, she repeatedly contradicted him and made sarcastic comments, letting him know that she hadn't forgotten what he'd done and planned to make him pay for it. His usual response—"Shut up, Leanne"—only added to the friction between them.

Over time, Sam and Leanne could have restored their marriage and eventually enjoyed an intimate, loving relationship. Instead, Leanne's bitterness over Sam's breach of trust was never resolved. It robbed them both of what could have been much happier years together.

Dr. David Allen, a Christian psychologist and author, describes the effect of bitterness this way:

> Whatever the causes of our injuries, if we do not work through them, the hurt begins to harden our hearts. The hardness contaminates us. We are less able to feel and touch and make connection with others. In other words, the resentment and hurt in our heart produces alienation within ourselves and also alienation from those around us.[2]

Wounds inflicted by others, when they fester and grow into bitterness, destroy our ability to communicate on a meaningful level—not just with the person who's wounded us, but with everyone. A bitter heart poisons *all* relationships.

The curse of bitterness is not alone in its ability to impose terrible damage. It has a twin just as devastating named *guilt*.

A Lifetime of Guilt

Elaine sat alone in her living room, fingered the photograph in her hand, and tried to hold back the tears. The image showed a mother and her five-year-old daughter with their arms around each other, beaming for the camera. The mother was Elaine's niece. The five-year-old was the first granddaughter of Elaine's sister. Elaine could see the family resemblance in the little girl's smile. It reminded her of her sister, even a bit of Elaine herself.

I could have been a grandmother now, Elaine thought. *That could be my daughter and granddaughter smiling at the camera. On holidays, I could have had a houseful of children and grandchildren gathered around the dining room table, and my husband—*

Elaine couldn't hold back any longer. The tears flowed down her cheeks. She made no attempt to wipe them away. *If only...*

It had happened forty years ago. She'd been sixteen at the time and living in Ohio. When Elaine had learned she was pregnant, she didn't know what to do. She wasn't ready to be a mother. Her parents were so disappointed and ashamed. Elaine herself was overwhelmed, nearly distraught. An abortion seemed the only solution. She didn't tell her parents until it was over, after that horrible visit to the clinic downtown.

From that point on, everything in Elaine's life changed. Her parents still insisted she marry the father. That union lasted only a few months; Elaine had it annulled. She graduated from high school and met an older, studious boy named Steve. He wanted to teach. They fell in love, married when Elaine was nineteen, and moved to the west coast when Steve graduated from college.

Thirty-six years later, Steve was a professor of history at an Oregon university. They'd tried without success to have children. It was a deep and mostly unspoken disappointment for both of them. An even greater strain on their marriage was the guilt Elaine carried with her over the abortion. Night after night, the terrible conversation with her conscience continued. *What was I thinking? I killed my child. I threw away the only chance I'll ever have for a son or daughter. How could I have been so blind? What will I tell my precious boy or girl when we meet in heaven? How can I ever explain or justify what I've done?*

Then came the day when Steve gently confronted her. Their relationship had no life to it, he'd said. They'd grown apart. He'd found someone else, a woman who worked at the university. The marriage was over. He was moving out.

For Elaine, Steve's departure simply added another layer of guilt. She realized her constant brooding over the years had corroded their marriage. She felt she'd driven Steve into the arms of another woman. Elaine lost all hope of happiness. She was drowning in guilt. She rarely went out and hardly spoke to her friends. She didn't try to find a job. She no longer went to church. What was the point?[3]

Like bitterness, guilt—if allowed to flow unchecked—will seep into every corner of our lives, eroding our joy and our bonds with others. In Elaine's case, her guilt over her abortion when she was a teenager was like an acid that burned away for decades at her marriage. After her marriage broke up, it also prevented her from seeking comfort from friends and people she knew at her church. Elaine had trained her mind to focus almost daily on what she'd done. She was subconsciously punishing herself.

I have seen the effects of guilt in my own family. My brother David once asked my father if he ever felt so depressed and disappointed in himself that he wanted to kill himself. My father, who'd battled depression on and off throughout his life, said "Yes." He went on to explain how he'd felt many years before, and exactly how he would have used a shotgun to end his life. David eventually used that same technique for his suicide.

My father carried a burden of guilt over this conversation for the rest of his years. "I killed my own son" was a phrase he uttered on more than one occasion. A few months before he died, he said to my brother Dunbar:

> "When I look back at my life, I regret nothing. Nothing. I have no regrets." His voice was strong, emphatic, militant. Then he would pause. His voice would soften and crack: "Except the death of David. Except the death of David."[4]

It is difficult for me to judge the toll that this burden exacted on my father. I do know that from time to time my father wrestled with doubts about his faith and his role as a minister and leader. For him, these were almost challenges from God.

Doubt, as we have seen, can be a healthy aspect of faith. Many of the saints portrayed in the Bible struggled with their belief in and commitment to God. But in the case of my father's guilt, it would not surprise me in the least to find that it hindered his relationship with the Lord. For just as guilt and its twin, bitterness, damage our relationships with other human beings, they also impair our relationship with our Father in heaven.

The problem is exacerbated when we reject—consciously or not—the God-designed solution to our anguish. We have a way out if we would only choose to follow it.

For As Long As It Takes

Jesus was as clear and emphatic about this "solution" as He was for any spiritual issue He addressed during His time on earth. The answer is *forgiveness*.

When Peter came to Jesus and said, "Lord, how many times shall I forgive my brother when he sins against me? Up to seven times?" (Matthew 18:21) he spoke for all of us. We like the idea of forgiveness—as long as it's within reason. Surely, we think, there is a limit, an expiration date, a point beyond which our obligation to forgive expires. Some things are unforgiveable, right? Certainly we can't be expected to keep on forgiving repeated offenses!

Yet Jesus leaves no ambiguity here. His answer to Peter, "I tell you, not seven times, but seventy-seven times" (Matthew 18:22), isn't meant to be taken literally. Jesus is making a point. He's essentially telling Peter, "Forgive for as long as it takes, and keep forgiving even then." No injury is so terrible as to be unforgiveable: "I assure you that any sin can be forgiven" (Mark 3:28 NLT).

To state that forgiveness is hard is like saying that the sun is a little bright. How can we forgive the pain caused by a spouse's affair? The violence perpetrated by a rapist? The brutal carelessness of a drunk driver who takes the life of our child? Why would Jesus put this burden on us? Why would He expect us to follow a course that conflicts with everything we feel in our hearts?

Because He loves us—and He knows what will happen to us if we *don't* forgive.

When we hold onto bitterness or guilt, the hate and anguish build inside us until we're consumed with it. We grow so focused on our misery that we can no longer communicate, no longer maintain a healthy relationship, no longer love. Instead, what comes out of us is anger and sorrow.

This may be why Jesus said, "In prayer there is a connection between what God does and what you do. You can't get forgiveness from God, for instance, without also forgiving others. If you refuse to do your part, you cut yourself off from God's part" (Matthew 6:14-15 MSG).

Our lack of forgiveness severs our connection to God's mercy and love. It throws a roadblock the size of Hoover dam into our relationship with Him.

When we do forgive, on the other hand, everything changes. In many cases, we experience instant release from our turmoil. We find that we can again enjoy the company of others, and vice versa. We rediscover the joy and peace that flow from intimacy with the Lord. We sense the reality that we ourselves are forgiven by our Creator.

Elaine, the woman suffering from guilt over her abortion, believed in God and knew from her reading of the Bible that she needed to seek forgiveness. What she failed to understand, however, is that the Lord does not ask for repeated penance. Elaine confessed her mistake repeatedly to God. She knew that the Lord forgives and forgets, but she was not willing to forgive herself. She never allowed *herself* to forget.

It wasn't until Elaine met with a pastor that she began to see how she'd been a slave to guilt. Rather than embrace the Lord's forgiveness, she'd rejected it so she could keep on punishing herself. During that meeting, hope flickered in Elaine's eyes. There was relief there too, even a hint of joy. For the first time in many years, she pictured the guilt-free path God wanted for her life.[5]

Remember Bob, the man who'd been swindled by his brother and was filled with bitterness? He found a different form of relief.

A few years after the death of his mother and disappearance of his brother, Bob's health declined significantly. Undoubtedly, the toll from his resentment contributed to his worsening condition. He soon entered a hospital. He was dying.

Bob didn't believe in God. His nephew Dennis, knowing that time was running out, confronted him in the hospital. "Bob, you know you're going to die one of these days," he said. "The

Lord in His grace has spared you this long. You've got to get right with Him. Why won't you?"

"I can't," Bob said. "It's because of the bitterness I have toward Ma and Eldon. I hate 'em. I can't expect God to forgive me if I won't forgive them."

"You can forgive them," Dennis said. "You can let that out right now."

Bob lay quietly in bed for a few moments. Then he said in a low voice, "I have to go to the cemetery. I have to ask for Ma's forgiveness."

It was a crazy idea, but Dennis eventually persuaded the hospital staff to allow him to transport Bob to the cemetery in his old blue Cadillac. Dennis located the correct tombstone and pushed Bob in a wheelchair to the spot.

Bob sat there shaking. Finally, in a loud, clear voice, Bob spoke: "Ma! I forgive you! This is Bob."

On the drive back to the hospital, Bob prayed and invited Jesus into his life. He died a few days later.[6]

Bitterness and guilt will destroy your heart and your relationships. Forgiveness, however, will free your heart and restore your connection to humanity and the Lord. This is the core of our next secret:

Forgiveness enables profound communication with others and God.

No one understood this better than Jesus. It is why, in His dying moments on the cross, He made sure to eliminate any trace of anger or bitterness: "Father, forgive them, for they do not know what they are doing" (Luke 23:34). By offering forgiveness, Jesus left His earthly life knowing the joy of intimate, uninterrupted communion with His heavenly Father. By embracing forgiveness, you and I can and must do the same.

Finding My Way to Forgiveness

If our hearts are filled with bitterness or guilt, forgiveness doesn't just "happen." There is a process to reaching the stage of consuming resentment or overwhelming guilt, and there is also a process to becoming a person who wholeheartedly forgives. If forgiveness were easy or natural, I don't think Jesus would have said so much about it!

For me, that process has involved three stages over the course of my life. When I was younger, the love, wisdom, and example of my parents introduced me to the concept of forgiveness. I was able to let go of my anger over certain incidents, but it was often a struggle. My ability to forgive was far from mature.

As a college student, I developed my own brand of forgiveness, an approach that usually included a dose of revenge. This was far from the type of forgiveness that Christ advocated. It was only after I'd invited Jesus into my heart that I began to understand the significance of forgiveness, the trust required to fully implement genuine mercy, and the joy that could result.

I still remember a shocking and frightening incident from my early years at Central Institute for the Deaf. I was about nine when Miss Nicols, a housemother at CID, found a drawing of a nude woman in my locker. I knew immediately which of the other students had put it there, a boy who was often stirring up trouble.

"Why did you draw this?" Miss Nicols nearly shouted at me. "Why did you hide it?"

"I didn't draw it," I said. "I didn't hide it!"

Miss Nicols refused to believe me. She dragged me to my locker and pointed to where she'd found the drawing. I happened to have a picture of Jesus pasted on a slab of wood in my locker, so I picked it up and shouted, "I am telling the truth! I didn't draw it. I didn't put it in my locker." I held up the picture of Christ as if I were warding off Dracula with a cross.

This made Miss Nicols even angrier. She raced to her room and returned with a wooden paddle, which she used to repeatedly hit me. Throughout this attack I held up the picture of Jesus, trying to keep this monster off me, but she only paddled harder for it. Soon her paddle broke, but she continued whacking me on my left forearm with the paddle's broken end.

The sight of blood smeared all over my lower arm finally broke the spell, and Miss Nicols stopped. She seemed to suddenly realize what she'd done and took me to the infirmary. I was shaken and afraid she would strike again.

It was hard for me to be around Miss Nicols in the following weeks. I was angry and didn't trust her. Yet I was comforted by the thought of my parents and their love for me. In their words and actions, they'd always made it clear how much they cared about me. They'd told me many times that they didn't like sending me to school so far from home, but that it was the only option if I was to receive a good education. I believed this and sensed their deep and genuine love.

This knowledge was the resource I drew on to let go of my anger over what Miss Nicols had done. My parents' love was stronger than my fury about the injustice of what had happened. Eventually, I was able to go through my days without worrying about or dwelling on Miss Nicols and her attack. This may not have been fully realized forgiveness, but it was the beginning.

Releasing Resentment

Later, my parents again played a key role in helping me see the value of releasing resentment. There was the high school event where the girl I asked to dance bluntly rejected me, saying she didn't want to because I was deaf. It was a devastating moment for me. I left the dance and went home, where my father talked with me.

"Why are you so obsessed with this girl?" he asked.

"She's pretty. She's cute. She's blond!" I said. I was so upset that I told him I wanted to quit school.

"Over this?" my father said. "Over a girl you don't even know? Maybe this is a person who has a problem, who is ignorant about deaf people. She may be immature. You don't know enough about her to be so offended. You have to let it go."

My father insisted that I go back to the dance and meet other people. At that moment, it was the last thing I wanted to do. But he was right. I returned to the dance, met a new group of students, and had a good time, forgetting about the cheerleader. The idea that someone better might be out there was an important one, as was the concept that I didn't know all the reasons behind this girl's decision to reject me over my deafness. For me, it was a lesson in common sense and another step toward understanding forgiveness.

I had a harder time understanding my father's point of view during a discussion in my senior year of high school. He was counseling a husband and father going through a crisis. This man—I'll call him Rick—and his wife had three children. The wife had an affair and was pregnant by her lover. Rick didn't know what to do. He asked my father, "Should I move out? Should I divorce her? Should I blame my wife for this? Am I being punished?" Rick was angry, hurt, and confused.

My father said, "You have to think about the children." He was talking about both the three children this couple had already had together and the one on the way. He advised Rick to go back to his wife, forgive her for the affair, and raise the child as his own. Eventually, that's just what Rick did.

I discussed this issue with my parents a great deal. I told them that if I were in Rick's place, I would never forgive the wife. I felt angry with her and with the counsel my father had offered. I didn't acknowledge the Bible verses that talked about God's forgiveness. When I saw this family together, moving on with life as if nothing had happened, I felt disgust.

It wasn't until years later, after I became a Christian, that my perspective began to change. I realized that Rick was actually courageous. If he had walked away, it would have virtually destroyed five lives. His wife most likely would have had to go on welfare and raise four children as a single parent. His three children would have been denied the daily presence and guidance of a father. The new baby might easily have been ostracized by the other children and also would have grown up without a father's influence. So much would have been lost.

Despite being betrayed, Rick decided to protect and preserve his family. The more I thought about it, the more impressed I became. Rick could have justified leaving. Instead, he chose mercy. Though I haven't kept up with this family, I suspect that today Rick's relationship with his wife and children—as well as with the Lord—is stronger than ever.

Personal Justice

Though I'd never consciously decided to develop a personal philosophy on how to respond to a wrong, by the time I was in college I'd nevertheless formed an approach that made sense to me. It was based less on love and more on making sure that my interpretation of justice was served.

I recall taking a summer graduate school class at the University of Illinois. Though I had an interpreter who signed the instructor's lectures to me in class, it was impossible for me to watch the interpreter and take notes at the same time. In the past, my solution to this problem had always been to approach someone in class and ask if they would be willing to share their notes. People were nearly always gracious and happy to do so.

During the first lecture of this graduate school class, I sat next to a school administrator about ten years older than me. This man—I'll call him Charles—seemed to be taking extensive and quite legible notes. I wrote a note that explained my situation and asked if he would be willing to share his notes, and handed it to him.

Charles read the note, turned it over, and wrote a one-word reply that filled the entire page: NO. He then got up and moved to a desk that was three or four seats away.

At first I was shocked. Then I was angry. Forgiveness was certainly not on my mind. Instead, I thought, *I am going to get back at him in some way.*

Later, it turned out that Charles and I had chosen the same topic for a research paper that was to be presented to the class. The instructor wanted everyone with the same topic to work together and present their findings as a team. Charles, however, went to the instructor and asked if he and I could work separately. He didn't want anything to do with me. The instructor agreed to this exception, making me even more furious.

When I learned about the presentation schedule and that I was assigned a day before Charles, I made a request of my own. The instructor allowed me to switch with Charles, so he would present on a Friday and mine would be the following Monday.

Charles' presentation was unimpressive. He used old research and did not list many examples to make his points. I decided to focus my energy that weekend on creating the best presentation possible. I spent hours at the library crafting my presentation. I'd never worked so hard!

When my turn came on Monday, I made sure the class understood that my research was more extensive and up to date. I even mentioned Charles' name and cited some of the research he presented, demonstrating that it was no longer relevant. I left little doubt that my presentation was far more thorough and polished. It earned an A+ from the instructor.

I must admit that initially, I felt so good about what I'd done. I'd triumphed over my "adversary," who'd sat through my presentation and showed no emotion. It was revenge on my terms—a way to make myself shine while belittling my opponent.

A few days later, however, my "victory" began to feel like a hollow one. I realized that my response had been shallow. I wasn't ready to forgive Charles, but I at least realized that something about my approach wasn't right. Today, I believe that Charles was most likely afraid of talking or working with a deaf person. He'd probably never had any experience with someone like me. Instead of getting angry, I could have tried to view the situation from his perspective.

Practicing Forgiveness

Once I became a Christian, I started to see that forgiveness was a significant spiritual matter. Verses such as Ephesians 4:32 spoke to my heart: "Be kind and compassionate to one another, forgiving each other, just as in Christ God forgave you."

This is a central point. God's love is so complete, so encompassing, that He always stands ready to pardon our sins against Him if we will only ask. Furthermore, our willingness to forgive is linked to this great mercy: "If you hold anything against anyone, forgive him, so that your Father in heaven may forgive you your sins" (Mark 11:25). Somehow, when we refuse to forgive those who have wronged us—or choose not to forgive ourselves—we block our access to God's compassion. The peace that can be found in God's forgiveness is available only when we extend mercy ourselves.

As my understanding of forgiveness deepened, the Lord gave me plenty of opportunities to practice my newfound knowledge. There was the time when I called a flower shop with the assistance of an interpreter, intending to make a large order. As soon as the interpreter stated that he was calling on my behalf, the flower shop attendant said "I don't deal with disabled people" and hung up.

I called back and asked to speak to the manager.

"That's me," the same employee said. *Click.*

I called a third time and asked to speak to the owner. Once again, she hung up on me.

I was surprised and disappointed, but I decided not to dwell on it. "Well," I said, "they just lost an order for my wife, my mother, and my mother-in-law." I let it go.

A few days later, I stopped at the flower shop and spoke to the same employee. I explained who I was, reminded her of what had happened, and said, "I'd like to educate you in a nice way." But she refused to talk with me. She either ignored my words and repeated "How can I help you?" or simply said "No."

Friends urged me to write a letter to the editor to pursue the issue further, but I decided to drop it. Though I didn't know what it was, there had to be a reason for this woman's strange behavior—ignorance, fear, a previous bad experience, who knows? In my mind, I forgave her.

I had the chance to practice more forgiveness after I joined the faculty at Fresno State. I was the only full-time deaf member of the faculty at the university. To my initial surprise, two other members of the faculty consistently opposed me and everything I tried to do. Their "old school" approach to education was to doubt new research and resist changes to the status quo. Since I was open to new findings and trends and was eager to push our program ahead, I apparently represented a threat to this pair. They resented my interest in and support for students who needed to be more prepared and trained professionally.

When I proposed a new class and measures to expand the Deaf Studies program, both of these faculty members worked to block it. One appeared to be seeking a reasonable solution when he said to me, "Let's meet with the dean." When he and I got together with the dean, however, I saw that through his comments he was subtly sabotaging my idea. The dean turned it down.

I revealed my frustrations about these two to Bill Ward. He said, "Paul, you're just going to have to forgive them."

"But again and again and again?" I asked.

That's when Bill showed me the passage in Scripture and Peter's question, "How many time shall I forgive...Up to seven times?" and Jesus' answer: "Not seven times, but seventy-seven times" (Matthew 18:21-22). It was a time of great struggle and prayer, but I realized what I had to do. Though it was hard, I did forgive these two—over and over.

What surprised me were the benefits I began to experience, all made possible by adopting an attitude of forgiveness. I talked with and learned much from my brother, Dunbar, and the founder of the university's Deaf Studies program, who suggested new strategies for dealing with the two faculty members. I learned how to work better with people, how to network, how to prepare better proposals, and to not grow complacent about my progress. I worked hard on a variety of committees and developed a strong relationship with the dean, to the point that when my two "adversaries" persuaded the personnel committee to deny my application for tenure—a terrible blow—the dean overrode their recommendation.

A few years later, just before he retired, one of the two faculty members proposed dramatic cuts in the Deaf Studies program that I led. In the past, I would have agonized over this action and made extensive plans on how to counteract his move. This time, however, I let it go. Several other members of the faculty, meanwhile, were shocked by this proposal and organized their own effort to preserve our funding. I didn't even ask them to do it. The proposal for cuts was never approved.

In 1995, sixteen years after I began my career at Fresno State University, I was named "Outstanding Professor of the Year" by the university's faculty, staff, and students, and nominated for the same award for the entire California State University system, where I placed second overall. It was a great honor, one that I realized was possible only because of the twin "thorns" that God had allowed in my life and because I had found a way to forgive.

It had been a long and arduous journey, but I was learning!

Justice and Trust

I've thought a great deal about forgiveness in the last few years. I've had a lifetime of dealing with public ignorance toward my deafness, as well as with the injustices that all people experience. The question that Peter wrestled with, and that you and I wrestle with today, is how do we react to these injustices?

Some of us respond inwardly, nursing our sense of wrong and turning it into either bitterness or, when we are the perpetrators, self-punishing guilt. We've seen how harmful this can be. Others respond by exacting a form of revenge, as I did with Charles in my graduate school class. Yet this choice soon proves to be unsatisfying as well.

We think a more measured, mature response is to avoid these and simply determine what is *fair*. Often we don't expect undue consequences. We just want the other person to "pay" for what he or she has done—no more and no less.

The problem with this approach, however, is that we appoint ourselves the ones to pick up the gavel, seat ourselves on the bench, make a judgment, and pronounce a sentence. Yet how do we know what is fair and just? Do we ever have all the facts? Are we impartial? Are we privy to the master plan for everyone's lives?

It is just as my father said to me all those years ago: "You don't know enough."

God understands how easily we are tempted to judge. This is why Jesus was so specific on the subject: "Do not judge, or you too will be judged. For in the same way you judge others, you will be judged, and with the measure you use, it will be measured to you. Why do you look at the speck of sawdust in your brother's eye and pay no attention to the plank in your own eye?" (Matthew 7:1-3).

Which brings us to the crux of the issue. The Lord, the alpha and the omega, is the only one qualified to judge sins. The rest of us are like fleas on an elephant—insignificant, unknowing, barely discernable. We are in no position to pass judgment because we cannot even begin to understand what is "fair": "Your thoughts—how rare, how beautiful! God, I'll never comprehend them! I couldn't even begin to count them—any more than I could count the sand of the sea" (Psalm 139:17-18 MSG).

God is all-knowing. We, in comparison, are nothing.

Why, then, do we resist the idea of leaving judgment to the Lord? Perhaps it goes back to the matter of trust.

One thing I've noticed in my study of Scripture is that forgiveness is almost always linked to love, mercy, justice, and trust. Paul, for instance, writes:

> Therefore, as God's chosen people, holy and dearly loved, clothe yourselves with compassion, kindness, humility, gentleness and

> patience. Bear with each other and forgive whatever grievances you may have against one another. Forgive as the Lord forgave you. And over all these virtues put on love, which binds them all together in perfect unity. (Colossians 3:12-14)

Love cannot exist for long without each of these other elements. Forgiveness—along with my relationship with the Lord—breaks down when I choose not to love, not to extend mercy, to take justice into my own hands, and not to trust Him.

The difficulty for me is that love and forgiveness do not always lead to justice that I can *see*. The offender often appears to go on with life as if nothing has been learned, nothing is changed. I don't experience the immediate satisfaction I desire. There is no tangible evidence that God is at work.

For me, this creates a dilemma. When I've been injured or see another person wronged, such as the time when Rick's wife had the affair, it has always been an emotional struggle for me to forgive. My desire is to see justice—right now!

Over the years, however, I've gradually learned to turn this dilemma over to my intellect. I remind myself that the Lord operates on His timetable, not mine. The very definition of faith is trusting when I do not see. I do know from experience that God has been trustworthy in the past, that so far *everything* He has promised in Scripture has proven to be true. When I yield to the logic of this and renew my confidence in His ability to take care of those who've injured me, I find that love and mercy flow through my life. It is a rational decision I must make each time I am hurt. The more I focus on God as the only one qualified to judge, the easier it is to forgive.

I also discover that the weight of responsibility for judgment is lifted, leaving me feeling lighter and relieved: "Take my yoke upon you and learn from me, for I am gentle and humble in heart, and you will find rest for your souls. For my yoke is easy and my burden is light" (Matthew 11:29-30). It is, then, a decision and condition of both the mind and the heart to embrace forgiveness and accept God's justice. When we do so, our connection to our Father in heaven grows steadily stronger.

On October 2, 2006, Terri Roberts was eating lunch with a friend on the patio at her workplace near Strasburg, Pennsylvania. It was a beautiful, sunny day. Their lunch was interrupted by the sounds of sirens and helicopters. Terri offered a short prayer: "Whoever's involved in this, Lord, just be with them, bring healing."

After lunch, when Terri and her friend walked back into the office, they found the phone ringing. It was Terri's husband. "I need you to come down to Charlie's house right away," he said.

Terri jumped into her car and drove the short distance to where her son, Charlie, lived with his wife and three children. On the way, she turned on the radio and heard there'd been a shooting at the one-room Nickel Mines schoolhouse operated by the Amish. Terri's son drove a milk truck and served many of the homes and farms in that area. *Wow,* she thought, *don't tell me Charlie was around when this was happening and tried to help with the rescue or something and got shot!*

She arrived and discovered news beyond her worst fears. That morning, her beloved Charlie had entered the schoolhouse and taken ten girls hostage. Apparently, he'd never forgiven God for the death of his first daughter just after she was born. He told the girls, "I'm angry at God and I need to punish some Christian girls to get even with Him." He then shot all ten of the girls—five would die—before shooting and killing himself.

Nearly as shocking for Terri Roberts was the response of the Amish. Her husband was devastated, unable to even lift his head. Henry, an Amish neighbor, came to the house that evening, put his hand on the grieving father's shoulder, and said, "Roberts, we love you. We forgive you." That same evening, three Amish men found Marie Roberts, Charlie's widow, along with her children, at her parents' home. They talked about their sorrow over what had happened and said they didn't hold anything against the Roberts family.

The next day, Marie's grandfather visited one of the bereaved Amish families. "I knew the father and grandfather of the children who were killed," he said. "We met in the kitchen and shook hands and put our arms around one another. They said there are no grudges. There's forgiveness in all of this. It was hard to listen to, and hard to believe."

The Amish would continue to express grace in the days and weeks to come. Many stopped at Marie's house to offer gifts, condolences, and forgiveness. Several of the parents of the slain children invited the Roberts family to attend their daughter's funeral. At his granddaughter's funeral, an Amish man said to the children around him, "We shouldn't think evil of the man who did this." When Charlie Roberts was buried, more than half of the seventy-five mourners were Amish. Some, including parents of Charlie's victims, even offered condolences and hugs to Marie.

Later, after financial support for the grieving Amish families poured in from around the world, the Amish committee established to manage this benevolence voted to present a portion to Marie Roberts and her family.

Two days after the shooting, the grandfather of two slain sisters succinctly summarized the Amish approach to forgiveness in a brief conversation with a TV reporter:

> "Do you have any anger toward the gunman's family" she asked.
>
> "No."
>
> "Have you already forgiven them?"

"In my heart, yes."

"How is that possible?"

"Through God's help."[7]

Impossible as it seemed, the remaining victims of Charlie Roberts's warped and violent revenge plot almost immediately put aside their anger and desire for justice and trusted instead in the will of God. He supplied the amazing power to forgive. Through heartfelt words, hugs, and acts of grace, they took a mighty step toward the loving God of the universe and an eternity of peace.

The Lord stands ready to help you and me as well. The choice is ours.

Paul was honored as "Outstanding Professor of the Year" by Fresno State University President John D. Welty and Academic Senate Chair Melanie Bloom in 1995.

12

HEAVENLY CONVERSATION

The value of consistent prayer is not that He will hear us, but that we will hear Him.

William McGill

Relationships are a bit like gardens. To thrive, they require a steady, nurturing hand. They do best with just the right amount of "water" and "fertilizer." They attract "weeds" that can expand and take over if they're not rooted out quickly. And when carefully cultivated, their beauty and bounty can be enjoyed for a lifetime.

Finding the time to properly tend to our gardens is not easy, however. We so often get caught up in the busyness of our lives. We think, *I really should spend a few minutes in the garden today, but I'm too tired. I'll get to it tomorrow*. Before we know it, a day stretches into two, and then a week. And our garden starts looking like something out of an Amazon jungle.

The same thing happens to our relationships—even the most important ones of all. Mike McManus, author and co-chair of Marriage Savers ministry, recalls the day he attended a marriage seminar and realized he'd allowed his relationship with his wife to drift.

> I was taking my wife, Harriet, for granted. I was doing nothing consciously to strengthen our commitment to one another. We had been married ten years, had three sons, and were active in a spiritually nurturing church. But I had become so involved in my work that I spent little time with her, and I was doing nothing to nurture her as a person…"You love your work more than you love me. You are neither a husband nor a father," she said on our Marriage Encounter. Her opinion shocked me. However, when I looked at how many hours I was working—and how little time I was spending with her or with our boys—I realized that I needed to change.[1]

So many things distract us from staying connected to those we care for. Overtime at the office. Transporting kids to basketball practice and dance classes. Church activities. Volunteering at school. Hobbies. Renovating the house. Surfing the Internet. Coaching the Little League team. Movies or television. Simply keeping up with daily responsibilities. When we devote most of our time and energy to other interests, our relationships suffer. Unless we're careful, our spouse, kids, family, and friends end up saying, like Harriet McManus, that "You love everything else more than you love me."

In the case of Mike McManus, his decision to take action turned his marriage around.

> Marriage Encounter recommended that we devote twenty minutes every day exclusively to each other. I resolve to do that. Each morning, we rise a little earlier than our demands of the day require. We begin by simply talking about whatever it is that we are concerned about. We enjoy coffee, observe the changing trees through our bedroom skylight, or watch birds at a feeder

> outside our window. Then I read from a couple-commentary and from Scripture.[2]

Their solution wasn't particularly innovative or complicated, but it worked. Mike and Harriet McManus have been happily married now for more than forty years. The change in routine that they made more than three decades ago may very well have saved their relationship.

I find two parts of their revised routine especially significant. One is that they start each session with "simply talking." The other is that they are committed to setting aside this time for each other *every day*.

When we first married, Anne and I did not understand the importance of making a regular practice of simply talking. It wasn't until our fourth year together that a friend at the modern Quaker church we attended asked us, "Do you have a regular date night?" When we said no, she explained how vital it was to a close relationship. Anne and I decided to try it.

Our friend was right. We soon found that meeting at least once a week to simply talk and connect made a tremendous difference in our marriage. We made a point of getting out of the house and going someplace where we were "stuck" with each other—a restaurant or favorite spot in the woods about an hour from our home. We didn't bring something to do or anything to distract us. We just sat and faced each other.

Sometimes we had little to say at first. We'd been around each other throughout the week, so it seemed we'd already covered all the little things that a married couple must manage. But regularly giving ourselves time and space to be together allowed us to delve into more profound subjects: ideas for the future, concerns about our own relationship or family and friends, thoughts about where God was leading us. Sometimes we reflected on the past, which gave us a new appreciation for what we'd both been through and a fresh perspective for going forward. Frequently, our conversation led us into opportunities to pray. The result was that we each found a deeper understanding of the other's heart. It brought us closer together.

Like a fragile flower, the vitality of each of our relationships is precarious. Left unattended, they will not survive. The good news, however, is that the power to renew them rests in our hands.

This brings us to our next secret, one that is both simple and profound:

To thrive, a relationship requires continual communication.

How is the garden of your relationships? Are you regularly setting aside time for the people you love so that your bond can grow deeper and stronger? Are you consistently looking for ways to cultivate these connections? When you do, you'll find your relationships flourishing like never before.

As we have seen with secrets in previous chapters, this one also applies to more than your interactions with other human beings. It is equally vital to success in your spiritual relationship with the Lord. The key is that mysterious intersection between heaven and earth, between God and man—the practice of holy conversation we know as prayer.

Our Link to the Lord

People are hungry for a connection to God. I vividly recall the morning of September 11, 2001. As I prepared for my morning drive to the Fresno State campus, Anne called me to the television. In shock, I watched the morning's footage of Boeing jets crashing into the north and south towers of the World Trade Center. I was worried. My niece lived in New York City. Her husband worked across the street from the World Trade Center.

When I arrived on campus for my 9:30 a.m. General Education class, I found my students watching the classroom TV in silence. Many had stunned or worried expressions on their faces. Some were crying. I wondered, *What do I say?*

I moved to the front of the room and, through an interpreter, asked, "Do any of you have family or friends in New York?" A third of the class of forty-five students raised hands. We talked for a minute about their concerns. Though it was the beginning of the term and I didn't know these students well, it didn't take long for me to realize what I should say next.

"Would any of you like to pray?"

Everyone nodded their heads or answered "Yes." I was well aware of state requirements about separating religion from teaching. On this morning, however, that didn't seem to matter to the people in front of me. "Okay," I said. "Let's pray."

We stood, gathered in a circle, and held hands. I asked God to take care of our loved ones in New York. It felt natural. It was an opportunity, through the Lord, to comfort my students during a time of tragedy. Many tears were shed. The students hugged each other when we finished.

Later, after the course was over and grades turned in, I read my students' written evaluations of the class. I was surprised that a number said our 9/11 prayer time was the highlight of the class. One student wrote that our group prayer set the tone for the class. I realized then that so many people are seeking a spiritual connection. We understand, either consciously or not, that prayer is our link to the Lord.

When Philip Yancey decided to explore the subject of prayer, he read accounts of noted pray-ers in history. Bishop Lancelot Andrews, for example, devoted five hours a day to conversing with God. Charles Simeon got up at 4 each morning to begin his four-hour prayer routine. Martin Luther was known to daily dedicate two to three hours to prayer. Jonathan Edwards wrote of "sweet hours" spent on the banks of the Hudson River, where he was "rapt and swallowed up in God."[3]

When Yancey queried modern men and women about their prayer practices, however, their answers offered a striking contrast.

> Typically, the results went like this: Is prayer important to you? *Oh, yes.* How often do you pray? *Every day.* Approximately how long? *Five minutes—well, maybe seven.* Do you find prayer satisfying? *Not really.* Do you sense the presence of God when you pray? *Occasionally, not often.* Many of those I talked to experienced prayer more as a burden than as a pleasure.[4]

Perhaps the problem is that we treat prayer as a task to be checked off the list, like doing the bills or taking out the garbage. We either try to work it in when we can (which isn't all that often) or we approach it as a perfunctory duty. Yet time with God is so much more than a chore on a checklist!

Some parents debate whether it's more important to devote quality time or quantities of time to their children. For me, the answer is clearly *both* quality and quantity. No relationship is going to grow if we devote just five minutes to it daily, no matter how focused those five minutes are. Similarly, we can't expect to bond with our kids—or with our Lord—if we spend hours in the same room with them, but have the TV on the entire time. I'm certain that Bishop Andrews and Martin Luther did not try to multi-task during the hours they spent on their knees in prayer, with one eye on conducting church business or writing letters. They understood that nothing trumped being fully engaged with the Creator of the universe—not for five minutes, but, if at all possible, for five hours. Conversing with God was not an afterthought they attempted to crowd into the schedule. It was instead the main event.

Preparing to Communicate with God

With tongue in cheek, C. S. Lewis has written out strategies for impeding the presence of God, thereby preventing a thriving relationship.

> Avoid silence, avoid solitude, avoid any train of thought that leads off the beaten track. Concentrate on money, sex, status, health and (above all) on your own grievances. Keep the radio on [or the computer in today's world]. Live in a crowd. Use plenty of sedation. If you must read books, select them very carefully. But you'd be safer to stick to the papers. You'll find the advertisements helpful; especially those with a sexy or snobbish appeal.[5]

Just as noise, distractions, and busyness impede our human relationships, they also obstruct our connection to our heavenly Father. We need calm and silence in order to communicate beyond a superficial level.

I was fascinated by a recent article indicating that neuroscientists have for decades completely misunderstood an important function of the brain. Previously, experts believed that when people were lying about doing nothing and thinking about nothing, their brains were in "default" mode, also essentially doing nothing. New research is showing, however, that the opposite is true.

"This default activity, to everyone's surprise, is no mere murmur in the background of a large symphony," writes Sharon Begley in *Newsweek* magazine. "It *is* the symphony, consuming twenty times as much energy as the conscious life of the mind." The article states that one of the purposes of all this activity appears to be preparing the brain to handle and react to future sensory information.[6]

I believe it is also preparing us to hear and respond to communication from God. When we give our brains this default "rest" time, we find it easier to reach out to the Lord and to "hear" what He's telling us. That won't happen in a period of five minutes. Scripture describes this approach succinctly: "Be clear minded and self-controlled so that you can pray" (1 Peter 4:7).

Jesus demonstrated this for us during His earthly ministry. We know that while staying at Peter and Andrew's home, Jesus healed many people, probably late into the evening. Nevertheless, "Very early the next morning, while it was still dark, Jesus got up, left the house and went off to a solitary place, where he prayed" (Mark 1:35). He must have been gone a long time, because He was missed: "Simon and his companions went to look for him, and when they found him, they exclaimed: Everyone is looking for you!" (v. 36).

We also know that on another occasion "Jesus went out to a mountainside to pray, and spent the night praying to God" (Luke 6:12). And we can read that after the miracle of feeding more than five thousand people with only five loaves of bread and two fish, Jesus dismissed the crowd and "went up on a mountainside by himself to pray" (Matthew 14:23).

In other words, Jesus made prayer a bigger priority than fellowship with His closest followers, than resting during the night, than preaching to and healing a huge crowd of people. The success of His mission depended on continual, fervent communication with His Father through extended, solitary, quiet times of prayer.

Mother Teresa once wrote, "We need to find God, and He cannot be found in noise and restlessness. God is the friend of silence. See how nature—trees, flowers, grass—grows in silence; see the stars, the moon, and the sun, how they move in silence. We need silence to be able to touch souls."[7]

Airplane Prayers

I too have found that my best prayer sessions take place when I am calm and quiet and can devote uninterrupted time to communing with God. For years, my most effective prayer times occurred on airplanes. When I am in the sky at thirty thousand feet, I feel separated from my problems on the ground and closer—figuratively and literally—to the Lord. It's always a great opportunity to settle my mind, read, pray, and listen to what God has to say.

I wasn't always so calm on airplanes. As I have described, in my early years at Central Institute for the Deaf, flying back to school after a vacation at home was traumatic. I loved being with my family and resisted returning. It was always a distressing moment to watch the image of the airport containing my parents recede in the distance.

My prayers during those years did not occur in the sky but in the Sunday school classrooms at CID. These were not sessions I looked forward to. Rather than seeing prayer as a privilege or opportunity to renew a cherished friendship, it felt like an obligation. I did it because it was expected of me and to please my housemother, but I didn't feel any spiritual connection. It was a one-way conversation. I talked to God, but didn't stop to "listen" and sense anything God might be telling me.

When I was home, I observed my parents praying with dinner guests, and when I was in high school, they sometimes prayed before a meal. But I didn't pray with my parents. We often discussed God and why He did this or that, but I never really talked *to* Him. I knew that in my absence my parents prayed for me, and I liked knowing that I was covered by their petitions to God, but this didn't make a major impression at the time. It was much later that my mother told me she sensed my lack of faith when I was young and prayed for my salvation. I'm so thankful now for the impact of those prayers on my life.

It wasn't until my high school years and time with the Quakers in the Appalachian Mountains that I caught a glimpse of the true power of prayer. The Quakers seemed to have a direct phone line to God, which fascinated me and which I admired. Their example encouraged me to be more open to discovering what prayer was all about.

During college, when I embarked on my period of intense searching, I recall sitting and thinking, *God, are you really hearing me? Are you there? Where are you? Show me.* So many people did not believe in God at Antioch, but for me it almost seemed that He was stirring something in my heart. These were my first true, tentative attempts at conversation with my Creator.

Then came November 1976 and the day I invited Jesus into my heart. It wasn't as if the floodgates suddenly opened and I had a constant flow of communication with the Lord. It was more like a cell phone conversation where (as I'm told) the signal often breaks up. I began learning how to set aside quiet times and to listen, and I did sense His presence on occasions. These were wonderful moments of spiritual connection. It felt as if I was being welcomed into His family.

At other times, though, it seemed that God was cutting me off. Particularly during the turbulent first three years of my marriage, I had trouble reaching and maintaining contact with Him. He seemed to come and go, and was absent more than present. Initially, I blamed God for this and wondered why He would so often abandon me after I had committed my life to Him. Eventually, however, I realized that *I* was the one putting up barriers. I was dealing with so many problems. It was as if a thousand ping pong balls were bouncing in front of me, distracting me from what was important. I was trying to watch the ping pong balls instead of focusing on God. I allowed my busyness, stress, and lack of trust to come between us. I wasn't giving God my full attention.

My best prayers continued to be when a work obligation or family visit put me on a plane and took me away from my distracting problems. In the sky, my "cell phone to heaven" always seemed to have good reception. Meetings with the Wards, or with a counselor or our Bible study, also seemed to make the "ping pong balls" stop bouncing. Ever so slowly, I learned through repeating memorized Scripture passages and by dedication and practice to insert regular periods of calm into my days. Not coincidentally, the better I became at this, the better I was able to discern the voice of God.

A Fifth Sense

I don't mean to imply that I literally hear God's voice—after all, I don't hear anyone's voice! But the more I talk to the Lord, the more I sense thoughts from Him popping into my head. I feel His presence with me. It's a little like "hearing" with my whole body.

I know people who say they receive clear directions from God. They wake up in the morning and hear Him say this or that. That's not how it is for me. My communication with the Lord is more abstract. I don't interact with Him through any of my four senses, though I'd like to. It's more like an extra sense that allows me to detect His presence. Maybe, like so many people, I *do* have five senses—one is just a little different than the rest!

A hymn written by Lanny Wolfe, "Surely the Presence of the Lord Is in This Place," helps describe the feeling. It includes the lyrics, "I can feel His mighty power and His grace. I can hear the brush of angels' wings." It is difficult to describe, but I know it when He's there.

My prayer schedule would best be described as erratic. Some weeks I sit down each morning for ten or fifteen minutes to read Scripture and pray. In other weeks it's not until the evenings that I find a few minutes of quiet, private time to spend with the Lord. Occasionally, Anne and I will sit together and pray for a full hour over issues that we, family, and friends may be facing.

More common is for people to stop me during the day and ask me to pray for them. It might be a friend, a student, or a colleague. They know I'm a Christian and that I believe in the power of prayer. We might ask God for a solution to a health problem or for His will to be done regarding a job interview. It's almost guaranteed that we both feel better and closer to God by the time we're done.

Though I heartily advocate making time for the kind of quiet, contemplative prayer we've been discussing, your prayer life does not have to be confined to these reflective meetings with God. I believe He wants to hear from us throughout our days, not just when we've set aside a block of time in our schedule. He loves us and longs for fellowship with us. He desires to hear from us no matter where we are or what we're doing.

The apostle Paul wrote, "Pray continually; give thanks in all circumstances, for this is God's will for you in Christ Jesus" (1 Thessalonians 5:17-18). For me, this means talking to God regularly as I go through my daily routine.

I engage in what could be called a running dialogue with the Lord. When I'm driving, I might see someone on the street and say, "Lord, he looks like he's having a hard time. Would you encourage him today?" I might do the same for someone standing in line ahead of me at the grocery store. It's an opportunity to do something for that person.

I know from Scripture that my prayers do have influence in this world. "This is the confidence we have in approaching God," the apostle John writes, "that if we ask anything according to his will, he hears us. And if we know that he hears us—whatever we ask—we know that we have what we asked of him" (1 John 5:14-15). When I pray for someone in this way, I feel like an instrument of God.

I also seek His counsel when I have a decision to make. I recall being on a flight into the Denver airport a few years ago.

The weather was awful as we made our descent, with almost no visibility. Just before we reached the runway, the plane suddenly pulled up and banked sharply to the left. We were sideways! I felt the engine strain as every loose item flew around the cabin and toward the side of the plane. My heart pounded.

We finally straightened out of the curve and eventually landed. I was horrified to learn that we'd almost collided with two planes.

On the ground, my fellow passengers were upset and angry. Half of them got off the plane and refused to re-board for the continuation of the flight to San Francisco. They demanded a different flight on a different airline.

I too was bound for San Francisco. I didn't know what to do. Should I stay on the plane and trust we would make it or, like many of the other passengers, try to negotiate something else? I was alone. Everyone was so distressed that it was difficult to ask questions or communicate with anyone. I was upset myself. I decided to ask the Lord for help.

God, what should I do? I prayed. *I don't know if I should stay on the plane and continue to San Francisco or get off. I have no one to talk to.*

Then I thought of trying to speak with a flight attendant. I approached one who had been on our harrowing flight. "Excuse me," I said. "Do you have a few minutes?"

"Oh," she said, "you're deaf." She wasn't put off by this discovery—in fact, she seemed almost pleased. I understood when she explained that she knew sign language. Much to my surprise, she told me she used to be a teacher of the deaf!

The flight attendant was easy to talk to. She blamed the Denver airport for the landing mixup. "We have the right pilot," she said. "I know him. He's one of the best. If we'd had a different pilot, who knows what would have happened? I feel safe with him. I suggest you stay on the plane and continue on to San Francisco."

I took a deep breath of relief. God had answered my prayer and shown me what to do. I stayed on the plane and arrived home without further incident.

Of course, part of seeking His guidance is being willing to accept His answer. That wasn't so easy for me after I agreed to chair one of the committees charged with organizing a Billy Graham crusade in Fresno in 2001. Each of the chairs of all the committees was asked to lead Billy Graham's staff, including Billy's grandson, through a session of biblical teaching.

I didn't want to do it. The idea terrified me. Naturally, I took it to the Lord.

"God, surely you don't want me to do this," I prayed. "I can't teach them anyway. I'm deaf." (This was my usual excuse when I really wanted to get out of something.)

I sensed that He wasn't going for this approach. "Can you ask someone else to do it for me?" I said. "Wouldn't Billy Graham's people be more blessed if someone more qualified did the teaching?"

I felt as if God was saying, "Nope, nope, you're going to do it."

I had to give in. "All right, God," I said. "What do you want me to talk about?"

The answer I received was, "Your life."

A few days later, I woke up with the idea of teaching on one of my favorite sections of the Bible, the Book of Ecclesiastes. I did lead the session, and actually enjoyed it. It never would have happened if I hadn't conversed with the Lord and (reluctantly) followed His instructions.

Discerning the will of God can, of course, be a tricky exercise. Some people pray frequently and are confident that the voice they hear in their head is from heaven. Yet they spend so little time reading from the Word that I fear they may be easily fooled by darker influences. They lack a Scriptural foundation that allows them to check what they're "hearing" and feeling.

Others are well-versed in the Bible's teaching, yet are so focused on following the details of rules and laws that they miss the bigger point. Jesus castigated the Pharisees for just this flaw, saying, "Woe to you, teachers of the law and Pharisees, you hypocrites! You give a tenth of your spices—mint, dill and cumin. But you have neglected the more important matters of the law—justice, mercy and faithfulness. You should have practiced the latter, without neglecting the former. You blind guides! You strain out a gnat but swallow a camel" (Matthew 23:23-24). I see Christians today who remind me of these Pharisees, more concerned about behavior and rules than about demonstrating the love of Christ.

To truly understand and live out God's will, I believe we must combine a strong scriptural foundation with consistent prayer—*and* link these with fellowship with other, mature believers. Jesus also said, "If two of you on earth agree about anything you ask for, it will be done for you by my Father in heaven. For where two or three come together in my name, there am I with them" (Matthew 18:20). Though God certainly hears our solitary prayers, there is something special about praying with fellow believers. It facilitates our communication with our Father and enables our understanding of His plans for each of us.

Binding Hearts to the One in Heaven

At the beginning of this chapter, we talked about the critical importance of continual communication to a thriving relationship. For a married couple, nothing promotes this steady connection better than prayer. When we join hands in marital harmony and present our praises and petitions to heaven, we discover something special that can't be found anywhere else.

Our unified prayers honor the Lord's creation of the institution of marriage and our status as a single and holy unit in His eyes: "Has not the LORD made them one? In flesh and spirit they are his" (Malachi 2:15). Praying together is a way of coming before God and affirming our love and commitment to Him and His ways.

When we invite the Lord into our marriage in this manner, we also begin to discern His will for our lives together: "Call to me and I will answer you and tell you great and unsearchable things" (Jeremiah 33:3). Our prayers open a window to heaven, allowing a direct view of the heart of our Father.

Equally significant, when we reveal our deepest feelings to each other and to the Lord in prayer, our hearts are bound in a way that holds firm against even the strongest test. Scripture says, "One standing alone can be attacked and defeated, but two can stand back-to-back and conquer; three is even better, for a triple-braided cord is not easily broken" (Ecclesiastes 4:12 TLB).

Of all the benefits to praying together in marriage, however, the most important is planting and cultivating a tender, heartfelt, intimate relationship between husband, wife, and the Lord. It creates a spiritual connection, accountability, and a holy bond that brings strength and stability. It often allows us to communicate about sensitive issues that might otherwise never come out—issues that can be discussed and prayed over in a spirit of humility and purity of motive.

Pastor and author Stuart Briscoe and his wife, Jill Briscoe, have written, "Praying together binds on earth two people whose hearts are bound to the One in heaven. It is one of marriage's deepest joys and greatest blessings."[8]

Another pastor and author, Bill Hybels, has recorded his own take on what prayer means for our spiritual lives.

> During the flows and ebbs, however, I remember that the most fulfilling byproduct of a life of prayer is not the satisfaction of checking off a daily to-do—perfect attendance in your prayer closet doesn't always equal deep fulfillment. The most fulfilling byproduct is also not receiving miraculous answers to the actual prayers prayed, although those are wonderful when they occur. What I have discovered along the path of prayer-life cultivation is that the greatest thrill to a life of prayer is the *qualitative difference made in one's relationship with God.*[9]

I wholeheartedly agree.

13

Broken Blessings

God will mend a broken heart if you give Him all the pieces.

Aesop

If you check out the religion section in your local Barnes & Noble, you'll find a host of titles that promise to change your life. These books offer bestselling advice on every conceivable desire—how to be a better wife, husband, parent, child, sister, brother, neighbor. How to succeed in business and ministry. How to get more out of the Bible. How to pray. How to find the right church. How to sing like David. How to eat like Jesus. How to be happy and fulfilled every minute of every day.

What you're less likely to find, however, is a book that will show you how to be broken.

Most of us look to improve our lives. We strive to be stronger, faster, healthier, and wealthier. We want to be more attractive and more intelligent. We desire to raise our self-esteem. We want to be more spiritual.

The idea that we might seek to be broken, that brokenness might be good for us, does not fit this picture. Most of us aren't even sure what brokenness is. Few of us wake up in the morning thinking, *I hope I'll find a way to be more broken today.*

And if something *does* happen to knock us to our knees, we certainly don't plan on acknowledging it. It's more common for us to either ignore the problem or work as quickly as we can to put it behind us, pretending that nothing awful ever happened.

I know of a woman named Zena whose life changed dramatically during her junior year of college. First, she lost one of her closest confidants when her grandmother died. Then Zena was raped.

For the next eighteen years, Zena attempted to forget that terrible year. Even after she developed an eating disorder to numb her pain, Zena tried to convince herself that everything was fine. Only after hearing a professional counselor speak at a conference did Zena allow herself to face the truth—that she was a broken woman. She started seeing that same counselor and, one day at a time, began facing her past and living again.[1]

Becoming aware of our brokenness—as undesirable as this appears to be on the surface—is actually to our benefit. It is a vital step toward healthy living and healing. It is also one of the qualities that draws us closest to our Lord.

According to the prophet Isaiah, God says, "I live in the high and holy places, but also with the low-spirited, the spirit-crushed" (Isaiah 57:15 MSG). This verse tells us that God dwells in two places—in the high and holy heavens, and with the lowest of the low, those whose spirits have been ground into the dirt.

After King David had an affair with Bathsheba, arranged for her husband to be killed in battle, and was confronted by the prophet Nathan, David was distraught. He realized that he'd been the instrument of great sin—and that he'd created great distance between himself and God.

David understood that no amount of animal sacrifices or good deeds would allow him to work his way back into God's good graces. His only hope was to turn to the Lord with a humble heart and ask for forgiveness: "Have mercy on me, O God, according to your unfailing love…You do not delight in sacrifice, or I would bring it; you do not take pleasure in burnt offerings. The sacrifices of God are a broken spirit; a broken and contrite heart, O God, you will not despise" (Psalm 51:1, 16-17).

Because he came to the Lord with a broken spirit, David's relationship with God was restored. It was the key to his redemption. It just might be the key to yours as well.

Our world is filled with broken people. Many are so discouraged by their circumstances that they've entirely lost hope. The difference for the broken believer is remembering that God can use our crushed spirits to create something new, powerful, and beautiful.

Allow me to share about my experience with brokenness.

A Shocking Loss

A man named Michael was one of my best friends. His wife, Miriam, and Anne had been close for years, and through them I got to know Michael. He was a successful executive for a Fortune 500 firm. He traveled often from his home in the Pacific Northwest to China, northern Europe, and other locations around the world on company business.

Michael and I had deafness in common, but I was fascinated by the differences between his life in business and mine in academia. I enjoyed comparing views of people and human nature with him. We often celebrated birthdays together. The friendship between Anne and me and Miriam and Michael grew to the point that they asked us to be the godparents of their two children. We happily accepted.

What Anne and I didn't realize, at least at first, was that there was trouble in Michael and Miriam's marriage. That's why we were both stunned and disappointed to learn that Michael was leaving Miriam for a woman fifteen years his junior. Michael and Miriam soon divorced.

My relationship with Michael changed. Though I still spent time with him, he grew more guarded and tried to convince me that the choice he'd made was better for him and his family. I pointed out that many of the marriages I was aware of between people with such a wide age range did not last. Michael seemed to realize that in many ways he was starting life over. He appeared stressed. Later, I learned that he was having troubles at work and with his new fiancée.

Michael was not a believer. In the past, I'd tried to share my faith with him, but he had always resisted. With the new tension between us, I no longer tried.

The final shock came in a phone call from Miriam in February 2005—Michael had downed half a bottle of vodka and then intentionally stabbed himself in the throat, underarm, and groin, choosing spots where he would most likely find a main artery and bleed quickly to death. Though paramedics had arrived in time to keep him alive and whisk him to a hospital, the Michael I knew was gone. He was brain dead.

Anne and I flew up to be with Miriam and the kids. Miriam confirmed with the rest of the family that Michael would not want his life prolonged. When doctors removed life support equipment and allowed him to die, Anne and I were in the next room. Only Miriam stayed with Michael.

Miriam and her children were devastated. They had lost a husband and a father.

I also deeply felt the loss of my friend. I realized I had not known Michael as well as I thought I did. He shared only his happy and successful side with me. I had not known about the struggles he faced at work, and his guilt over what he'd done to his family. I wondered if I had failed him, if things would have been different if I had pushed harder to talk about my faith. I would never know.

At the same time, though, I felt more prepared for Michael's suicide than I had for similar losses in the past. I'd dealt with the trauma of my brother David's suicide. Twice, I'd handled the heartbreak of discovering that students of mine had taken their own lives. I'd survived the experience of learning that a beloved uncle, who was caring for a wife with Alzheimer's, killed my aunt and then himself after learning that he had a very short time to live.

All of these deaths left emotional scars. Yet because I loved and trusted in God, I still had hope. Moreover, in the years preceding Michael's suicide, I'd grown stronger spiritually. I felt connected to the Lord. I believed that I could face this moment with this inner strength grounded in my Christian faith.

Michael had been so broken, so despondent, that he felt ending his life was his only option. Now Miriam and the kids were broken too. Anne and I decided to do everything we could to support them and restore their hope in God and the future. I felt I was prepared to be God's minister and messenger of comfort.

What I didn't know was that God had a message for me as well.

A Walk in the Desert

After Michael died in the hospital, Anne and I flew home. We returned two weeks later, however, for the memorial service. We returned again for the summer, living in our vacation home nearby, and went back again a week after that when Miriam became ill from a hard-to-treat infection. Though Miriam was a Christian and she leaned on God's help, the shock of losing Michael coupled with the divorce and her new role as a single mother took its toll on her. Anne and I willingly made it a priority to be there for Miriam and the kids.

Miriam gradually recovered from the blows that she'd suffered and entered school to finish her doctorate. Anne continued to experience a thriving relationship with the Lord. I, on the other hand, entered a new and uncomfortable phase.

For me, God was silent.

It's difficult to put those days into words. Before Michael's suicide, I felt I was in a thriving relationship with God. I talked and He listened. I listened and He impressed His will on my mind. I praised and worshipped Him. I felt the joy of regular give-and-take with my heavenly Father.

Then, suddenly, that was cut off. I discerned no holy presence, no connection. I felt vulnerable. My spiritual life was dry. It was like walking alone through California's Mojave Desert. More than ever before, I identified with some of the laments that David expressed in the Psalms: "How long, O Lord? Will you forget me forever? How long will you hide your face from me? How long must I wrestle with my thoughts and every day have sorrow in my heart?" (Psalm 13:1-2).

This went on for two years. I didn't understand. I was tempted to give up on God, to go my own way. If He was going to ignore me, why shouldn't I ignore Him?

Perhaps you've had this experience yourself. No matter how much you seek the Lord, He seems absent. You feel frustrated, angry, and abandoned. Truthfully, you also feel scared. This isn't the joy-filled Christian life you signed up for.

In the midst of my spiritual drought, however, I found some solace. I recalled an idea I had heard once, that when God is silent, we should try to go back to our last conversation with Him. Though I didn't remember the details of this last communication, I knew it had to do with the theme that even though there will always be people against me, the Lord is always for me. It was a needed reminder of His love and support.

Since that time, I've also begun to consider that the times when God appears to be absent may actually be when He does His most important work for us and in us. Jim Daly, Focus on the Family president, has described it this way:

> It's a little like being a child in your bedroom at night. It's dark, and so black that you can't see anything. Your door is closed, so you can't hear anything outside your room. Yet your favorite pillow and nightstand are still there. Your parents are nearby too. They haven't left you. In fact, your mother is in the kitchen preparing lunch for the next day. She's humming as she works, because she's baking chocolate chip cookies to surprise you.
>
> It's a simple illustration, but you get the idea—circumstances may make it hard for us to sense God's presence, yet He's still there. He hasn't left us. And more often than we realize, His "hiddenness" allows Him to work on our behalf in a way that wouldn't be possible if we could see Him.
>
> To take the analogy further, if you're a child in bed at night, you could jump out of bed, turn on the light, and rush into the kitchen to make sure Mom is still around. You could do that all night long. But that isn't what's best for you, is it? It would leave you exhausted the next day, and it would spoil the surprise of the chocolate chip cookies. You'd be far better off to trust that Mom is there, that she has things under control, and that all you need to do now is go to sleep.[2]

Larry Crabb, a Christian author, counselor, and psychologist, has also commented on this situation:

> [God] vanishes from our sight to do what He could not do if we could see Him. In the spiritual journey, I know of nothing so difficult to believe. But it's true.
>
> Think of those three hours of darkness on the cross. Jesus screamed in agony, "God, where are You?" God said nothing. But it was during that exact time that God was in the Son reconciling the world to Himself.
>
> Imagine the comfort we would experience and the hope we would feel if we realized that during His felt absence, Jesus is working to cut the chain from our ankles, to remove the weight that keeps us from flying.[3]

If we are willing to trust the Lord, we will realize that there is hope even when life is bleak and He seems far away. Though we may not sense it, He *is* still there, and He *is* still working on our behalf.

Looking back on this period of spiritual drought in my life, I see now how responsible I was for distancing myself from God. Anne and I were so focused on supporting Miriam and her family that we neglected our relationship with the Lord. We didn't pray as often as before. We didn't attend church as often—in fact, we changed churches during this time. I was overly confident of my ability to deal with Michael's suicide. I didn't acknowledge, at least at first, that I too was grieving the loss of my friend.

Difficult as it was, I determined to wait on God, to keep trusting and praying. Finally, in November 2007, my wait ended.

Discovering My Brokenness

I'd been to a conference in the San Francisco Bay area and was staying overnight at the home of a close family friend.

That evening, she handed me a present, saying, "This is the perfect book for you." The title was *Life of the Beloved,* by Henri Nouwen. I started reading it almost immediately.

Nouwen's words touched me deeply. He said that each of us is uniquely created and beloved by God, and that we must daily live and practice our "belovedness" to fully realize it. He also discussed four movements of the Spirit, symbolized by his actions as a priest before meals—taking bread, blessing it, breaking it, and giving it to those with him—and by our lives as Christians and human beings.

To be *taken,* Nouwen said, means we are chosen, loved, and accepted by God. We must rise above self-rejection, ignore the negative messages of the world, and affirm the truth that we are precious in God's eyes. Being aware that we are chosen also involves being aware that we are *blessed.* Prayer and meditation help us to hear the voice of God, reveal our blessings, and empower us to bless others.

Each of us, according to Nouwen, is *broken* in a unique way. "The deep truth is that our human suffering need not be an obstacle to the joy and peace we desire," he wrote, "but can become, instead, the means *to* it."[4] Our response to our brokenness should be first to face and embrace it, rather than avoid it, and second to accept it as part of our blessing. Finally, Nouwen said that we are taken, blessed, and broken not just for our own sakes but so that we may be *given*—that is, so that we may share, forgive, spread joy and faith, and love others. Every moment of love shared with another flows in wider and wider circles, like ripples in a pond, extending beyond what we might imagine.

I woke up the next morning at my friend's home in San Francisco with these ideas swirling in my head. I also noticed that physically, I wasn't feeling my best. We said our goodbyes before another friend, Marie, picked me up. The plan was for

Marie to go out to breakfast with me, and then she would drop me off at the airport.

Over buckwheat pancakes smothered in pure Vermont maple syrup, I learned that Marie was in a period of crisis. Her marriage was on the rocks. She was also the caregiver for one of her children, a disabled adult, which was causing conflicts in her relationships with her other children.

The correlation to what I'd just been reading seemed obvious. *Marie is broken,* I thought. *There are so many issues in Henri Nouwen's book that she could relate to.* I pulled *Life of the Beloved* out of my backpack and handed it to Marie, saying, "You need to read this."

Marie dropped me off at the airport, where I was to catch a flight to the Midwest for a fundraising event. I marveled at the timing. *God just gave me this book last night, and now I run into someone who needs it. Maybe after all this time we're reconnecting.*

I was excited at this prospect—but also concerned about my physical condition. My backpack felt heavier than usual. More worrisome was that my heart seemed to beat erratically, occasionally adding an extra beat. I hadn't experienced anything like it before, which made me think it wasn't related to my heart valve issue. I got on the plane hoping the problem would go away.

Instead, it got worse. As was so often the case, I prayed throughout the flight, but this was not my usual session of peaceful reflection and communion with God. When the plane landed in Phoenix, where I was supposed to connect to another flight, I texted Anne to explain what was happening, then took a taxi to an emergency room.

The ER staff admitted me right away, and also arranged to meet my request for a professional interpreter. I answered a barrage of questions and submitted to a host of tests.

Several hours later, with me hooked to a heart monitor and IV machine and oxygen tubes plugged into my nose, a doctor entered my room. He explained that I had an ascending aortic aneurysm—a balloon-like bulge in my aorta, near my heart. It was a dangerous condition. If the bulge was another half centimeter larger, it would warrant immediate surgery. If the aneurysm ruptured, it could easily prove fatal.

I'd dealt with a variety of health issues throughout my life, but this was a huge blow. I was lying in a hospital bed, alone in a strange town, facing my mortality like never before.

Lord, I truly am broken, I prayed. I began to cry.

Through my interpreter, I called Anne and told her what the doctor had said. It was an emotional conversation. We both realized that my heart was degrading. I had mentally prepared my whole life for the idea that I would eventually need to slow down and be less independent. Now, at age fifty-eight, it appeared that moment had arrived. This time we both cried. We also prayed—and in my brokenness, I did perceive that God was with me. In the midst of one of the most distressing days of my life, He was my life preserver.

We're All Broken

During my prayer with Anne, I noticed that my interpreter, a woman named Pamela, was familiar with the hand signs common to a prayer. I'd already come to appreciate her presence. When Pamela had arrived at the hospital, she'd told me her shift would end after four hours and that a new interpreter would take her place. I dreaded starting over with another stranger. Yet when the time for her shift to end approached, Pamela said, "I'm willing to stay if you want me to." I quickly agreed.

Now, after ending my conversation with Anne, I wondered about Pamela and her fluency with our prayer. "You must be a believer," I said.

"Yes."

"Do you pray a lot?"

"Yes."

We began to talk further, and I learned that we had much in common. Her dark brown hair was about three inches long, making it appear it'd been shaved recently, so I suspected she'd been dealing with a major health issue. Pamela confirmed that she'd just completed her final round of chemotherapy treatments for cancer. She was trying to put her life back in order and wondering how she would get through it all.

Here, I thought, *is another broken person. Henri Nouwen is right. We* are *all broken people.*

I told Pamela about the book I'd just read. She identified right away with the ideas that God chooses and blesses us, and that each of us is broken in some way. I realized that talking about our unique, yet common brokenness established a rapport between us. I felt that Pamela was a kindred spirit, a child of God who was also journeying through life and discovering His plan a day at a time. I was thankful that He had provided her at a time when I was alone, in a crisis, and needed both a professional interpreter and someone to share with.

Though Pamela was a highly competent interpreter, it was her struggle that allowed me in an unexpected way to be comforted by her presence. I knew she understood the questions and fears I was confronting. Was I going to die soon? How was my life about to change? How would this affect the people I loved? That she had the courage to face her own mortality and briefly share her circumstances with me gave me encouragement.

Pamela ended up spending eighteen hours with me at that ER in Phoenix, serving as my interpreter until I was discharged with a plan for medical treatment and follow-up appointments back home. I will always be grateful for her professionalism, steady presence in a time of crisis, and friendship.

Though I didn't think of it at the time, my connection with Pamela helps introduce our newest secret:

Accepting and sharing the knowledge that we are uniquely broken before God enables a strong and spiritual connection with Him.

The upheaval that leads to being broken is much more than an unwelcome intrusion in our lives, as I was soon to discover. It is in fact a critical link point between hurting human beings—which is all of us—and between us and God.

A Renewed Life

One of the common experiences of life is that we must deal with the unwanted effects of aging. You've probably heard a few of these lines before, as in "You know you're getting old when…"

- Your back goes out more than you do.
- A fortune teller offers to read your face.
- Your idea of weight lifting is standing up.
- It takes twice as long to look half as good.
- You don't sleep with your teeth.
- You try to straighten out your socks and discover you aren't wearing any.

Everyone, as they grow older, finds that their body isn't what it used to be and they must give up certain activities. Because of my health issues, I faced this reality sooner than many. I love folk dancing, for instance, but while going to graduate school I found I could no longer keep up with the other dancers because of my heart condition. I had to stop.

Now, with the discovery of the aneurysm, Anne and I understood that major changes were required. I began taking medication designed to keep the bulge in my aorta from enlarging. It left me weak. I found that I was uncomfortable lifting objects that weighed more than eight pounds. I was disappointed to realize that I had to give up my newest hobby, flying radio-controlled airplanes. I just didn't have the strength to carry the planes.

The biggest change, however, involved my career. To reduce the stress on my body, I decided to retire from my position as a full-time professor at Fresno State, though I did stay on as a part-time instructor. I was pleased when the administration named me a professor emeritus. Nevertheless, it was a hard adjustment for Anne and me. I was keenly aware of my brokenness. Teaching had been a central focus of my life for nearly thirty years. How would I contribute now? What would I do with my extra time? I feared that my new circumstances would leave me feeling discouraged, unhappy, and useless.

It turned out, however, that the opposite was true. The sudden open periods in my schedule allowed me to spend more time with friends and acquaintances. I found myself more open about my faith. I prayed more frequently, both alone and with others. Though my physical condition had deteriorated, the rest of my life experienced a renewal. Unexpectedly, I felt more blessed and more thankful.

You know what? I told myself. *It's okay to be broken. It is part of what makes us unique. It's brought me closer to God and made me more excited about my relationship with Him. God isn't against me. He's just using my situation to get my attention.*

I realized that because of my brokenness, I was serving the Lord more effectively than ever before. My attitude toward friends was, "Hey, guys, I want you to know about God and how amazing He is. I don't want you to miss out." He was shaping me into the person He had in mind from the beginning.

According to Scripture, the Lord once said to Jeremiah,

> "Go down to the potter's house, and there I will give you my message." So I [Jeremiah] went down to the potter's house, and I saw him working at the wheel. But the pot he was shaping from the clay was marred in his hands; so the potter formed it into another pot, shaping it as seemed best to him.
>
> Then the word of the LORD came to me: "O house of Israel, can I not do with you as this potter does?" declares the LORD. "Like clay in the hand of the potter, so are you in my hand." (Jeremiah 18:2-6)

Like the pot described above, we too are marred. Yet if we trust in the expertise of God, the master potter, He will take our ugly and useless form and make it into something beautiful and valuable. By embracing our brokenness and allowing Him to combine the experience of our flaws with His artistry, we become a new creation.

I believe that if I'd read Nouwen's *Life of the Beloved* when I first became a Christian, I would have reacted to it differently. I probably would have felt that I was just a "little" broken. I never saw my deafness as a terrible handicap. I am thankful my parents taught me that being deaf was not a big issue. Other people might have trouble with it, but that wasn't my problem. I viewed the rest of my difficulties as inconveniences, things I had under control.

The reality, however, is that I've *always* been broken—again, not because I am deaf, but for other reasons: my health; the problems I've encountered in life; my frustrations and insecurities; the distance I've sometimes created between myself and the Lord. Others are broken in their own unique ways. Anne and I know of many people who are battling drug and alcohol addictions. Others fight depression, disease, bitterness, guilt, and anxiety.

The point is that we are all broken in some way. These debilitating experiences are an enormous part of who we are—and are critical to our intimate relationship with God and others. It is our brokenness that attracts the potter: "The Lord is close to the brokenhearted and saves those who are crushed in spirit" (Psalm 34:18).

Today I feel thankful for all God has given me—including my brokenness. He has blessed me.

Broken to Give

In 2010, a friend made a painful request. He was a member of a group called Survivors of Suicide (SOS). He knew of my experiences with suicide, and wondered if I would speak to the group. I realized that it was exactly fifty years since my brother David had ended his life.

I agreed to do it.

Not long after this request, I pulled out a binder of papers and sat down. I read through the letters that David had written just before his death to each member of our immediate family and to his closest relatives. I was amazed. It was the first time I'd gone through the letters without breaking into tears. I suspected that my new attitude toward brokenness had something to do with it.

I'd never shared the letters with anyone before, but I found myself contacting a friend and fellow professor named George. During forty years of teaching, thirteen of George's students had taken their own lives.

George and I met for dinner, where I read aloud David's letters to God and to me. George mostly listened as I talked. It felt good to open up after all these years. Because of his own brokenness over his experience with losing so many students, I knew he understood what I was trying to say.

A few days later, I appeared before the SOS group and talked about my brother and what happened to him and our family. Among the letters from David that I shared were these:

> Dear God,
>
> Forgive me. I can't think at all. I'm so sick.
>
> Dear Paul,
>
> I love you very much. You are a wonderful brother, and I am lucky to have had such a loving and good boy for a brother.
>
> You are interested in many things and you will be a fine man some day. I hope your life will always be happy, not sad like me.
>
> Remember to love others more than anything else in the world and you will be happy.
>
> Do not be sad that I am gone. Be happy with Jonathan and Dunbar; Annegret [Dunbar's wife], Mother, and Dad.
>
> We had many good times together. You were very good to me. Thank you for praying for me every night. Thank you for wanting my headaches to be well. I hope that you never have any headaches.
>
> I hope you will always have many friends.

The group members welcomed me and responded warmly to my comments. It was so satisfying to have the opportunity to talk about David and his death. I felt honored to be invited and pleased that my presentation seemed to have a positive impact.

Later, I realized that with the SOS group, I was living out the progression outlined by Henri Nouwen. I'd been taken (chosen) by God, blessed, and broken. Now I was being handed opportunities to give out of my unique experience—my personal brokenness.

I *was* broken—and that was okay. In fact, because it was part of God's plan, it was better than okay. It was just right.

14

True Contentment

He is the richest who is content with the least.

Socrates

I was more than twenty thousand feet in the air, flying in a commuter jet over California's Death Valley. The name seemed appropriate, because I thought I was going to die.

It was only a few days before that I'd had the heart palpitations that led to discovery of the aneurysm in my aorta. Anne had flown down to Phoenix to join me. Earlier in the day, we'd shared an uneventful flight to the Las Vegas airport, where we'd planned to wait a couple of hours before boarding a U.S. Airways flight bound for Fresno and home.

The weather in Las Vegas was stormy, however. Lightning frequently split the dark November sky, prompting three delays in our scheduled departure. Finally we ascended steps to the jet's cabin, found our seats and, amidst wind and rain, took off.

It wasn't long before I wished we'd never left. As we climbed higher, massive gusts blew the plane sideways. The jet began to shake consistently. Reading or walking in the aisle was out of the question. Anne and I held hands and concentrated on staying in our seats. I thought, *We'll be fine as soon as we get above this storm.*

As we flew higher, however, the weather seemed only to get worse. Our "ride" turned violent as we passed over the Sierra Nevada mountain range. I felt my bones crack as we rattled around in our seats. From my window seat, I saw that we were encircled in a menacing blackness. I looked at the other passengers ahead of and behind us. Some covered their ears or heads. Others had their eyes closed. A few stared straight ahead, their faces white.

Surprisingly, I wasn't frightened. Though I certainly wasn't enjoying the journey, I felt a strange, benign calm.

Part of the reason for my peace was Anne's presence. Sharing the experience with my lifelong partner made it so much easier to bear. When she mouthed to me, "This is terrifying," I responded, "It's okay, we're going to be all right."

I also sensed God's presence. Anne and I prayed together, asking for the Lord's protection and comfort. Remembering that He was in control gave me a feeling of serenity.

I traced my sense of peace to another factor as well. My new understanding of my brokenness had combined with acceptance of the aneurysm and my increasingly fragile health. I added to our prayer, "God, if this is to be our last moment, that's fine. We trust in You and Your plan." I was beyond broken. I was ready to accept my circumstances and trust them to God.

Because of the terrible weather, our plane was diverted to Bakersfield. We finally landed without incident. I saw the overwhelming relief of the one hundred passengers on board. When we got off the plane, two or three of them dropped to their knees and kissed the tarmac.

My reaction to surviving the harrowing flight was less dramatic. I simply turned to Anne and said, "I guess God isn't finished with us yet."

I realized there was an overriding reason for my unexpected peace in the midst of our truly terrifying flight, one that both encompassed and rose above the others: I was content.

Godliness with Contentment

When people talk about contentment, most think in terms of achieving a level of satisfaction with status, possessions, or circumstances. Perhaps after years of striving, we accept that we aren't going to become the company president or a multimillionaire. We come to terms with the fact that our body is aging and that we can't run, throw, or stay as trim as we once did. We decide we're okay with letting go of that dream to live in Europe for a year.

We can speak of being happy with what we have, about accepting our lot in life, about being at peace with the person we've become. For me, however, true contentment runs deeper than this. It is a spiritual state. It means fully recognizing and resting in the presence of God.

The Bible offers many verses that speak to contentment, including:

- Keep your lives free from the love of money and be content with what you have. (Hebrews 13:5)
- Do not fret because of evil men or be envious of those who do wrong; for like the grass they will soon wither, like green plants they will soon die away. (Psalm 37:1)
- Consider it pure joy, my brothers, whenever you face trials of many kinds, because you know that the testing of your faith develops perseverance. (James 1:2-3)

- "Therefore I tell you, do not worry about your life, what you will eat or drink; or about your body, what you will wear. Is not life more important than food, and the body more important than clothes?" (Matthew 6:25)

These passages bring us closer, like steps on a descending staircase, to the depth of contentment that I imagine is possible. It is the apostle Paul, however, who speaks most eloquently to my heart on the topic. In his letter to Timothy, Paul wrote: "Godliness with contentment is great gain. For we brought nothing into the world, and we can take nothing out of it. But if we have food and clothing, we will be content with that" (1 Timothy 6:6-8).

The key is Paul's initial phrase: "Godliness *with* contentment is great gain." I believe it's one of the grand understatements in the Bible. Godliness—behaving in a way that honors and is approved by the Lord—is the fulfilling, visible, physical demonstration of our commitment to following Him. Contentment, meanwhile, is an inner state of being. It is embracing God with our souls—becoming one with Him.

When we combine godliness with contentment, we do indeed discover "great gain." We become the fulfillment of God's unique design for each of us.

Paul, a Roman citizen and Christian-persecutor-turned-advocate, discovered this state of being. Perhaps surprisingly, it was hardship that led him there. This is a man who, after his conversion to the cause of Christ, was beaten with rods, stoned, beset by storms while at sea, shipwrecked, chased by bandits and political and religious opponents, and imprisoned. He frequently found himself hungry, thirsty, cold, and naked. He also suffered from a "thorn in my flesh," an unidentified malady that may have been malaria, epilepsy, a speech disability, or even migraine headaches.

In so many ways, Paul had a difficult life. He was a broken man. Yet he did not regret his trials. Instead, he celebrated them:

> To keep me from becoming conceited because of these surpassingly great revelations, there was given me a thorn in my flesh, a messenger of Satan, to torment me. Three times I pleaded with the Lord to take it away from me. But he said to me, "My grace is sufficient for you, for my power is made perfect in weakness." Therefore I will boast all the more gladly about my weaknesses, so that Christ's power may rest on me. That is why, for Christ's sake, I delight in weaknesses, in insults, in hardships, in persecutions, in difficulties. For when I am weak, then I am strong. (2 Corinthians 12:7-10)

Paul found power and strength in his brokenness—not from within, but by relying on the Lord. Moreover, he learned that God's power is "made perfect in weakness." In a supernatural way that I don't fully understand, the fusion of our brokenness and the Lord's power establishes something greater than would exist separately, makes it, in fact, "perfect." Perhaps God uses this word to describe it because it is the purpose of His power—to be linked with His creation, which is inadequate by itself.

All of us must endure hardship and suffering in this life. Rather than curse our troubles, however, I propose that we view them from a different perspective. From the watchtower of eternity, our suffering serves a purpose. It makes us fully aware of our brokenness, which leads us deeper into communion with God and contentment.

Pastor and theologian John Piper has written:

> This is God's universal purpose for all Christian suffering: more contentment in God and less

> satisfaction in the world. I have never heard anyone say, "The really deep lessons of life have come through times of ease and comfort." But I have heard strong saints say, "Every significant advance I have ever made in grasping the depths of God's love and growing deep with Him has come through suffering."[1]

This appears to have been Paul's experience. Despite his "weakness," he found the courage and strength to become one of the most influential leaders of the early Christian movement, repeatedly risking his life until he was eventually martyred. His trials allowed him to use his newly discovered power to move beyond acceptance of his circumstances and a sense of peace. He found the essential ingredient for true contentment:

> I have learned to be content whatever the circumstances. I know what it is to be in need, and I know what it is to have plenty. I have learned the secret of being content in any and every situation, whether well fed or hungry, whether living in plenty or in want. I can do everything through him who gives me strength. (Philippians 4:11-13)

In recent years, I have begun to glimpse the kind of contentment Paul talks about. Getting to this point, however, has been a long journey.

As Long As We're Together

All my life, I have struggled with the feeling of needing to hurry, to accomplish as much as I can while I still have time. It is an Ogden family trait, which carries with it both benefits and drawbacks. Certainly it has propelled me in my career, allowing me to earn a certain amount of recognition and respect as a professor. Yet too often it has also served to distract me from pursuing my relationship with God. Perhaps you understand what I'm talking about.

As I've said, I wasn't close to God during my high school years. I was not a patient youth either. During my junior year, I applied for early acceptance to one college: Antioch. We were supposed to be notified within two weeks. When that period passed without a letter from the college, my anxiety skyrocketed.

"The letter didn't come today?" I said. "It's supposed to be here. I can't wait. I have to know. I have to plan the rest of my life right now!"

My mother injected a dose of calm into my increasingly frazzled state. "Paul, it's all right," she said. "Just wait. The letter will come. God knows what to do."

A couple of days later, I arrived home from school and found in the hallway a folding chair with a card in it. The card had an arrow pointing to the left and the words, "Go this way." I obeyed the instructions and came to another chair with another arrow and the directions, "Now go this way."

Three more chairs followed. Finally, with my patience nearing its end, I walked into the family room and discovered yet another chair, only this one contained a letter. My mother was there too. Her face did not display a hint of anxiety. Rather, her expression seemed to say, "Okay, let's just see what it says."

Though my father had taught me to open envelopes carefully with a letter opener, this time I grabbed the letter and ripped it open with my fingers. It was from Antioch. I'd been accepted for enrollment the following year.

"It's not surprising," my mother said. "That's good news."

As always, my mother was the calm counterpoint to Ogden family striving. She demonstrated this again a couple of years later when my plans to work at Wayne State University for three months suddenly collapsed. She had a way of encouraging me, my brothers, and my father to slow down, to breathe, to listen.

When I was younger and upset about an upcoming move to a new town or other family changes, my mother would say, "It doesn't matter what happens or where we go as long as we're together. We have God and each other." Years later, after my father died, the message was the same: "We're still together," she said. "God is still with us." Her quiet faith was always an example for us to follow.

More than any of us, my mother understood the advantages of genuine contentment. Not surprisingly, one such benefit is the way in which contentment impacts communication.

Great Expectations

Most men and women enter marriage with a set of unspoken expectations. They may not even be aware they have them. These expectations may be as minor as which way the toilet paper should unroll or as significant as how many children they should have. A husband might assume that his wife will happily do all the cooking and laundry each week. The wife might assume her new husband will have no problem with her scheduling a ladies night out every Tuesday. Both expect to easily resolve questions about how to spend their income.

Frequently, we unconsciously bring another expectation into our marriages—that our new husband or wife will make us happy. We hope that this person will complete us. We believe that they are the piece we've been missing, and that by joining our lives, we will become fulfilled and content.

I believe that in the most successful marriages, however, husbands and wives find contentment not in each other but in the Lord. It is when we *enter* a relationship with this kind of contentment that our union thrives.

In the case of a couple named Randy and Marilyn, the issue that exposed their differing expectations was Saturday mornings. Marilyn awoke each Saturday with a full day's agenda planned in her head and anticipated that Randy would join her in every activity. Randy, meanwhile, was used to sleeping in every Saturday and spending the rest of the day working out, watching sports, and relaxing.

How did Randy and Marilyn resolve their differing expectations of Saturdays? They started with communication. They avoided the pitfall that plagues many couples—they didn't dig in their heels and expect the other to do all the changing. Rather, they began by respecting the other's view and accepting it as perfectly legitimate.

Letting go of the idea that our partner should make us content dramatically improves our ability to communicate with him or her. When Randy and Marilyn talked about their Saturday dilemma, there was no finger pointing or arguing. They listened to each other and accepted their spouse's point of view. They quickly moved into a discussion that centered on compromise and deference. The result is that they plan their Saturdays in advance, negotiating which tasks to tackle and which to leave for another day, while also setting aside part of the day for fun and relaxation. Their Saturdays get started a little later than Marilyn is used to and are busier than Randy is used to, but they are content with the new arrangement.[2]

I have found that in similar discussions I've had with Anne, being content with God and His plan for me makes all the difference in how I "hear" what she's telling me. When I am unhappy with myself, Anne, my circumstances, or God, my focus is usually on my problems and what needs to be done to fix them. I find it difficult to absorb what Anne is saying to me—not so much the words, but the depth of urgency or concern behind them.

Conversely, I am a much better listener when I am content. I feel more patient and ready to hear the whole story. I am willing to ask follow-up questions to explore the details of what Anne is saying. I can more easily accept that Anne is upset or worried about something because I'm less concerned about how it affects me. If I'm conversing with someone else and there is a communication breakdown—a common occurrence when I'm talking with a hearing person—it's easier to let it go if I am content. When I reach this state of peace, I talk less, listen more, and can see the bigger picture.

Anne and I have discovered that when we are having problems and growth is needed in our relationship, rather than try to change each other, it's best to be open to God's guidance and allow Him to be the agent of change. It is another way of being content with Him.

Not surprisingly, this approach also leads to more successful interaction with the Lord.

The Gentle Whisper of Heaven

When we're anxious, angry, fatigued, or focused on taking care of our "needs," it's difficult to hear and heed the gentle whisper of heaven. Searching and striving do not deliver us into contentment. Instead, they distract us from the source of peace.

When I was growing up, my times of contentment were rare and probably lasted about ten minutes. Like many young people, I was not at peace. As I matured, however—especially after I gave my heart to the Lord—these brief periods of contentment grew longer and longer. As my foundation in and relationship with God expanded, so generally did my sense of peace.

It helped to read about the example and wisdom of saints from centuries past. For instance, in the 1600s, Brother Lawrence served as a menial kitchen employee in a monastery for most of his life. Yet he determined that while there, he would be content with his position, perform his work to the best of his ability, and thereby more easily commune with God: "The time of business does not with me differ from the time of prayer; and in the noise and clatter of my kitchen, while several persons are at the same time calling for different things, I possess God in as great tranquility as if I were upon my knees at the blessed sacrament."[3]

I have also found inspiration from a current example. The Old Order Amish reject television, the Internet, car ownership, and other technological advances that they believe will detract from their community life and faith. They strike me as far more content than their modern neighbors across the country. I believe they are on to something.

I have read that the sweeping technological advances we've experienced in the last twenty-five years equal the advances society experienced over the previous three thousand years. Our world is changing more quickly than our ability to adapt to the changes. In our frenzy to keep up, it is easy to lose touch with our Creator. Perhaps this is why, at this writing, Anne and I still have not switched from analog to digital television, and I still own my 1995 pickup truck. I am satisfied with what I have. In fact, we downsized a few years ago by moving to a smaller house. In small ways, we are trying to hold back the flood of "new" and remain content.

Probably my most effective strategy for trusting the Lord and embracing contentment, though, is immersing myself in His Word. Time with Him and in the study of His wisdom breeds a sense of calm and peace. In turn, the greater our sense of peace, the more easily we connect with God.

This passage from Deuteronomy reminds me that He is the source of all my talents, possessions, and blessings: "You may say to yourself, 'My power and the strength of my hands have produced this wealth for me.' But remember the LORD your God, for it is he who gives you the ability to produce wealth" (Deuteronomy 8:17-18). Nothing I have achieved or "own" is truly mine, so I have no reason to take pride in my accomplishments or hold tightly to my possessions.

One of my favorite Scripture passages is an encouragement to be satisfied with the life I know today and a reminder of what can happen if I am not:

> Two things I ask of you, Lord; do not refuse me before I die: Keep falsehood and lies far from me; give me neither poverty nor riches, but give me only my daily bread. Otherwise, I may have too much and disown you and say, 'Who is the LORD?' Or I may become poor and steal, and so dishonor the name of my God. (Proverbs 30:7-9)

When I keep these words in mind, I feel, like Paul, that "I can do everything through him who gives me strength." I also find it easier to detect God's will for my life.

This was the case during a conversation I had early in my career at Fresno State. It was graduation day, always a joyous time of celebrating an important milestone with students, their parents, other family, and friends. It was also an opportunity to visit with faculty members I rarely see.

On this particular day, I sat under a bright sun with the rest of the faculty on folding chairs arranged on Jim Sweeney Field, inside the football stadium. Next to me was a woman named Glen Doyle, a member of the university's nursing department. As we talked, I told her about a dream I'd harbored for some time—to move to San Francisco Bay and join my brother Dunbar on the faculty at the University of California at Berkeley.

When I revealed my thoughts, Glen arched her eyebrows. "Do you really want to lock yourself in the ivory tower?" she said. "It's true, you could do all the writing and publishing you want. But you'd have limited contact with students. You'd be focusing on yourself—that doesn't seem like you.

"I've known you just a short period of time," she continued, "but you seem to belong in this area. You can share so much more of yourself here. People love you. People need more role models like yourself. You seem to be the kind of person who thrives on being with people. Why would you want to take yourself away from here?"

I sat back, stunned. I sensed that God was talking to me—not in a whisper, but in a deafening shout. I knew that my life had again taken a dramatic and permanent turn.

Later, when I explained Glen's comments to Anne, she was quick to embrace the idea as well. It confirmed what my heart already told me. Everything Glen said made sense. More importantly, I had a strong impression that it was from God.

It would have been easy to resist the suggestion. Who wants to give up on a dream? Yet because I was content, I was able to hear and receive the message. My sense of peace with life and with God allowed me to absorb the idea thoughtfully, without feeling threatened or fearful. I didn't see it as a directive to give up something. I viewed it as an opportunity to remain aware of God's will, on a course that was best for me and His plan.

I believe you will have the same experience, encapsulated in our next secret:

We communicate best—with people and with God—
when we are content.

Dead End Signs

Over the years, I have gradually (and sometimes reluctantly) learned to allow God to direct my life. This has grown easier because as I look back, I've begun to see how problems and setbacks, so disappointing at the time, were actually God's way of protecting me.

I remember that for most of my freshman year of high school, I had a crush on a very pretty girl named Marcia. We did much together—we talked often, we both served on the yearbook staff, we danced together at dances. She was an excellent communicator. Yet whenever I asked Marcia out, she always turned me down, saying we were just friends. It was hard to accept—I wanted her to be my girlfriend!

At our high school's twenty-five-year reunion in Charleston, West Virginia, I saw Marcia again. I decided it was time to find out about all those rejections.

"We had such a good relationship," I said to Marcia. "We were good at communicating with each other. Yet whenever I asked you out, you said no. Would you mind telling me why?"

Marcia looked down for a moment and sighed. "Paul, you were working so hard to be successful, to make something of your life," she said. "You had such great, stable parents. I really admired them. You know how I never let you visit me at home or meet my family? It's because my parents were both alcoholics. My home life was awful. It was totally messed up. I had a lot of problems. I just couldn't drag you into my life knowing how messed up my world was. I had to protect you."

Marcia's words hit me hard. I had no idea about the difficulties with her family. I also was amazed that she would reject me out of concern for me.

Upon more reflection, I realized that God had protected me too. I realized that when God says no to a question or desire, it's best to not challenge it and simply let it go. I began paying more attention to the times when things didn't work out in my life. Instead of attempting to overcome them, I tried to just accept them and be content with where God led me.

This was the case when out of nineteen thousand faculty members in the California State University system, I was second choice for the Outstanding Professor of the Year award. Though it would have been a tremendous honor to win, it also would have required me to do a great deal of traveling and speaking, adding stress to my life and distracting me from my family, friends, and students. It could have easily compromised my health. I also feared being chosen because I was deaf. I wanted to be known as a strong teacher and communications professor, not as the "deaf professor." Finally, when I saw the accomplishments of the winner, I felt that he was the right choice. I did not want to win ahead of someone more deserving. In multiple ways, God showed His wisdom by allowing me to finish second instead of first.

Similarly, when one of the two Fresno State professors who consistently opposed me recently proposed a major change in the Deaf Studies program, I did not shift into high-stress mode and formulate a battle plan to stop him. Instead, I prayed and was content to let God show me the solution. Without me saying or doing a thing, several colleagues spoke out against the cuts. The proposal ultimately failed. These are a few among many, many examples of times I've found God protecting me from what I thought was best.

I encourage you to look back over the years at the problems and disappointments in your life. Is it possible that if God granted your desire, it would have led you down the wrong path? Maybe the obstacles you encounter are actually "Dead End" signs from the Lord, pointing you back in the right direction. I believe you'll find the road easiest to navigate when you're content and relying on God's GPS system.

Refusing the Pill

My life has changed significantly since discovery of the aneurysm in 2007. Because of the medication I take, I have less energy than before. It used to be that I operated with a long list of goals to accomplish. I rushed around with many details pressing on my mind. Now, with only a part-time teaching load, my life has slowed down. I find I have more time to chat with friends and students, and that more and more people are requesting to talk with me. I feel I am more patient with everyone and that I listen better. Though I miss some of the things I've given up, my new life provides great opportunities to share my faith and spend time with others and God.

A number of my family and friends took the news of my aneurysm harder than I did, including Anne. I did feel distressed and sad at first. But now I focus on my blessings and the fact that I've had—and am having—a great life. I'll just let God decide what's next. I once feared death, especially after seeing and experiencing all the confusion and pain surrounding my brother David's suicide. Today, however, I'm not afraid to die. It is another step in the journey.

One of the questions people ask me most is, "If someone offered you a pill that allowed you to hear, would you take it?"

I have three answers to the question. If you had asked me when I was sixteen, I would have said, "Sure." At that age, I was searching for new and better ways to grow, to advance, to gain advantages for my life, relationships, and career. I would have grabbed the opportunity to join the hearing population.

Today, if you offered me a pill that gave me the ability to hear for twenty-four hours, I would again happily take it. What fun it would be to hear the lilt of Anne's voice, to enjoy a classical symphony, to go to the beach and discover the sound of wind, waves, and birds, to go to Berkeley and hear my brother Dunbar give a lecture to his students at UC Berkeley! After all these years, I think I would be happy to satisfy my curiosity and understand what so many others experience.

If the pill you offered me was for a one-time, lifelong, irreversible change to hearing, however, my answer would be "No thank you." I've lived a long time and worked hard to get where I am. If I could hear, I would have to start over, learning to recognize unfamiliar noises and sounds. I'm comfortable with who I am and with my personal challenges and issues. I'd rather not trade them in for a new set of issues.

The truth is that I'm grateful for my deafness. I think it's strengthened my faith by keeping me humble. I might have otherwise grown arrogant and unwilling to depend on anyone else, including God. It has also given me greater empathy for those who struggle with their own unique challenge in communication. It is a foundational part of who I am. I find it hard to imagine who I would be or what my life would be like if I was not deaf. I am satisfied with who I am.

I don't mean to imply that I exist in some kind of nirvana-like state where every problem wafts past me like a soft breeze. I do get frustrated, irritated, and angry at times. I have bad days. But these moments are rarer than they used to be, and I find it easier and easier to return to a state of contentment.

I go through my days attempting to maintain a grateful attitude toward God for my life and my blessings, including the "thorns" that don't go away. I can honestly say that quite often—with His help—I truly am content.

I wish you the same.

15

The Mystery Of God

Mystery creates wonder and wonder is the basis of man's desire to understand.

Neil Armstrong

We've talked throughout this book about the significant role communication plays in determining the quality of our relationships with each other and with the Lord. I've spent a lifetime studying the art of how we interact with each other, and concluded that our ability to express thoughts, feelings, and ideas—and receive them in return—has everything to do with living a fulfilling life and developing a profound faith.

With this in mind, I have dedicated myself to understanding and improving my ability to communicate. I would encourage everyone to do the same. From my perspective, few pursuits are more significant.

As we strive to master our grasp of communication techniques, however, all of us eventually come across a locked gate. No matter how hard we try, we can't open the gate and discover what's on the other side. Because we live in a complex and unfathomable world, perfect communication and complete understanding are simply not possible.

This is true for even the closest of human relationships. Some couples spend a lifetime together. They are true soul mates, sensing each other's thoughts, finishing each other's sentences, knowing each other as intimately as two people can. Yet even when this is the case, one partner does not understand the other completely. Surprise and mystery are still part of the relationship.

I, for one, am glad this is so.

At this writing, Anne and I have been married for thirty-five years. Emerging from the tumultuous period that marked the beginning of our marriage, we have steadily built a relationship characterized by trust, respect, mutual faith in God, and unquestioned love. Anne is my steady companion, lover, partner in faith, and best friend. All of this has been made possible by our shared commitment to consistent and effective communication.

For one thing, we are better today at patiently listening to each other. When I try to explain an idea and can't find the words, Anne will give me the time I need to order my thoughts. Frequently, when one of us struggles to put words into coherent sentences, we will say, "Can you help me explain this better?" That's something we never said to each other even five years ago.

We're also far less defensive. We feel so safe with each other that we know the other does not mean to hurt with words. We are simply trying to offer a new perspective or concern.

In addition, we've improved at summarizing the other's thoughts and repeating them back. When I do this, it lets Anne know that I am listening and working to understand her intent. All of these techniques express respect and love and help establish intimacy. When I proposed to Anne by listing the principles in "The Marriage Creed," we both saw them as ideals, almost a fantasy. Today, after traveling so long on the journey of marriage together, we feel there are times when we actually live up to the dream we envisioned all those years ago.

Even with the deeply felt closeness we've achieved in our relationship, however, Anne and I are still making new discoveries about each other. I've realized recently that Anne is more loving today toward people who are difficult to love than she was thirty years ago. She says that I'm more forgiving and understanding, that I'm talking less and listening more.

We are continually changing, which means we are continually adapting to one another. Anne's father was a medical doctor who'd served in the military during World War II and was a constant support for her. When he died late in 2010 of aspiration pneumonia, she was naturally grief-stricken. She was also angry. At the hospital, one of her father's doctors inserted a tube through his nose that damaged his throat, leading to the aspiration pneumonia. Anne and I both felt that the pneumonia could have been prevented.

A few months after her father's death, however, I began to see a change in Anne. We talked about it during a weekend retreat at the coast. She still grieved, but she also was beginning to embrace the fact that she'd had a good life with her father and was thankful for her years with him. She was determined to handle her grief in a new way.

For me, watching Anne go through these stages of grief has injected a sense of the unknown in our relationship. I'm not sure how she will respond to the new feelings and ideas she's exploring, and how that will affect our interaction. The uncertainty is not a bad thing. It is an invitation to evolve with her as we face the future together. It's an example of what we all go through in relationships.

The striving for total understanding that we experience in our human-to-human interactions is even more pronounced and elusive in our relationship with our Creator. God is the ultimate mystery.

A Big God

As we have already observed, we were created to seek and experience an intimate relationship with God. He is the ultimate source of our daily provision, joy, and purpose. He is the solution to our proclivity toward sin and need for salvation.

The depth of our need for God is matched, however, by our inability to wholly know Him. It is virtually impossible to comprehend our insignificance as compared to the power and vastness of God. If we imagine Him as a human being and ourselves as fleas only dimly aware of His presence, we still fail to fully describe the gulf that separates us. He is the great I Am, the one who has always existed, the beginning and the end. To put it in the simplest terms, God is big—really, *really* big.

Augustine, one of the most influential early Christian writers, once glimpsed the futility of trying to understand and explain God.

> Saint Augustine walked the seashore one day, pondering the majesty of God. He saw a small boy who had dug a hole in the sand. The boy kept scooting down to the ocean, scooping up water in a seashell, and scrambling back to pour the water in the hole.
>
> "What are you doing?" Augustine asked him.
>
> "I'm going to pour the sea into that hole," the boy said.
>
> *Ah,* Augustine thought. *That is what I have been trying to do. Standing at the ocean of infinity, I have tried to grasp it with my finite mind.*[1]

Our "finite minds" do serve us to a point. The memories of moments when I experienced a strong awareness of the presence of God sustain me to this day. When I first invited Jesus into my heart back in my little graduate school apartment in Illinois, I perceived an unmistakable and nearly overwhelming sensation of the Lord's love for me, as if He had wrapped me in a warm, tight embrace. It was an "aha" moment—I felt that I suddenly saw how to complete the ten-thousand-piece jigsaw puzzle before me. That sense of His love and presence has comforted me many, many times since.

Yet there have also been frequent occasions when the Lord was silent and appeared to be absent. Certainly, my recent two-year "spiritual drought" was a time of testing for me. That experience and others have shown me that *we*, rather than God, may be to blame for the lack of spiritual connection.

The apostle Paul aptly describes the continuing struggle we each have with our sinful nature: "I do not understand what I do. For what I want to do I do not do, but what I hate I do" (Romans 7:15). We allow ourselves to be distracted by selfish desires and worldly influences, wasting our lives in shallow pursuits that prevent us from cultivating a relationship with the Lord: "Love of the world squeezes out love for the Father. Practically everything that goes on in the world—wanting your own way, wanting everything for yourself, wanting to appear important—has nothing to do with the Father. It just isolates you from him" (1 John 2:15-16 MSG).

At other times, however, it seems it is the Lord Himself who prevents the connection. Even our most fervent prayers may be "ignored" for days, weeks, months, or years. At other times, meanwhile, we may be fully aware of the Lord's answer—but we surely don't understand His reasoning.

This was the case for Anne and me a few years after our wedding. We had looked forward to having children and parenting together. Despite our efforts and prayers, however, the years passed without success. It was both stressful and deeply disappointing.

One day a good friend came to Anne and me with a unique proposal. Her daughter was pregnant. Sadly, the daughter had multiple sclerosis and was not expected to live long. "Everyone in our family loves you," our friend said to us. "Would you adopt our grandchild?"

Anne and I were tempted to say yes immediately, but we decided to pray about it first. It seemed the perfect solution to our situation, as well as an explanation for our inability to have a child of our own. Here was an unexpected need that met our desire. The request seemed to come straight from God.

The only problem was that the more Anne and I prayed about it, the more unsettled we felt about the idea. Each of us, individually, sensed God saying that we should decline. We were terribly disappointed, but also certain that God had spoken. The mystery was why He'd said no.

Fifteen years later, we received our answer. We met our friend again and saw a picture of the boy, now a teen, and his adoptive parents. They looked like a wonderful family. More importantly, we learned that the boy had a severe learning disability. The parents who eventually adopted him were both special education teachers. They had the background and training that Anne and I lacked.

When we first heard this news, Anne and I exchanged an amazed look. We realized that God must have had this couple in mind for "our" baby from the beginning. His plan was best. We were so glad that we heeded His direction.

Anne and I never did have children. After eleven years of attempting to conceive and pursuing adoption avenues that led to closed doors, we realized that God was saying to us, "Your life is so rich. It's time to let go of the idea of starting a family. I have a different ministry and path in mind for you."

We wondered for years about why God would steer us away from adopting our friend's grandchild, and then we learned why. On the other hand, though we can see the freedom to serve Him that it offers us, we still don't fully understand why we have been denied the opportunity to become parents. It brings us to our final communication secret, one that we must accept if we are to stay faithful and sane.

God is too big for us to ever fully understand.

We who are on this side of heaven have no choice, then, but to remember that our Father loves us, and to trust in His guidance.

Why, God?

These are but a few examples of the questions that arise from dealing with an invisible and, at times, seemingly shy God. Why do so many prayers appear to go unanswered? Why must evil exist?

We have already examined some of the benefits of struggle that leads to brokenness. Yes, these struggles can bring us closer together, and yes, they frequently move us closer to God. But are these benefits truly enough to justify the suffering, bloodshed, and heartache that have plagued humankind throughout our history?

Why in the midst of such struggles does God so often hide himself from our sight and minds? As author Ron Hansen has noted, "God gives us just enough to seek him, and never enough to fully find him."[2] The miracles that would so easily announce His presence seem to be in short supply. Events such as the burning bush witnessed by Moses and the transfiguration of Jesus observed by Peter, James, and John are encounters apparently reserved for a select few. Would it really disrupt the eternal plan so much to allow us modern Christians to experience even one of these life-altering exchanges?

I won't pretend to have all the answers, because I don't. God's purposes are certainly far beyond the reach of my humble musings. Yet as a seeker still on the journey toward understanding, I will at least venture a few theories.

I must first operate on the assumption that God's actions or inactions are intentional and for our ultimate good. I believe with all my heart that His love for us is boundless. He has proved it by giving us life, by sacrificing His Son for our eternal salvation, by the countless ways both large and small that He has blessed you and me, though we do not deserve it. I must conclude that He has a good purpose in all that He does.

Thomas Keating, a Trappist monk and priest, has written, "God's first language is silence. Everything else is a translation."[3] I get what he is saying. Even when the Lord speaks, His meaning is often obscured or couched in riddles. I have read that in the Gospels, people approached Jesus with a question 183 times, yet He replied with a direct answer in but three instances. His responses instead took the form of another question, a story, or some other indirection.[4]

Scripture makes plain that we will not always be aware of the Lord or comprehend His purposes. Solomon states, "It is the glory of God to conceal a matter" (Proverbs 25:2). Isaiah writes, "Truly, you are a God who hides himself" (Isaiah 45:15). Moses says, "The secret things belong to the LORD our God" (Deuteronomy 29:29).

The disciples themselves, though they walked and talked with the Lord, were frequently confused about Jesus' words and intent. Though inspired by His radical message, the disciples and crowds that followed Jesus misunderstood. They yearned for political revolution, for a king who would deliver them from their earthly position of inferiority and transfer them into a ruling class. Instead, Jesus offered a revolution based on love, grace, and forgiveness—yet He frequently allowed the confusion among His followers to remain.

What are we to make, then, of a God who is so often intentionally silent, hidden, and mysterious? Why would He behave this way?

The answer, I suspect, has to do with our faith and our readiness to absorb and understand His teaching.

A God who is presented fully and matter-of-factly to us will not inspire deep-rooted love, trust, and faith. Like any knowledge or truth, it must be experienced and integrated over a lengthy period of time before it sinks into our soul and becomes a permanent part of us. Quality relationships are not forged in a day but hammered out in increments, blow by blow, over a lifetime.

My sense is that the Lord wants us to work out our faith on our own, in conjunction with fellow travelers in a community of faith, so that we will "own" it. It is the same reason that He gives us the freedom to choose Him or reject Him. God has the power to force us to praise and worship Him like robots, but how meaningful is that? As we have discussed, the depth and quality of our faith is of the utmost priority to our Father. When we work through it and embrace it of our own free will, it takes on a life, power, and significance that glorifies Him.

It is our suffering and struggle that renews our faith and moves us into relationship with the Lord. Scripture describes the woman who suffered from bleeding for twelve years. Doctors were unable to cure her malady. Her existence must have been miserable, for she would have been shunned because she was ceremonially unclean. Yet when she heard about Jesus, her faith swelled. She approached Him in a crowd and touched His garment, thinking, *If I just touch his clothes, I will be healed* (Mark 5:28).

When she touched Jesus' cloak, the woman's bleeding stopped immediately. Jesus then turned around and asked, "Who touched my clothes?" (v. 30). The healing was already complete, but Jesus wanted to affirm the woman's faith and their new relationship. His words also affirm for us what can happen when we nourish our faith and enter into relationship with Him:

"Daughter, your faith has healed. Go in peace and be freed from your suffering" (v. 34).

I believe there are other reasons God does not fully reveal Himself too us. I would venture that as finite creations of the Creator, we are simply not equipped to take in the totality of all that God is. Does a parent try to explain Einstein's Theory of Relativity to a baby? For the most part, the awesomeness of God passes over our heads. We can only faintly glimpse the wonder. If He were to reveal all that He is, we would be overwhelmed, perhaps to the point of death: "You cannot see my face, for no one may see me and live" (Exodus 33:20).

Our almighty Father is to be honored, worshipped, and reverenced. It is the reason why many Jewish people refuse to speak His name aloud, and why some write His name "G-d" or "G_d." It is a form of respect for the Most High, a reminder that even the use and meaning of His name is beyond us.

When I was a senior in high school, I wanted to map out a plan for my life. Despite my limited experience, I wanted to decide on my future college and future career right then. It was important to me to have these issues settled in my mind.

Today, however, I am content to let God unfold the future before me as He sees fit. None of us knows how much time we have left on this earth, but especially because of my health issues, I wonder if my time is short. It may be many years or it may be much less than that. Either way, I am fine with not knowing. If God revealed the date of my last breath in advance, I fear it would awaken the old Ogden drive inside me. I might feel pressed to make a personal list of goals to accomplish in the time I had left. I imagine I would be stressed as I counted down my days.

I think God has a better plan. I try to simply allow Him to lead my steps each day. I don't know where He's taking me, but I am confident it is in the right direction.

Hide and Seek

Perhaps I should clarify something. I don't mean to appear as if I'm advocating that Christians close their eyes and wait for God to transport them to a land of milk and honey. We have an important role to play, one that requires total commitment on our part and brings us full circle back to the theme of this book.

If we are to enter into relationship with God and establish a profound, lasting faith, we must do so through the process of communication. The final, and perhaps most important, reason that God hides from us may be that He is inviting us to seek Him. He gave us the gift of curiosity and the desire to learn. I believe He expects us to "solve" the mystery by continually attempting to connect with and discover Him.

> Belden C. Lane remarks that he used to fret about how his children played hide-and-seek. His son would bellow out "Ready!" when he had found a good hiding place, which of course instantly gave him away. Lane, the father, kept reviewing the point of the game—"You're supposed to hide, not give your position away!"—until one day it dawned on him that from his son's perspective *he* had missed the point of the game. The fun comes in being found, after all. Who wants to be left alone, undiscovered?
>
> "God is like a person who clears his throat while hiding and so gives himself away," said Meister Eckhart. Perhaps God also feels pleasure in being found?[5]

When communication works—when we overcome the obstacles, failures, conflicts, misunderstandings, and breakdowns that seem to inevitably crop up—we experience the deep pleasure of "finding" each other. When, through prayer, listening, reading the Word, meditating, worship, and fellowship with other believers, we "find" God, we know a truly deep joy.

I believe that as our faith—and our ability to communicate—matures, we have the opportunity to grow in knowledge and understanding. More and more often, we catch hints of His true glory and wisps of knowing. These alone can be enough to take our breath away. We begin to really see the depth of love, grace, and mercy that characterize our God.

The apostle Paul wrote, "For now we see only a reflection as in a mirror; then we shall see face to face. Now I know in part; then I shall know fully, even as I am fully known" (1 Corinthians 13:12). I look forward to the day when I "shall know fully," when the obstacles to perfect communication are swept away and I can commune without interruption or confusion with my Lord. I do not expect to hear sounds in this heavenly place—this silent Eden—because communication is about far more than the ability to hear. I anticipate, instead, finding a joy that lasts forever, because I will *understand.*

My prayer is that you too will one day discover this joy, and that we will understand together.

Photo of Paul and Anne with their Belgian sheepdog, "Chelsea," their first professionally trained, fully certified hearing dog from Paul's book, Chelsea: The Story of a Signal Dog (Boston, MA: Little, Brown, 1992)

Students and the Deaf Education faculty, Nan Barker, Karen Jensen, Susan van Gurp, and Paul, with the sign language interpreter, Suzanne Conway, at the annual gathering in the Spring of 1998.

Anne celebrates with Paul in 2008, when he retired as director of the Deaf Studies program. The program grew and evolved to include the large Deaf Studies faculty.

Anne Ogden at the end of her 40-year career as an R.N. For the previous 20 years she worked as a Nurse Manager/Nurse Educator/Nurse Staff at the San Joaquin Valley Rehabilitation Hospital, Fresno, California.

Paul's mother with her three living sons: (L to R) Dunbar, Jonathan, and Paul in 1998.

Secrets From My Silent Eden

- Successful communication requires reaching out on the other person's terms.
- We were made for deep relationship—with each other and with God.
- Good communicators adopt an attitude of inclusion.
- Lousy communicators usually make lousy Christians.
- When we love the "least of these," we link our hearts to God's.
- Doubt is often the path to deeper faith.
- Faith combined with effective communication leads to strong relationship.
- Open, honest communication leads to trust and intimacy.
- God speaks to us through Scripture, His love letters to His children.
- Forgiveness enables profound communication with others and God.
- To thrive, a relationship requires continual communication.
- Accepting and sharing the knowledge that we are uniquely broken before God enables a strong and spiritual connection with Him.
- We communicate best—with people and with God—when we are content.
- God is too big for us to ever fully understand.

NOTES

Chapter 1

1. Jokes Unlimited website, http://www.jokesunlimited.com/jokes/funny_classified_ads.html
.

2. "Tragic 'Misunderstanding' in West Virginia Mine Accident," ABC News website, January 4, 2006, http://abcnews.go.com/US/story?id=1469171.

3. Jack Welch, *Winning* (New York: HarperBusiness, 2005), 68.

4. Science Daily website, November 5, 2009, http://www.sciencedaily.com/releases/2009/11/091105092607.htm.

5. L. S. Koester and K. P. Meadow-Orlans, "Parenting a Deaf Child: Stress, Strength, and Support," *Educational and Developmental Aspects of Deafness* (Washington, D.C.: Gallaudet University Press, 1990), 311.

Chapter 2

1. Peter F. Drucker, *Management: Revised Edition* (New York: HarperCollins, 2008), 485.

2. John Gray, *Mars and Venus in the Workplace* (New York: Harper Collins, 2002), 95.

3. Gary Chapman, *The Five Love Languages of Teenagers* (Chicago: Northfield, 2000), 123-24.

4. Marlo Schalesky, *Empty Womb, Aching Heart* (Minneapolis: Bethany House, 2001), 113-116.

5. Philip Yancey, *Reaching for the Invisible God* (Grand Rapids, Mich.: Zondervan, 2000), 148.

6. Kenneth Barker, general editor, *The NIV Study Bible* (Grand Rapids, Mich.: Zondervan, 1985), 115.

7. Frederick Buechner, *Wishful Thinking* (San Francisco: Harper & Row, 1973), 46.

8. Yancey, 123-24.

9. Ibid, 125.

10. Frederick Buechner, *The Magnificent Defeat* (San Francisco: Harper & Row, 1985), 47.

Chapter 3

1. John McCain with Mark Salter, *Faith of My Fathers* (New York: Random House, 1999), as excerpted in John B. Letterman (editor), *Survivors: True Tales of Endurance* (New York: Simon & Schuster, 2003), 390-97.

2. Clive Thompson, "Brave New World of Digital Intimacy," *The New York Times*, September 7, 2008, http://individual.utoronto.ca/kreemy/proposal/07.pdf.

3. Lori H. Gordon, "Intimacy: The Art of Relationships, *Psychology Today*, December 31, 1969, http://www.psychologytoday.com/articles/199309/intimacy-the-art-relationships.

4. Brennan Manning, *The Ragamuffin Gospel* (Sisters, Ore.: Multnomah, 1990, 2000), 46.

Chapter 4

1. Dunbar H. Ogden, *My Father Said Yes* (Nashville, Tenn.: Vanderbilt University Press, 2008), 28.

2. Ibid, 29.

3. Brother Lawrence, *Brother Lawrence: The Practice of the Presence of God* (Google ebooks), 37.

Chapter 5

1. Brennan Manning, *The Ragamuffin Gospel* (Sisters, Ore.: Multnomah, 1990, 2000), 31.

Chapter 6

1. Dunbar H. Ogden, *My Father Said Yes* (Nashville, Tenn.: Vanderbilt University Press, 2008), 92.

2. Patrick Morley, *The Man in the Mirror* (Grand Rapids, Mich.: Zondervan, 1997), 116-17.

3. Jim Wallis, *God's Politics* (New York: HarperCollins, 2005), 214.

4. Philip Yancey, *Soul Survivor* (New York, N.Y.: Doubleday, 2001), 192.

5. Ibid, 192-93.

6. Ibid, 198-99.

Chapter 7

1. Sally Fitzgerald (editor), *Letters of Flannery O'Connor* (New York: Vintage, 1979), 476.

2. Philip Yancey, *Reaching for the Invisible God,* (Grand Rapids, Mich.: Zondervan, 2000), 37.

3. Blaise Pascal, *Pensées* (Sioux Falls, S.D.: NuVision Publications, 2007), 61.

4. Yancey, *Reaching for the Invisible God,* 46.

Chapter 8

1. David and Jan Stoop, *When Couples Pray Together* (Ann Arbor, Mich.: Servant Publications, 2000), 68-70.

2. Philip Yancey, *Reaching for the Invisible God,* (Grand Rapids, Mich.: Zondervan, 2000), 108.

Chapter 9

1. *Merriam Webster's Collegiate Dictionary,* Tenth Edition (Springfield, Mass.: Merriam-Webster, 1997).

2. Conrad Smith, *Best Friends* (Colorado Springs, Colo.: NavPress, 1989), 107.

Chapter 10

1. Ginny and Manny Feldman, "The Marriage Creed," http://www.poofcat.com/m2.html.

2. Billy Graham, "Billy Graham: Bible Is God's 'Love Letter" to Us," Seattle Post-Intelligencer, September 6, 2007, http://www.seattlepi.com/news/article/Billy-Graham-Bible-is-God-s-love-letter-to-us-1246557.php.

3. Angela Winter, "The Science of Happiness," *The Sun Magazine,* May 2009.

Chapter 11

1. Dennis Kizziar, *Hope for the Troubled Heart* (Bend, Ore.: Maverick Publications, 2008), 47-48

2. David F. Allen, *Shattering the Gods Within* (McLean, Va.: Curtain Call Productions, 2004), 161.

3. Kizziar, *Hope for the Troubled Heart*, 35-36.

4. Dunbar H. Ogden, *My Father Said Yes* (Nashville, Tenn.: Vanderbilt University Press, 2008), 146-47.

5. Kizziar, *Hope for the Troubled Heart*, 44-45.

6. Ibid, 58-59.

7. Donald Kraybill, Steven Nolt, and David Weaver-Zercher, *Amish Grace* (San Francisco, Calif.: Jossey-Bass, 2007), 44-45, 191-92.

Chapter 12

1. Les and Leslie Parrott, *Becoming Soul Mates* (Grand Rapids, Mich.: Zondervan, 1995), 215.

2. Ibid.

3. Philip Yancey, *Prayer: Does It Make Any Difference?* (Grand Rapids, Mich.: Zondervan, 2006), 14.

4. Ibid.

5. C. S. Lewis, *Christian Reflections* (Grand Rapids: Eerdmans, 1967), 168-69.

6. Sharon Begley, "The Hidden Brain," *Newsweek* magazine, June 7, 2010, 24.

7. Mother Teresa, QuotationsBook website, http://quotationsbook.com/quote/36248/#axzz1KrQM8gWg.

9. Parrott, *Becoming Soul Mates*, 76.

10. Bill Hybels, *Too Busy Not to Pray* (Downers Grove, Ill.: Intervarsity Press, 2008), 16.

Chapter 13

1. Pam Vredevelt, *Angel Behind the Rocking Chair* (Sisters, Ore.: Multnomah, 1997), 15-19.

2. Jim Daly, *Stronger* (Colorado Springs, Colo.: David C. Cook, 2010), 100-01.

3. Larry Crabb, *Shattered Dreams* (Colorado Springs, Colo.: WaterBrook, 2001), 158-59.

4. Henri J. M. Nouwen, *Life of the Beloved* (New York: Crossroad, 1992), 95-96.

Chapter 14

1. John Piper, *Desiring God* (Sisters, Ore.: Multnomah, 2003), 265.

2. Randy Hicks, "Great Expectations, Sure—But Are They Realistic?" *The Daily Tribune News*, http://www.daily-tribune.com/view/full_story/7750398/article-Great-expectations--sure---But-are-they-realistic-.

3. Brother Lawrence, *The Practice of the Presence of God*, as quoted in Richard J. Foster, *Prayer: Finding the Heart's True Home* (New York, HarperCollins, 1992), 124.

Chapter 15

1. RBC Ministries, "Beyond Our Understanding," *Our Daily Bread*, June 11, 1995.

2. Ron Hansen, *Mariette in Ecstasy* (New York: HarperPerennial, 1991), 174.

3. Thomas Keating, *The Sun Magazine*, September 2010, http://www.thesunmagazine.org/issues/417/sunbeams.

4. Philip Yancey, *Prayer: Does It Make Any Difference?* (Grand Rapids, Mich.: Zondervan, 2006), 205.

5. Philip Yancey, *Reaching for the Invisible God*, (Grand Rapids, Mich.: Zondervan, 2000), 116.

Acknowledgements

I wish to thank Tracy Van Zanten for planting the seed to write when she handed me Henri Nouwen's *Life of the Beloved*. The turning point took place when Mark and Laura Stager watered the seed and nurtured the idea of undertaking an ambitious writing project. My wife, Anne, immediately became the most enthusiastic fan of the project, providing all the support a writer could dream of.

Heartfelt gratitude goes to Lindsey Johnson Krebs and Erin Uribe Ruiz for their interpreting services and friendship. I enjoyed working with patient and thoughtful readers who provided insightful comments and constructive criticism, including: Ron and Karen Coles, Brian and Kerry Nicols, Dr. George Diestel, Dr. Alan Sortor, Dr. Diane Blair, Mark and Laura Stager, Melinda Pate, Kathy Yoshida, Dunbar and Annegret Ogden, John Franz, Susan Shanks, Melanie Silva, Jeanne Glad, and Stephen and Isle Osier. I deeply appreciate the professional expertise of Andy Baldwin and Kari Boydstun-Baldwin throughout the publication process.

Special thanks to two individuals: Melinda Pate for her prayers and many discussions about the writing project and Dr. George Diestel for inspiring me to continue the project and to make many decisions which have been incorporated into this volume. I do appreciate his insights and creative suggestions.

I must say that *Secrets from My Silent Eden* would not exist without the constant enthusiasm and practical perseverance of Jim Lund. Besides Anne, I thank him most of all.

About The Author

Paul W. Ogden has spent a lifetime exploring what it means to be an effective communicator. He is an educator, author, mentor, scholar, and advocate for the deaf and hard of hearing. Born deaf into a hearing family, Paul is the youngest of four sons, including one who was also born deaf. Paul grew up in the South during the tumultuous years of the Civil Rights movement. As a boy, he met Martin Luther King Jr. in the Ogden home and was old enough to appreciate his father's bravery and compassion when Dunbar Ogden led members of the "Little Rock Nine" through a white mob to Central High School.

Paul earned a bachelor's degree in mathematics and computers from Antioch College and master's and doctoral degrees in educational psychology and deaf education from the University of Illinois, Champaign-Urbana. For more than thirty years, he has served as a professor of Deaf Studies at California State University, Fresno, where he is currently Professor Emeritus. He uses his knowledge and talent to teach students to be advocates for the deaf, serve as a support system for parents, and be a resource for children, families, and other key individuals in the lives of deaf and hard-of-hearing children. Paul was named **Outstanding Professor** of the Year at Fresno State and placed second overall for the same award for the California State University system comprised of 23 campuses.

Among his major publications are *The Silent Garden: Understanding Your Hearing Impaired Child; Chelsea: The Story of a Signal Dog; The Silent Garden: Raising Your Deaf Child,* and *El*

Jardin Silencioso: Criando a Su Hijo Sordo, a Spanish translation of the first five chapters of *The Silent Garden*. Gallaudet University Press lists both volumes of *The Silent Garden* as classics. Among Paul's recent honors is the Lifetime Achievement Award, conferred in 2012 at the annual conference of California Educators of the Deaf.

Paul lives in Fresno with his wife, Anne Keenan Ogden, one of the first members of the deaf community to become a registered nurse. She retired as a certified registered rehabilitation nurse in 2011 after forty years of service.

Author Paul W. Ogden

On the rear cover you will note images of butterflies. Butterflies are precious and beautiful icons for my deaf friends because butterflies have no hearing ability during their short lives of 8-10 weeks.

CPSIA information can be obtained at www.ICGtesting.com
Printed in the USA
BVOW10*1225101113

335868BV00002B/2/P

9 781618 636058